With thanks to Jack McGinn,
whose original idea is still going
strong after more than 40 years.

First published in 2007 by
HEADLINE PUBLISHING GROUP

Celtic View would be happy to hear from readers with their comments on the book
at the following e-mail address: tictalk@celticfc.co.uk

1

Cataloguing in Publication Data is available from the British Library

ISBN 978 0 7553 1583 3

Designed by Fiona Andreanelli (www.andreanelli.com)

Printed and bound in Great Britain by
Butler & Tanner

Headline's policy is to use papers that are natural, renewable and recyclable products and made from
wood grown in sustainable forests. The logging and manufacturing processes are expected to conform to
the environmental regulations of the country of origin.

HEADLINE PUBLISHING GROUP
An Hachette Livre UK company
338 Euston Road
London NW1 3BH

www.headline.co.uk
www.hodderheadline.com

www.celticfc.net

The Best of

The 100 issues that made you laugh, cry and cheer

Paul Cuddihy
Joe Sullivan

headline

Contents

The cream of the crop

From the very first issue of the *Celtic View* on 11 August 1965 to the first issue of season 2007–08, we had to choose the 100 best covers… and here they are together at last. The *Celtic View* has reported on the best of times for the club and, on occasion, the worst of times. The front cover has provided the most powerful image for each of these stories. Some of them will be well known to you while others may be less familiar. But each one tells a little piece of Celtic history for you to enjoy.

Introduction

A book which highlights one hundred memorable front covers of the *Celtic View* is not just a celebration of the oldest and biggest-selling weekly club magazine in football. It is also a chronicle of Celtic Football Club itself.

Since 1965 the *View* has recorded the highs and lows of the club, from the birth of Celtic's domination under Jock Stein through to the centenary season, then on to the dark days of the early nineties and the near demise of Celtic. More recently, the club's official publication has reported on Celtic's domestic dominance and re-emergence as a serious contender in European competition.

The *View* has become an integral part of Celtic's identity and provides a vital link between the club and its supporters. Over the years that relationship has not always been smooth. In fact, more often than not, the quality of the relationship has been dependent on the success of the club at the time. A winning Celtic team has also provided a boost to the *Celtic View*'s circulation. In simple terms, it has meant that sales soar after a victory over Rangers and slide following a defeat.

The idea for a club publication came from Jack McGinn, who was working as a circulation representative with the *Daily Express* newspaper. Back in 1965, the number of column inches devoted to football was a fraction of what readers are served up now, while the Internet, Teletext, nightly radio phone-ins and 24-hour rolling sports news on satellite TV were probably not even the stuff of science fiction.

McGinn, thinking as a Celtic supporter as much as a newspaper man, believed that a club newspaper would provide supporters with more information about the club. However, it's difficult not to believe that there was also a nod to the 'paranoia' that Celtic fans are reputed to possess in great abundance when it comes to the Scottish press. An official publication would be able to give the club's '*View*' on any given matter at any given time without distortion.

After two presentations to the Celtic board, Jack McGinn attended a board meeting in early 1965 when the final decision on the project was made. It also happened to be the meeting at which Jock Stein's appointment as Celtic manager was confirmed. The new boss vowed that the Scottish Cup would be on the front page of the paper when it first hit the newsstands at the start of the 1965–66 season and he was true to his word, as Celtic defeated Dunfermline Athletic 3-2 to win the trophy.

The Celtic board gave McGinn the princely sum of £600 to set up the *Celtic View* and the first issue went on sale on Wednesday 11 August, priced 4d (2p). It sold just over 31,000 copies. Regardless of the sum involved, the investment still represented a gamble for the Celtic board and, given the success and longevity of the publication, it must be congratulated for backing Jack McGinn's plan.

With the benefit of hindsight, it also appears appropriate – fated even – that the *View* began at almost the same time as Jock Stein's reign at Celtic, and the club's newspaper was able to report on nine league championships in a row, eight Scottish Cups, six League Cups and, of course, the 1967 triumph in Lisbon when a club originally founded to raise money to feed the poor Irish immigrants in the East End of Glasgow became the Kings of Europe.

Jack McGinn himself remained as editor until 1979, when he was appointed the club's commercial manager. Two years later he was made a director, subsequently becoming chairman in the period which spanned the centenary season of 1987–88. By then, of course, the *Celtic View* had well and truly established itself as part of the club's identity with a faithful, if not uncritical, readership.

In one respect the centenary season represented the pinnacle of the 'old' Celtic, when the club was privately run by a handful of directors, most of whom had family links going back to Celtic's formation. Moving into the nineties, football was changing irrevocably, specifically in terms of finance, and by 1994 Celtic's failure to predict those changes, and to react to them once they had occurred, had left the club almost fatally wounded.

During those years, when it was becoming obvious to many supporters that the club was in the midst of decline – though few, if any, could have imagined that the decline would threaten to become terminal – the *Celtic View* suffered accordingly. It was, in the eyes of many supporters, guilty by association.

It was also at this time that fanzines began to emerge, not only at Celtic, but at football clubs throughout Britain. In Celtic's case, *Not the View* was easily the best and most popular of the new fanzines, and it labelled the official club publication Pravda, a reference to the state newspaper of the Soviet Union. The implication, of course, was that the *View* was simply the mouthpiece of a board in which supporters had lost faith.

While it was both humorous and cutting, in some respects the 'Pravda' reference went straight to the heart of the *Celtic View*'s *raison d'être*. As a publication it has to appeal to the Celtic board, the manager and the players, while, at the same time, remaining relevant and interesting to supporters. At all times, however, the *View* has to remember that it is the official publication of Celtic Football Club. That means that it cannot, and should not, provide a platform for the type of criticism of the team or the club that is all too prevalent in the various forums available to supporters today.

This undoubtedly turns some supporters off buying the *View*, but with so many external media outlets happy to criticise Celtic whenever it suits them, it makes no sense for the club's own publication to join in as well. That doesn't mean the *View* won't report on bad results – it will always record the facts – but it won't make personal criticisms of performances or tactics. On the rare occasions that this did happen in the past, it didn't reflect well on the magazine and didn't help it in any way. Everyone who works on the *View* is a Celtic supporter – they were before they joined the magazine and will continue to be long after leaving the magazine – so defeats and poor displays hurt the staff just as much as any other supporter.

Over the years, players and managers who have come and gone at Celtic have all appreciated the *View* and what it is trying to do. That is particularly true in this media-intense age, when what is said is not always what is subsequently reported in other outlets. What is said is published in the *View* without spin or twist. This is one of the *View*'s great strengths and also helps to build up trust in the club's publication. The *View* has to be doing something right, because newspapers 'steal' its stories on a weekly basis, sometimes acknowledging the original source, but quite often failing to do so.

As well as recording the history of Celtic since 1965, the *View* also offers a unique insight into the changing face of publishing in this country. The first issue of the *View* – which is also the first cover chosen for this book – was a four-page, broadsheet newspaper, produced almost entirely in black and white. The hundredth cover in this book – the first issue of the 2007–08 season – is a seventy-two-page, full colour, A4 magazine.

Along the way, the *View* has evolved, adding extra pages, more colour and glossier paper, before changing from a newspaper to a magazine. The pagination has grown to its present level and, on occasion, has exceeded it, most memorably in 2002 when a 148-page, perfect-bound (i.e. with a spine rather than stapled) issue was produced ahead of the World Cup.

Even the way in which events are reported on has evolved, from the understated manner of the sixties to the colourful brashness of the twenty-first century. Over the years, and thousands of issues, a whole range of different features have been introduced, with varying degrees of success.

The challenge of producing 45 issues of a magazine every season about one specific subject – Celtic – is to try to remain interesting and innovative season after season. Celtic's present will always remain the primary focus of the *View*, but the club's rich, varied and unique history will also continue to be mined for useful sources of stories. The fact the *View* remains a popular publication over 40 years after its inception is testament to the hard work of everyone who has worked on it.

Choosing which covers and relevant excerpts from that same edition to include was a labour of love and the difficulty came in deciding what to leave out. There have been so many important events in the club's history, as well as many eye-catching covers. This is particularly so in the 'magazine era' of the *View*. In looking through this book, you are taking a journey through over 40 years of Celtic history. I hope the covers will entertain and inform you, triggering memories of favourite moments of your Celtic-supporting years, or dredging up ones you'd thought you had managed to bury forever. I make no apologies for that – it is all part of our history.

For those of you lucky enough to have been alive during the Stein years, you'll be transported back to the sixties. Think of the victories, the great players you cheered from the Jungle, your journey to and from the ground which would, more likely than not, have involved public transport.

For supporters who idolised Danny McGrain and Kenny Dalglish in the seventies there is the good (winning nine in a row), the bad (Atletico Madrid at Celtic Park) and the ugly (the awful clothes you wore, which, at the time, you considered fashionable).

The eighties was the decade of drama; the 1985 Scottish Cup final, Love Street a year later and then the centenary season. Billy McNeill said there was a fairytale surrounding Celtic Football Club and the 1987–88 season proved his point.

It was all downhill from there as the early nineties brought tears and turmoil. It also brought Fergus McCann to Paradise and for that we should be eternally grateful. Henrik Larsson also came to Celtic in that decade, though he would prove to be the perfect twenty-first-century Bhoy as Celtic, under Martin O'Neill, took Scottish football by storm and reclaimed the domestic top spot.

And then there was Seville… Was that a triumph or a tragedy? For the fans, and what they did to enhance the name of Celtic in world football, it was a triumph. Yet, we still lost the final and who can honestly say they've ever watched that game again? Relive those moments and hope we'll see their likes again.

Celtic's dominance has continued under Gordon Strachan, who also guided the club further in the UEFA Champions League that anyone before him. The future is bright and the latest in Strachan's shrewd signings graces the final cover of this book. Italian midfielder Massimo Donati has that honour and he is another indicator of football's evolution. Back in 1965 when the *View* began, Celtic was a team full of Scots-born players. In 2007, the first-team squad is a veritable league of nations. It makes you wonder what the *Celtic View* front cover will look like in 2050.

Paul Cuddihy
Editor
Celtic View

THE HOOPS
No 331
© GF 18/10/01

SINCE MARTIN HAS BEEN HERE THE TEAM HAS BEEN LIKE HIS GARDEN.... HE'S PRUNED SOME OF IT BACK, PUT IN SOME OF HIS OWN STUFF AND NOW ITS BLOSSOMING AND PRODUCING FRUIT.... IS THAT HOW YOU SEE IT ?

HINGMY AIRPORT
FOR TORR -AN PORTO'S GROUND

YES... AND UNFORTUNATELY THE GARDEN...

...GOT TURNED OVER BY PORTO... SIGH!

OK SO WE GOT A BAD RESULT IN EUROPE.....BUT ACCORDING TO SOME OF OUR "EXPERTS" WE HAVEN'T BEEN OUTCLASSED AND OUTPLAYED SINCE.... SINCE EH.. SINCE...

SINCE WE WERE AT.....

we... eh the Gers fans are furious... to give so much and for us to lose... it's a travesty

7-1

DEAD EARLY EDITION !!! PORTO 3 CELTIC 0 CHANCE TO SLATE CELTS !!

...IBROX?

WE JUST NEED TO PUT THAT RESULT OUT OF OUR MINDS WHICH WILL BE VERY DIFFICULT !

GLESGA CUSTOMS
NO BOTHER !!!
CLUNK! CLUNK!
KIT BAG

WELL I DUNNO COS CELLIC FOLK DO HAVE A REPUTATION FOR OCCASSIONALLY MENTIONING PREVIOUS ONE-SIDED....

CELLIC 2 INTER 1 1967

GLESGA CUSTOMS
SIGH!!

...THREE GOAL MATCHES PLAYED IN PORTUGAL !!!

"Well Joe, I'm very flattered — isn't Paul McStay marvellous — that you should pay me this honour".

"Agnes, d'you hear me? I forgive you!"

AUGHEN ROVERS FC
NOTICES
MANAGER

"If you consider £500 a week an insult, we'll pay you monthly and that way you won't be insulted so often!"

AND WHO WAS THE WEE HUMORIST WHO GAVE AUNT AGATHA A SUBSCRIPTION TO 'THE CELTIC VIEW' FOR HER 80TH BIRTHDAY, THIS YEAR ?

LISBON OR BUST
PORTUGAL FRANCE
CELTIC
CELTIC

McP

You have to laugh, don't you?

You're a Celtic supporter, so if you don't laugh you go mad, but just when things threatened to get out of hand in the hilarity stakes, there was always the *Celtic View* cartoon to wipe that smile off your face. It's amazing how times and acceptable humour have changed, but listen to any Scottish post-match phone-in and the pundits will still be using the forty-year-old patter of the mysterious McP.

The CELTIC VIEW

ISSUE No. 1

AUGUST 11, 1965

PRICE FOURPENCE

PURPOSE OF THE NEW PAPER

THE Celtic board of management are now publishing the club's own newspaper. Today is the first issue of a project never before attempted by a football club in Scotland. We believe that our legions of faithful supporters and all who have Celtic at heart will welcome the novelty and that every Wednesday of the football season they will find in the "View" much to interest and delight them.

Our first job, of course, as a football club is to field a team worthy of your support, a team to win the major honours of the game and keep winning them, a team to restore to the full the glorious name of Celtic. That we believe we are in the process of doing.

But we think that a newspaper such as this, an almost exclusively Celtic newspaper, will help the support to enjoy even further such triumphs as may come. We shall provide information and talking points that the nations' press cannot give because of the much greater demands on their space.

We wish to emphasise that we have no intention of competing with the press, with whom we are on excellent terms.

"The Celtic View" will be of special value to our many supporters outwith Scotland and even abroad. Constantly we get requests for news and views of Celtic from the exiles. Our newspaper will satisfy this demand.

Through the medium of the paper we hope to form a closer relationship with the supporters and to work as a great Celtic team on and off the field.

We wish you good reading and the very best of watching.

Saturday, August 14

SCOTTISH LEAGUE CUP

DUNDEE UNITED
v.
CELTIC

(at Tannadice Park, kick-off 3 p.m.)

RESERVE LEAGUE CUP

Celtic
v.
Dundee United

(at Celtic Park, kick-off 3 p.m.)

McBRIDE'S MAGIC WORD

Of all the Celtic newcomers for the new season by far the best-known is Joe McBride. Joe scored almost 75 goals for Motherwell in the past two seasons. It is his ambition to score many more for Celtic.

Says Joe: "I really believe I am starting a new football life with Celtic. I always wanted to play for them. I have enjoyed playing for Motherwell. But this is different. Celtic is a magic word for me. I shall do my utmost to justify their confidence in me."

Scottish Cup Winning team, April 24, 1965—Back row: Young, Gemmell, Fallon, Murdoch, McNeill, Clark, and Front Row: Chalmers, Gallagher, Hughes, Lennox, Auld.

SCOTLAND TEAM BOSS AND CELTIC

THE news of the appointment of Jock Stein, Celtic's manager, to take charge of the Scottish international team, has surprised some of the club's supporters. It will be recalled that Celtic not long ago emphasised to the S.F.A. that the club had granted permission for their manager to act for Scotland only in connection with the two World Cup matches that were played in Poland and Finland in May of this year.

Mr. Robert Kelly, the Celtic chairman, takes this opportunity of putting the supporters fully in the picture.

"They are entitled to know the reasons," he says "why the directors have agreed to the new appointment of Mr. Stein, who will act as manager of Scotland only for so long as Scotland have an active interest in the current World Cup competition.

"There was a great deal of careful consideration of various angles before we consented to let Mr. Stein act as World Cup manager. We had to consider every possible implication.

"The fact that the S.F.A. asked for Mr. Stein's services despite the agreement with us that his term of office was over after the two World Cup games in May is very important. Clearly it is a great tribute to Mr. Stein and to the Club. Therefore we could hardly treat the further request lightly.

"All of us know that a successful Scottish International side can do nothing but good for the club game, our own included. Celtic Football Club will always be willing to do everything possible to foster the nation-wide game, so long as our club business gets proper attention.

"We know too, that the World Cup finals for which I hope sincerely Scotland under Mr. Stein will qualify, will be played at a time when the club season is over and we shall have no fixtures.

CONDITIONS

"But the most important aspect of our new agreement is that the S.F.A. were ready to meet all our conditions if they could get their man.

"We feel sure we have reached an ideal compromise that will be of help to all concerned and of disadvantage to no-one."

The key to the whole matter is in the first point of the agreement between Celtic and the S.F.A.—"that if there is any conflict between the Club's fixtures and those of the Association, Mr. Stein will remain with his club".

By Kerrydale

That clause in the agreement enables Celtic to have full power in an emergency of conflicting fixtures.

THE STEIN VIEW

Jock Stein himself has a most interesting and valid point to make. He told me when the news of his new Scottish appointment was announced last week:

"Naturally I am pleased with the honour. But I want all Celtic supporters to know that my interests will always be first and foremost Celtic's interests. It was my football ambition to return to Celtic. Everyone can rest assured that I wouldn't do anything likely to harm Celtic."

DEVELOPMENT FUND

The Celtic Development Fund welcome the advent of the club's own newspaper. It appreciates that "The Celtic View" will afford an unrivalled opportunity of informing the members of what is happening—not least in the prize-winning sense.

The Development Fund is looking for more agents for the Fund. Last month 15 of our agents and their partners enjoyed a holiday on the Continent because of their connection with the Development Fund. They were the lucky agents of the 1200 who went into a ballot for a bus-and-plane holiday in recognition of their services.

Continued on page 4

When the great Jock Stein first arrived at Celtic Park as manager in the later months of the 1964–65 season, he was told that the club would be publishing its own newspaper at the dawn of the forthcoming term.

It was then that he told Jack McGinn, the man behind the launch of the *Celtic View*, to keep a space on the front page for a photo of the team with the Scottish Cup, as he vowed to win the trophy and promised the *View* team they would get off to a flying start.

And so it happened. The new manager took charge of the Celts for the first time on 10 March 1965 and, just eleven games later, he fulfilled his promise as Celtic beat Dunfermline 3-2 in the Scottish Cup final. The *View* had its launch-pad front cover.

The aims of the new paper were set out in the very first paragraph, which proclaimed: 'The Celtic board of management are now publishing the club's own newspaper. Today is the first issue of a project never before attempted by a football club in Scotland. We believe that our legions of faithful supporters

ONE OF THE NEW BOYS

The youngest player on the staff is sixteen-year-old George Connelly, who joined us from Tulliallan and hails from Dunfermline.

George is the impressive height of 6 ft. 1 in., but for a very tall lad he is a skilful manipulator of the ball. He is an inside forward with no special preference for the right or left side of the field.

His older brother Joe plays for Valleyfield Juniors, the team for whom former Celtic favourite Jimmy Walsh played.

and all who have Celtic at heart will welcome the novelty and that every Wednesday of the football season they will find in the *View* much to interest and delight them.'

The price was 4d, or 2p in today's money, and the costs back then came in at a penny a page. The four pages contained only seven photographs, but featured no fewer than nineteen adverts, although these were mostly of the classified boxed type, such as those included on the front page (opposite).

Among the news stories, though, was a note that five Celtic players were in the Glasgow Select side to play Chelsea that night in the Glasgow Charity Cup match at Hampden. Those five players included skipper Billy McNeill, who was featured in that first edition proudly displaying the first ever Scottish Football Writers' Player of the Year award.

From little acorns… and it would seem that 1965 was a springboard for all and that the manager, the captain, the team and the *Celtic View* itself were destined to go on to bigger and better things.

THE CELTIC VIEW

ISSUE No. 40   MAY 11, 1966   PRICE 4d

BUSBY'S STARS PLAY AT CELTIC PARK

Manchester United here on August 6

THE first reward for Celtic supporters, to whom in another column Manager Jock Stein pays tribute for their help to the team in their league championship success, is a glamour game on the Saturday before the start of next season. Manchester United are coming to Celtic Park for a match on Saturday, August 6 — a match that will be treated by both clubs as a great challenge.

This is the first year in which Scotland's football authorities have permitted such a game in what is officially the close season. Celtic played Sunderland in a similar match last August and several thousands of Celtic supporters travelled to Roker Park. Now they will see one of the great clubs of Europe at Celtic Park.

FAMOUS NAMES

The name of Manchester United is famous throughout football. Matt Busby and his international players, Denis Law, Bobby Charlton, George Best, and former Celt Pat Crerand, are household words.

When Manager Stein fixed the August 6 match by telephone with Manager Busby last week he received a message of good luck for Celtic's two remaining league games. Mr. Busby hoped that Celtic would not in the end fail to get even one major honour as had happened to Manchester United.

United were considered hot favourites to reach the final of the European Cup and also of the English Cup. But they were eliminated in the semifinals within a week.

The Celtic-Manchester United match will be on the first-come-first-served principle of attendance. The prices will be:— Ground 4s; enclosure 8s; stand £1.

Mr. Stein thinks Celtic may see a big name in the United team when they come to Parkhead. Mr. Busby, he says, was disappointed that no trophy came to Old Trafford this season. A big United signing is likely.

Manchester United last played Celtic at Parkhead in April 1956 when they drew a charity match 2-2.

Congratulations

When last Wednesday night's league matches were over and it became known that Celtic would win the championship provided that they lost by no more than 5-0 at Motherwell on Saturday the majority of football enthusiasts considered that the race was at last over. The more cautious, however, did not dismiss the possibility of Rangers pipping Celtic on the post.

But on Thursday morning came two telegrams to Celtic Park which increased the confidence of Mr. Jock Stein. One was from Rangers vice-chairman John Wilson and it read:—

"The chase is over. This proves that the "Old Firm" are not infirm. Congratulations on winning the Scottish League. Best of luck in Europe next year."

The other, from Rangers manager Mr. Scot Symon read:— "Heartiest congratulations from all at Ibrox".

Those messages were most pleasing and courteous gestures from the "enemy".

WELSH SUPPORTER

One of the more recent enquiries as to how to become a member of a Celtic supporters club is from Glamorgan, Wales. The letter, from Mr. P. J. Stanbury, 14 Ffrwd Terrace, Llanbradach, Caerphilly, Glamorgan, has been passed to Celtic Supporters Association.

Among other telegrams of congratulation which have reached Celtic Park is one from Liverpool and one from former Celtic centre forward Billy McPhail, who wired:— "Congratulations to you all on a magnificent achievement."

Mr. Stein, the players, and the directors and other members of the staff wish through the "View" to thank everyone who sent good wishes.

Liverpool Sportsman

Much has been said and written about bad feelings caused by two European Cup-winners Cup semifinals between Celtic and Liverpool. It is therefore a great pleasure for us to publicise an act by a Liverpool supporter which deserves to be commended.

Mr. James Tobin of 90 Dervaig Street, Parkhead, Glasgow, called at Celtic Park at the weekend accompanied by a friend, Mr. John Rafferty, also of Parkhead. They produced a letter which included a postal order for £1. The letter, addressed to Mr. Tobin read:—

*1 Far Meadow Lane,
Irby,
Heswall,
Cheshire.*

*Dear Mr. Tobin,
Enclosed please find £1 in payment of our bet made at Anfield. I hope you are well, and who knows we may meet again next year in the European Cup.
The best of luck to you and Celtic in the future,
Yours sincerely,
K. Gill.*

The bet, Mr. Tobin explained, was made almost at the end of the semifinal at Anfield and after there was a disagreement as to whether Bobby Lennox's late goal should have been disallowed. Mr. Tobin told Mr. Gill that he thought Borussia Dortmund would beat Liverpool in the final. The bet was struck and addresses were exchanged.

"Mr. Gill is a real sportsman," says Mr. Tobin. "I've got to admit that I had forgotten all about the bet."

continued on page 4

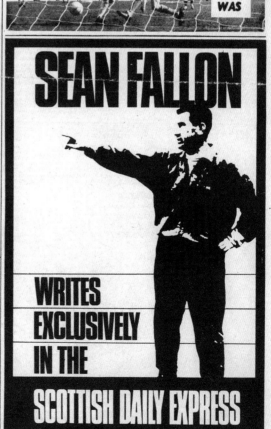

THE ONE THAT WASN'T

ABOVE: One of the chances Bobby Lennox missed in the match at Motherwell.
RIGHT: One that he didn't miss and the goal gave Celtic the league championship with a margin of two points over the runners-up, Rangers.

THE ONE THAT WAS

FROM THE BACKROOM
The Manager's Review

THE season of great hope and expectation has ended. I have never tried to conceal the fact that right from the start the league championship was our principal ambition. Now the flag will fly at Celtic Park at the start of the new season.

In early editions of the "View" I pointed out that we must at all cost seek consistency. Before I returned to Celtic the team had played many fine games but they had not been consistent enough to bring real honours to the club.

The signing of Joe McBride was an attempt to improve our goalscoring ability, and I think he has throughly justified his transfer fee. He is leading scorer in the league even though he has missed several matches both early in the season and at the vital late stage.

SEAN FALLON

WRITES EXCLUSIVELY IN THE SCOTTISH DAILY EXPRESS

It may not, according to this front page of the *View* anyway, look like Celtic Football Club have just clinched their first championship in twelve long and arduous years, but perhaps in those bygone days the official organ of the club was the master of the understatement.

A week earlier, the midweek scores ensured that Celtic would have to be beaten 4-0 by a Motherwell side who sat third bottom of the league for Rangers to have any chance of pipping the Bhoys to the title. However, on 7 May 1966, as 20,000 looked on, with many making use of the Fir Park terracing roof as a vantage point, the Bhoys left it late, with Bobby Lennox waiting until the last minute of the last game of the season before knocking in from close range to ensure Celtic won the title by two points over their Ibrox rivals. And yet it would seem that a banner headline proclaiming 'Champions' was not the done thing as far as the *View* custodians of the day were concerned.

The rampant Celts had already lifted the League Cup that season by beating Rangers, but had lost out in the Scottish Cup final to the same team after a replay. That 1-0 win over Motherwell clinched the championship, but the *View* revealed that congratulations had been forthcoming from Ibrox in the immediate aftermath of the previous midweek results.

A telegram from Rangers manager Scot Symon arrived on the morning of Thursday 5 May, saying: 'Heartiest congratulations from all at Ibrox.' Another, from the Ibrox club's vice-chairman John Wilson, said: 'The chase is over. This proves that the Old Firm are not infirm. Congratulations on winning the Scottish League. Best of luck in Europe next year.' The final line may have been added as nothing more than an afterthought, but those words were to come back and haunt some not-so-magnanimous followers of the Ibrox club's fortunes just twelve months later – and still do to this day.

The back page featured an advert with the *Sunday Mirror* trumpeting its upcoming coverage of Celtic's tour of North America. Little did anyone know just how much that transatlantic jaunt would mean to the club.

'MISS CELTIC'

"Miss Celtic" of 1966 is Kathleen English, of 2 Gilburn Road Kilmacolm, the representative of Port Glasgow No. 1 Celtic Supporters' Club. Kathleen was adjudged winner of the title at the final staged by Celtic Supporters' Association in the Locarno Ballroom, Glasgow on May 3. In the picture above she is being congratulated by Mr. John Bonnar, former Celtic goalkeeper of Coronation Cup fame, who is now secretary and organiser of the Celtic Development Fund.

THE CELTIC VIEW

Issue No. 91   MAY 3, 1967   Price 4d.

SCOTTISH CUP TRIUMPH

One of the sights many Celtic supporters would have enjoyed seeing after the Scottish Cup final victory—Willie Wallace, scorer of both Celtic goals, with the trophy won by his club for the nineteenth time.

Another Record Imminent

CELTIC are within one league point of creating yet another Scottish club record. Since the League Cup was stared in its present form 20 years ago the clubs in the Scottish League have been able to take part in three main competitions—the league championship, the League Cup, and the Scottish Cup. Rangers have twice achieved the feat of winning all three competitions in one season—in 1948-49 and in 1963-64. Now Celtic are about to equal that record.

But Celtic are also winners of the Glasgow Cup this season and Rangers in their two most successful years did not also win the Glasgow Cup (or, in the days when it was open to the Glasgow clubs, the Charity Cup).

So when Celtic win the 1966-67 league championship they will become the first club ever to win every home competition open to them in the last 20 years.

In addition, of course, there is the European Cup, in which Celtic are the first British club to qualify for the final.

1966-67 Details

Played	58

(League championship 31, League Cup 10, European Cup 8, Scottish Cup 6, Glasgow Cup 3).

Won	49
Drawn	7
Lost	2
Goals For	188
Goals Against	42

(Competitive matches only : up to and including April 29)

COMPETITION WINNERS

The six winners of one guinea in Competition No. 90 are:—
John Watson, 56 Laverock Terrace, Moodiesburn (age 14, St. Barbard's School, Muirhead), *Mary McLaughlan,* 28 Lang Avenue, Renfrew (age 13, St.

Margaret's Senior Secondary School, Paisley).
Agnes Fyfe, 109 Ryeside Road, Glasgow, N.1 (age 14, St. Roch's Junior Secondary School).
James McGunnigle, 475 Royston Road, Glasgow, N.1 (age 11, St. Roch's Primary School).
Thomas Maher, 23 Dunmore Street, Glasgow, C.5 (age. 14, Holyrood School).
Ann Dillon, 44 Elizabeth Crescent, Cumnock (age 9 St. John's Primary School).

'CELTIC BOYS'

This week's "Celtic Boy" is Martin Kerr, 10 Finn Park, Toronto, Canada. Martin is 12, and his favourite player is John Hughes. Martin is on holiday in Scotland and if he is still in the vicinity of Glasgow on Wednesday, he is invited to meet his favourite at Celtic Park before the league game with Dundee United. Last week's "Celtic Boy," John Casey, also should come to the official entrance on Wednesday night at 6.50 prompt.

"The Celtic View" having been registered at the General Post Office as a newspaper, copies of it published on and after October 26, 1966, are transmissible through the post in the United Kingdom at the newspaper rate of postage and to Canada (including Newfoundland) at the magazine rate of postage up to September 30, 1967.

A matter for regret—and warning

SUCCESS in the Scottish Cup final crowned a great week for Celtic and the directors and management of the club share the delight of the players and the supporters.

What a great pity it is that a great day did not end without a disturbing note.

The Celtic chairman, Mr. Robert Kelly, speaks for the club when he says:—

"We are sorry that once again a magnificent Celtic occasion was to some degree adversely affected by the misconduct of some of our "supporters"—first by their behaviour during the playing of the National Anthem before the match; second by the rowdiness of alleged supporters who had travelled from Belfast.

REPUTATION

"The directors and management of Celtic Football Club pay tribute to the splendid efforts of the team, who have ensured that Celtic's reputation stands high not only in Britain but all over Europe. Indeed it is greater now than ever it was.

"We are determined to do everything in our power to eliminate any conduct on the part of 'supporters' which in any way is liable to detract from the glory of Celtic's wonderful achievements."

The Celtic officials wish also to point out that though they can understand the crowd's disappointment that the Scottish Cup was not paraded by the team at the end of the match they are in agreement with the decision not to have what are known as "laps of honour" on such occasions. There is always the chance that some spectators allow their enthusiasm to get the better of them and invade the pitch, thereby giving those who are not greatly enamoured of a Celtic success the chance to be critical.

TONIGHT'S MATCH

The Scottish Cup will be prominently displayed tonight when Celtic play Dundee United with a 7.30 kick-off. There is an excellent chance of Celtic winning the league championship tonight, so the time for celebration will be ripe.

ALTERATIONS

Note—Because of reconstruction of the enclosure opposite the stand that section of the ground will not be open.

By KERRYDALE

LISBON

•

If you are going to see the final in Lisbon on May 25th do it right—take your wife and stay a few days at the

MIRAMONTE HOTEL
Praia das Macas

a British-owned, British-run country hotel 30 minutes coach ride from Lisbon.

You have no fear of a Lisbon tummy with us.

Apply :

Claygate House
Reigate 45741

PRAGUE DELIGHT

JOHN FALLON has not played a single first-team game for Celtic this season. But no one was more delighted than the man who has been deposed by Ronnie Simpson when the final whistle blew in the Juliska Stadium, Prague, and Celtic had qualified for the final of the European Cup.

Backroom experts Bob Rooney, Sean Fallon, and Neil Mochan along with Manager Jock Stein share the happy moment.

How times had changed in the very short lifespan of the *View*, as the first edition had contained an advert for Cotter's buses letting supporters' clubs know they had single- and double-decker coaches for hire.

Now, in only the *View*'s second season, this particular edition carried an ad by Preston Travel Service, proclaiming 'Aircraft available for Lisbon' with prices ranging from £27 15s per passenger for a seventy-two-seater to £40 19s per person for a forty-four-seater.

And the reason for this elevation to the upper echelons of transportation? Quite simple really, as this copy of the *View* pointed out in somewhat muffled terms in the bottom right-hand corner – a 0-0 draw in Prague's Juliska stadium with Dukla meant, at the first time of asking, Celtic had reached the final of the European Cup.

Lisbon was the key word in this issue and it was mentioned everywhere including in two adverts which rather craftily didn't mention the venue of the Portugal final, but offered personal loans! One

wonders why the companies felt the need to advertise their services in the *View* and how many readers applied without their other half knowing anything about it.

There was a perfectly viable reason why reaching the European Cup final was allotted that space in the bottom right-hand corner of the front page, though. The news was a week old after all and, in between times, the Celts had also lifted the Scottish Cup, after beating Aberdeen 2-0 at Hampden in front of a crowd of 126,102.

Front-page pin-up Bhoy Willie Wallace, or 'Oor Wullie' as the banner proclaims, netted both goals as the Celts claimed the trophy for the twenty-second time and now sat within touching point of another record. In the league they were one point away from claiming the title and doing so would complete the treble. Rangers had achieved this twice before, but failed to win the Glasgow Cup on both occasions. Celtic already had the three cups – Glasgow, League and Scottish – in the bag and were homing in on the title, so it was three down and two to go.

Five "Celtic Boys" with their favourite players in the boardroom at Celtic Park. They are, from left to right (favourite player in brackets)—Michael Irvine (Willie Wallace), James Sherry (Jimmy Johnstone), Tommy Gormley (Jimmy Johnstone), Denis McDonach (Bobby Lennox), Gerry Allan (John Clark).

The trophies in the background are, left to right, 1901 Exhibition Cup, St. Mungo Cup, League Championship Trophy, League Cup, Glasgow Cup, Coronation Cup, League Shield (awarded to Celtic for winning six league championships in succession from 1905 to 1910).

THE CELTIC VIEW

Issue No. 92   MAY 10, 1967   Price 4d.

The Jimmy Johnstone One-two

Jock Stein Says:

WELL, we've completed the clean sweep of the Scottish senior football competitions and I don't need to emphasise how happy I am. My first duty now is to give my great thanks to the players who have fought so nobly for the club and to the Celtic directors who have given me magnificent support in trying to build a team to enhance the club's reputation.

Never before in modern times have a Scottish club won all the competitions open to them. Now the league championship trophy remains in our boardroom and stands alongside the Scottish Cup, the League Cup, and the Glasgow Cup.

We have, of course, one more job to do. We cannot relax for long, for the European Cup final at Lisbon lies ahead and we are going to try to win this one just as hard as we did the others.

IBROX DECIDER

It was, of course, especially pleasing to win the title finally at Ibrox against the only team who have been challenging us for many weeks. It was also gratifying to see so good a match in such difficult conditions.

So heavy was the rain in the hours before the kick-off that I wondered if the game would go on. I think that if the torrential rain had continued for another half-hour there would have been a postponement. As it was we were fortunate in that while the rain did not cease throughout the match it became much less heavy.

What a mess the league authorities would have been in

(Continued on page 4)

Competition Winners

The six winners of one guinea in Competition No. 91 of the issue of May 3, 1967, are:—

Peter Degnan, 2 Moore Park Drive, Glasgow, S.W.2 (age 9, St. George's School, Penilee).

Marle Barr, 60 Hart Street, Linwood, Renfrewshire (age 8, St. Conval's School).

Peter McArthur, 118 Arnprior Road, Glasgow, S.5 (age 7, Dougrie Terrace School).

Marian Kelly, 1240 Royston Road, Glasgow, E.3 (age 12, Our Lady and St. Francis School).

Robert Verner, 20 Moss Avenue, Linwood, Renfrewshire (age 10, St. Conval's School).

John Kelly, 15 Fincraig Street, Dundee (age 9, St. Luke's Primary School).

European Cup Souvenir Issue

The ninety-third issue of "The Celtic View" will take the form of a special souvenir in connection with the European Cup.

Several of the usual features will be omitted in order to make room for articles and pictures relative to Celtic having reached the final.

The club colours will be much more freely represented in next week's edition and the Celtic directors and management are confident that all Celtic supporters will wish to be sure of a copy. You should make certain by ordering the "View" from your newsagent now, or applying to the "View" office for subscription copies to be mailed to you (see foot of page 2).

Jimmy Johnstone's goals in the 2-2 draw at Ibrox—the result that finally enabled Celtic to retain the league championship. Above—the first goal, here—the second. The latter, shot with his left foot after he had cut inside from a throw-in and beaten two Rangers players, is almost certainly his best ever.
The state of the ground after several hours of rain is shown particularly in the lower picture.

A RURITANIAN VIEW

THE Editor has received the following letter in connection with a matter that has caused some concern :—

7 Arundel Drive, Bishopbriggs.

Sir,

As further proof of Celtic's ever-growing European reputation, I enclose an excerpt from a Ruritanian newspaper which, despite one or two minor mistakes, reveals, as I am sure you will agree, a remarkable grasp of the state of Scottish football today:—

"The Scottish team manager, Mr. Helenio Herrera, has succeeded in arranging a fixture with North Borneo to be played in Sarawak on 24th May, eve of the European Cup final in Lisbon. He told reporters yesterday that his pool would include 27 Celtic players and that he would also need Messrs. Stein, Fallon, Rooney and Mochan to help sell programmes before the game.

"Explaining the rather large number of Celtic men chosen, Mr. Herrera pointed out that Rangers players are unavailable since they are to play a fourth division Madagascar side in a vital friendly that evening; he added that this was a prestige match, not just for Rangers but for Scotland and that therefore nothing must be done to impair Rangers' chances of success.

"Arrangements have been made to fly the Celtic contingent to Malaga immediately after the game, where donkeys will be waiting to carry them over the 300 miles of mountainous country to Lisbon. All going well, they will reach the stadium at 5.25, well in time to line up against Inter Milan at 5.30.

"No effort or expense was too great, said Mr. Herrera, to give Celtic every chance of bringing the Cup home to Scotland. All Scotland was proud of Celtic and Mr. Herrera was confident they would not let Scotland down. But we had to get our priorities right—first things first, and right now the main job is to beat the North Borneans."

There are admittedly some discrepancies in this report, but, apart from the completely pardonable mistake—shared, I may add, by many people in Scotland—that Mr. Herrera is responsible for picking the Scottish team it is surely a great tribute to Celtic in particular and Scottish football in general that even such remote corners of Europe as Ruritania should be so well informed, at least in essentials, about what is happening in Scotland.

Yours, etc.,

Patrick Reilly.

1966-67 RECORD

Played	... ...	60

(League championship 33, League Cup 10, European Cup 8, Scottish Cup 6, Glasgow Cup 3.)

Won	... ...	49
Drawn	... ...	8
Lost	... ...	3
Goals For	... ...	192
Goals Against	...	47

(Competitive matches only : up to and including May 6)

It was now four down and one to go, although, once again, you would never have guessed it from the *View* front page as there was no trace of triumphalism, *schadenfreude*, blowing of trumpets or banging of drums as Celtic claimed the title at Ibrox.

SUBSCRIPTION COPIES

If you would like a copy of " The Celtic View " mailed to you weekly (home or abroad) complete this coupon and send it to: The Editor, 48 Renfrew Street, Glasgow, C.2.

NAME ....
(block letters)

ADDRESS ....
(block letters)

....
(Total weekly cost is sevenpence)

RATES

	AIR-MAIL
	U.S.A. and Canada
	52 weeks £2 12s. 0d.
	13 weeks 13s. 0d.
SURFACE MAIL.	4 weeks 4s. 0d.
Great Britain and Abroad	Australia and New Zealand
52 weeks £1 10s. 4d.	52 weeks £3 0s. 8d.
13 weeks 7s. 7d.	13 weeks 15s. 2d.
4 weeks 2s. 4d.	4 weeks 4s. 8d.

Two chalk and cheese goals from Jimmy Johnstone on a rain-sodden pitch helped the Bhoys to a 2-2 draw as the team completed a clean sweep of all the domestic trophies available to them.

On 6 May 1967, almost a year to the day of their previous title win, Jock Stein's side kept the ball rolling with their second successive championship. With one game left to play, against Kilmarnock, it could have been all so different if Jinky hadn't managed those two goals, and it would seem that the powers that be in Scottish football at the time weren't doing their utmost to keep things on an even keel – or even boost the club's chances of glory in the European Cup.

In all, nine Celts were chosen for a Scotland friendly against the USSR, while Rangers, also due to play a friendly game, were excused international duty. Jock Stein said in the *View*: 'One of the real snags, of course, was the choice of no fewer than nine Celtic players for the pool of sixteen for the international tonight. Compare that with the situation regarding Rangers players and the game with Russia [sic].

'The international was arranged long before Rangers fixed up to play a friendly match in Toronto. Yet their players are released from international commitments while ours get the heavy bend of the stick. If the position weren't so serious it would be laughable.'

Seven Celts played in the 2-0 defeat under the captaincy of former Rangers player Jim Baxter.

All eyes were increasingly turned towards the impending European Cup final, but an advert on the front page showed that the Universal Travel Agency clearly didn't think that Celtic, or Inter Milan for that matter, would tie things up on 25 May. In the event of a draw, the replay was scheduled for Saturday 27 May at the same venue and the said travel agency asked: 'Why charter and miss the replay?' Oh ye of little faith!

THE CELTIC VIEW

Tradition . . .

By BOB KELLY

IT is no exaggeration to say that all of those who love Celtic are in happy, thankful mood—happy with the great successes in the club's greatest season, thankful that the players and the management have been blessed with fine health and spirit.

I as club chairman am, of course, particularly delighted—for three principal reasons. Having been reared in a Celtic family—my father, James Kelly, played in the very first Celtic team and when his playing days were over became a director and then chairman of the club —I am steeped in Celtic tradition.

In my father's day and in mine, Celtic have always preferred to play attacking football whenever it was possible. Who would say we have not maintained this tradition in the past season?

Chairman of Celtic

Secondly, though we have bought senior players when the need arose Celtic have always preferred to rear our own players.

The backbone of all our teams has been the young man brought up to believe in the club and to feel honoured in playing for the club. Again we have fully maintained the tradition.

Last, but not least important, is the third principal reason.

ALL SCOTTISH

Celtic will play in the European Cup final with an entirely Scottish eleven. It is often claimed that a club which reaches a final in European competition represents their country as well as club. I claim that Celtic can most fittingly represent Scotland because we are an all-Scottish eleven. Few if any of the famous teams of Europe, Real Madrid, Inter Milan, and the rest can make such a claim—in some degree they have been International clubs.

You will therefore understand why I and my directors and all at Celtic Park are very happy at this proud moment of Celtic's history.

Mr. Robert Kelly has been a director of Celtic since 1931 and chairman since 1948. He is a former president of the Scottish Football Association and also a former president of the Scottish Football League.

TV AND RADIO

The whole of the Lisbon final will be televised live by both B.B.C. and S.T.V.

The match will also be broadcast on the Light Programme of the B.B.C. at 5.30.

There will also be a second half radio commentary on the B.B.C.'s World Service.

1966-67 Record

Played	... ...	60

(League championship 33, League Cup 10, European Cup 8, Scottish Cup 6, Glasgow Cup 3).

Won	... ...	49
Drawn	... ...	8
Lost	... ...	3
Goals For	... ...	192
Goals Against	...	47

(competitive matches only: up to and including May 6)

Published by the Celtic Football and Athletic Co., Ltd., and printed by Civic Press Ltd., Printers and Stationers, 26 Civic Street, Glasgow, C.4. ("View" telephone DOU 0097).

European Cup

FINAL IN LISBON

Souvenir Issue

CELTIC THE FIRST

NOT only are Celtic the first team in Scotland to qualify for the final of the European Cup, they are the first in Britain to achieve that distinction. It is an especially worthy feat in that this is Celtic's first-ever entry to the foremost club competition in Europe.

The 1966-67 season has been one of "firsts" for Celtic. For the first time they won all three major honours in Scotland—League Championship, Scottish Cup, and League Cup. Having also won the Glasgow Cup, they are the first and only club since the League Cup was started in its present form in 1946 to win every national competition open to them.

The Hampden Record

THE biggest attendance in the 11 previous finals of the European Cup was 135,000 at Hampden Park in 1960. The results of the finals have been :—

1956	Real Madrid	4	Rheims	3	Paris
1957	Real Madrid	2	Fiorentina	0	Madrid
1958	Real Madrid	3	Milan	2	Brussels
			(after extra time)		
1959	Real Madrid	2	Rheims	0	Stuttgart
1960	Real Madrid	7	Eintracht	3	Glasgow
			(Frankfurt)		
1961	Benfica	3	Barcelona	2	Berne
1962	Benfica	5	Real Madrid	3	Amsterdam
1963	Milan	2	Benfica	1	London
1964	Inter Milan	3	Real Madrid	1	Vienna
1965	Inter Milan	1	Benfica	0	Milan
1966	Real Madrid	2	Partizan	1	Brussels
			(Belgrade)		

. . . Fitness

By JOCK STEIN

EVERYONE connected with Celtic knows how much effort the players have made in the past few months; they have done a magnificent job. They have one more effort to make—the greatest of them all—before they enjoy a well deserved rest. And make it they will.

I shall probably surprise many people by saying in the week before the European Cup final that capable players as the Celtic lads are they go into the final inferior in the skills of the game to their opponents. We in Britain are still behind the best of the European clubs in the arts and crafts of the game. That does not mean to say I am pessimistic about our prospects against Inter Milan in Lisbon on May 25—far from it.

It does mean that we shall have to play with all of our traditional spirit, to be able to play at the greatest pace we can find, and—most important of all—to be in 100 per cent physical condition, prepared to play till we drop for the club and the wonderful supporters we have.

It is a manager's dream to have a team of great skill and superb physical fitness. It would be foolish to say now that we have such a combination. But we are on the way—no one would deny us that. And our efforts to match the best in the world will be intensified whatever happens in Lisbon.

Inter have a clear advantage, of course, in that they have considerable experience of the great occasions in Europe. We are only beginning to get to know them.

Next Thursday night will make us much richer in experience and, who knows, perhaps champions of Europe also.

Manager of Celtic

Mr. John (Jock) Stein, was captain of the Celtic team who won the Coronation Cup in 1953 and the League Championship and Scottish Cup in 1954. When his playing career ended through injury he became Celtic's coach. Then he went to Dunfermline Athletic as manager and on to Hibernian in the same role. He became manager of Celtic a little more than two years ago.

REPLAY?

If the teams are level at the end of 90 minutes half an hour's extra time will be played. If a replay is necessary it will take place on the same ground on Saturday, May 27.

FIRST-TEAM POOL

Standing—Jim Craig, Tommy Gemmell, Billy McNeill (captain), Ronnie Simpson, Bobby Murdoch, John Clark, John Cushley, Willie O'Neill.

Sitting — Jimmy Johnstone, Charlie Gallagher, Willie Wallace, Steve Chalmers, Joe McBride, Bobby Lennox, Bertie Auld, John Hughes.

ISSUE No. 93

MAY 17, 1967   PRICE 4d.

Champions of Scotland

[Winners of League Championship, Scottish Cup, League Cup, Glasgow Cup]

This wasn't the final edition of the *View* before the Celts took to the sun-kissed turf of the Estadio Nacional in Lisbon, but to all intents and purposes it was the preview.

Another issue hit the streets on the eve of the final, but by then the green and white legions would have been well on their way to Lisbon and the main message of the *View* published on 24 May was, win or lose in Lisbon, stay away from Glasgow Airport when the team return on Friday – aye right! It should be said, though, that, although the *View* urged supporters to steer clear of Celtic's touchdown in Glasgow, it did conveniently let all readers know that the plane would arrive at 6.30pm!

This 17 May issue was the real deal as far as Lisbon souvenir specials go and there was a break with tradition with this one-off masthead, plenty of green type on the front and back pages, and no adverts at all throughout.

Inside there was a guide to Lisbon, although imparting the information that: 'Visitors must carry a valid passport. Application

EMPIRE EXHIBITION CUP
Celtic won this trophy, which is a replica in miniature of the tower that was a landmark of the Empire Exhibition in Glasgow in 1938, at Ibrox. Eight teams competed— Aberdeen, Celtic, Hearts, Rangers, Brentford, Chelsea, Everton, and Sunderland. Celtic beat Sunderland 3-1 (after a goalless draw and extra time), Hearts 1-0, and Everton (in the final) by 1-0 after extra time.

VICTORY IN EUROPE CUP
The Victory in Europe Cup was won by Celtic in May, 1945. The trophy was presented by the Glasgow Charity Cup committee, who invited Celtic and Rangers to play for it. Rangers declined, and Queen's Park, who deputised lost at Hampden by one goal and two corner kicks to Celtic's one goal and three corner kicks. Like the Empire Exhibition Cup of 1938, the Coronation Cup, the St. Mungo Cup, the League Shield and the Exhibition Cup (1901) this trophy is Celtic's permanent possession.

(with two passport photographs) to 14 Princes Square, Glasgow, G1, must be made in person' was probably a tad tardy.

Those who couldn't make the sabbatical would have to make do with the black and white images transmitted back from Portugal and some would have to settle for even less than that. The *View* stated: 'The whole of the Lisbon final will be televised live by both BBC and STV. The match will also be broadcast on the Light Programme of the BBC at 5.50. There will also be a second-half radio commentary on the BBC's World Service.'

But back to that guide to Lisbon and, among the handy hints, it stated: 'Climate at this time of year pleasantly warm; light clothing is best. The Portuguese are more formal than most in the matter of clothing; men do not go about without wearing a jacket; shorts are not encouraged.'

Page two of the *View* featured photos and info on ten of the trophies on show in the Celtic boardroom and, last of all, in the bottom right-hand corner, from May 1945 was the Victory in Europe Cup – an omen perhaps!

THE CELTIC VIEW

Issue No. 95   MAY 31, 1967   Price 4d.

European Cup Triumph

BY JOCK STEIN

Lesson of Lisbon

IT is my great privilege and pleasure to put on record through the columns of our own newspaper Celtic Football Club's congratulations to the players, manager, and staff who have completed the greatest season in the history of Celtic by winning the European Cup.

It is my particular delight that the majority of these players who have brought wonderful credit to the club are very young lads with us, imbued with the Celtic spirit which is essential.

British type

Naturally, of course, the winning of the European Cup has given me the finest hours

BY ROBERT KELLY

of my many years with Celtic. In spite of the modern trends of recent years I was confident that the old basic type of British football, attacking and entertaining, would return and again prove its worth. I visualised that concentration on defence and a win-at-any-price football would drive spectators away from the game. I was determined that Celtic would lead the way back to the old—admittedly a streamlined old.

I have always thought that football is the greatest spectator sport in the world and I was not going to have any part of encouraging its decline and latterly its ruination. Now our lads have put us in the forefront of world football by playing entertaining attractive football.

Lesson

Our supporters have, of course, played a magnificent part with their encouragement. Maybe some of them will think back to the days when they were not just so helpful but to some extent or another impatient.

From now on every team will be out to beat the European champions; it will be difficult to maintain our very high standard of the moment. But with the supporters' encouragement and the kind of help we have had in the glorious season now ended we shall move on to further success.

THE DAY OF GLORY

Reports of the superb display of Celtic in winning the European Cup have by this time gone round the world of football, but there still are many to whom Celtic Football Club is dear who have had but scant accounts of the manner of the defeat of Inter Milan. One must emphasise to these Celtic supporters in distant parts that the 2-1 score does not in the slightest give an indication of the disparity between the sides.

Though it took Celtic a full hour in the burning sunshine of Lisbon to neutralise the seventh-minute goal by Mazzola they had been so superior in the arts of attacking football that defeat seemed out of the question. When the winning goal came six minutes from time not only the 10,000 Celtic supporters but all the spectators except the disillusioned Italians hailed the new champions.

FATIGUE

Inter were so fatigued that they could not make even a token effort of trying to take the game into extra time. Indeed I am sure some of them would have collapsed exhausted had they had to undertake another 30 minutes of chasing and marking these wonderfully fit and fast Celtic players.

Manager Jock Stein in common with the majority of the great football managers of the world believes that if a team cannot make sufficient scoring chances they will not win much; even the defensively minded Inter Milans of the football world know they cannot always live on defence.

Lisbon pictures by courtesy Scottish Daily Express.

By KERRYDALE

That being so, one must pay tribute to the Celtic team who made so many chances against the perfectionist Italian defenders that had it not been for the inspired Sarti, who had more than the fair share of luck which hovers benevolently over all good goalkeepers Inter would have suffered a humiliating defeat.

Bertie Auld struck the crossbar and so did Tommy Gemmell, and had Celtic been awarded two penalty kicks they would not have been receiving more than their due. The foul of Sarti's when with both hands he gripped Willie Wallace's ankles almost on the goal-line was much more glaring an offence than that for that

(Continued on page 4)

ONE of the things we did at Seamill while we were making our final plans to try to win the European Cup was to watch from start to finish the film of that great match at Hampden in 1960 between Real Madrid and Eintracht in the European Cup final of that year. All of us had seen it several times, but none of us tires watching the very fine play that is portrayed in it.

Seeing it once again enabled me to urge the Celtic players to try to emulate the very high standard of attacking football, the entertaining football which made the match memorable. We of Celtic, I said, should try our utmost to emulate the teams and the players of that 1960 final.

Skill

Now on reflection I think we at least partly succeeded. I said in the recent souvenir issue of the "View" that, generally speaking, we in Britain were behind the top club teams in Europe in terms of skill and that we had to offset that disadvantage by being at our fittest, playing at our top speed, and showing our club spirit.

I think it is fair to say now that we beat Inter Milan in the way we thought we might but that we also matched them and even defeated them in the skills of the game. The reason for that is that we did not permit them to use the skill on which they have depended so much—the highly technical defensive skill which enables them to dictate the pace of a game and to strike suddenly in attack by means of the long ball.

I might add that Inter Milan's manager, Helenio Herrera, might have been better off if he hadn't come to see us playing Rangers when he did. That day he saw Celtic in dreadful conditions display their great stamina. I am sure he went home a very worried man, because weeks before the European Cup final he was preparing excuses. In the event we were the carefree side and the more famous, more world-wide experienced, Inter Milan the troubled one.

Madrid

Now our lads who have brought so much credit to the club have one more game before they go on a well deserved holiday. We play Real Madrid

(Continued on page 4)

This is Celtic's record for competitive matches in season 1966-67 :—

Played	62

(Scottish League 34, League Cup 10, European Cup 9, Scottish Cup 6, Glasgow Cup 3).

Won	51
Drawn	8
Lost	3
Goals for	196
Against	48

Two friendly games were played and resulted: Celtic 4, Manchester United 1 ; Celtic 0, Dinamo Zagreb 1.

The above picture was taken just before the full invasion of the Lisbon playing pitch at the end of the European Cup final. It typifies the real strength of Celtic—the happy combination of players (as represented by Billy McNeill), the men behind the players (Jock Stein) and the supporters. Ronnie Simpson is just behind the deliriously happy trio, with, we suspect, a tear or two of joy in his eyes.

In the picture below the wall of Inter defenders is penetrated by Tommy Gemmell (second from the left) for the equalising goal.

CUP RULE

Many requests have already been received at Celtic Park for the European Cup to be displayed outwith the Club's premises.

The directors regret that it will not be possible for this new and extremely valuable trophy to be on show anywhere but at Celtic Park.

Those who have already written should consider this notice as an official reply.

This is what the *View* was made for. When the idea of the newspaper was first mooted the club had been in the doldrums as far as silverware was concerned and now, at the end of its second year, every trophy available shone brightly in the Paradise boardroom as the front page proclaimed 'European Cup Triumph'.

Tommy Gemmell and Stevie Chalmers scored the all-important goals as Celtic defeated Inter Milan 2-1 in Lisbon to spark unbridled joy from Portugal to Parkhead. It would appear, though, that the trophy itself wasn't about to do the rounds, as the *View* stated: 'Many requests have already been received at Celtic Park for the European Cup to be displayed outwith the club's premises. The directors regret that it will not be possible for this new and extremely valuable trophy to be put on show anywhere except Celtic Park. Those who have already written should consider this notice as an official reply.'

The *View* also proudly proclaimed Celtic's record in all competitive matches – league thirty-four, League Cup ten, European Cup nine, Scottish Cup six and Glasgow Cup three. The record was:

P	W	D	L	F	A
62	51	8	3	196	48

One of those drawn games was a drab affair on a dreich day at lowly Stirling Albion and in a season when Celtic blazed a trail throughout Europe and won every single competition they entered, and in the wake of celebrating lifting world football's top club trophy at the first time of asking, the *View* marked the occasion by devoting the main story on page three to that dismal February draw at Annfield in Stirling! The back page noted that one of the youngsters who came up trumps in the competition from the previous *View* was a Liam Gallagher – it couldn't be, could it?

This issue also featured another link with Italy as the Scots College in Rome had just lifted the Gregorian Championship by beating the English College for the sixth year running. The Scots seminary won 4-2 and played the final resplendent in their Celtic green and white hoops.

SCOTS COLLEGE FOOTBALL SUCCESS

THE CELTIC VIEW

Issue No. 189   APRIL 30, 1969   Price 4d.

THE CUP FINAL

WELL, the match of the season is over — at least what so many people described as the match of the season, the Scottish Cup Final, is over. The last Saturday in April, the last Saturday of the Scottish Club season was to be the moment of decision for two clubs, the time when one or other was to gain the clear upper hand for the season.

The only accurate statement of these is the fact that the game was the Scottish Cup final. I can tell you with full conviction that though Celtic dearly wished to win this match and were determined to do so we treated it as we do all our other games; our approach was basically the same—to win by playing good, attacking, football.

Points of Fact

It has been said and written that Rangers had a lot more of the play than Celtic in the first half. That may be so, but I should like to point out that they had it in areas of the field which did not cause us any concern.

I am not overstating the Celtic case when I say that Celtic won in the fashion we intended. We had made our plans in the knowledge that our International wingers, both outstanding match-winners in their own right, were out of the team. And I was quite sure that we would have the necessary skill, strength and will to win to offset the disadvantage of playing without our regular wingers.

At the end of the day we could afford to be amused by remarks that the game was more tense than ever, more physical than ever. That is not Celtic's experience this season or in other seasons.

Those who attended Hampden must have noted, if they were willing to do so, that before quarter of an hour had been clocked, three Celtic players, Billy McNeill, John Fallon, and Bobby Murdoch had required the attention of our trainer after infringements, all of which were penalised by the award of a free kick and all of which had been committed by the same opponent!

I can say in all honesty therefore that if there was undue physical contact in the game Celtic were undoubtedly not responsible. I cannot but think of the saying that if you live by the sword you deserve to die by the sword.

The "Gifts"

A word or two now about the "gifts" we received. Anyone who has watched football regularly will agree that the team who make the fewer errors generally win the game. But because a team makes mistakes it does not follow that they have gifted goals to the other side.

All of our three first-half goals—the "gifts," as they have been described — needed considerable skill on the part of our players before they were scored.

Billy McNeill's goal, far from the first of its kind, was an object lesson in judgment of jumping and heading and further reward for long arduous practice of the corner kick move. Bobby Lennox displayed great skill and sense of purpose in taking advantage of George Connelly's fine tackle and interception, and young George himself could not have profited from a Ranger's mistake and scored the third goal had he not shown tremendous coolness and deft ball control.

Mind you, Celtic are not much bothered about how the critics saw the match. And if it has taken us 65 years to beat Rangers in a Scottish Cup final the wait has been well worth while, especially when the Scottish Cup victory follows the winning of the League Cup and the League championship.

Tributes

I wish to pay tribute to every man who wore the Celtic colours. I know that the rest of the team will not only pardon me but agree with me when I single out John Fallon, whose

> We do not intend to repeat the record of "firsts" that Celtic have achieved. But the feat to which we now refer is unprecedented or, if you like, unique.
>
> Never before have a Scottish club won all three major trophies within a month. This month Celtic have annexed the League Cup, the first-division championship, and the Scottish Cup.
>
> It is but fair to point out that this is the first time the League Cup final has been played in April—the usual October match was postponed because of the damage caused to Hampden Park through fire. Nevertheless because of the extra strain involved Celtic's is a magnificent achievement.

cutting out of the cross ball and lob was as excellent goalkeeping as I have seen for a long time, and George Connelly, for his general effectiveness on a nerve-racking occasion, for special mention.

I would like to pay tribute to the Celtic "fans" for their support. The acoustics at Hampden nowadays seem to favour the supporters at the other end and from the one where Celtic "fans" gather, yet the great encouragement for Celtic could not be missed.

Entertainment

We have had quite a few entertaining moments in connection with our recent successes.

(Continued on page 4)

Celtic's four goals in the Scottish Cup final on Saturday are pictured above. Billy McNeill (top picture) heads the opening goal, Bobby Lennox scores the second and above George Connelly and Steve Chalmers complete the scoring.

ABSOLUTE NONSENSE!

Billy McNeill has requested a little space in our columns of this issue to clear up a point in connection with a Sunday newspaper statement.

In this newspaper the Celtic captain is referred to in these words in connection with the Scottish Cup final :—

"Skipper Billy McNeill made the crack of the day when grinning all over his face he said—

'Maybe we should play without wee Jimmy Johnstone and Yogi every week'."

Billy not only never held such an opinion but—and this is even more important—he had no discussion or conversation with any reporter or writer on the subject of Jimmy Johnstone or John Hughes and how they were or were not missed.

"I know that both Jimmy and John appreciate that I made no such statement — not even jokingly—but I want the Celtic supporters to know this through the 'View'."

We agree wholeheartedly with Billy and are delighted to give prominence to his disclaimer. It is nothing short of a scandal that so much rubbish is published in the name of "quotes" from individuals prominent in the game.

RECORD 1968-1969

Played	56

(Scottish League championship 32, League Cup 10, European Cup 6, Scottish Cup 1).

Won	...	39
Drawn	...	12
Lost	...	5
Goals for	...	164
Goals against	...	49

(Competitive matches only)

Foundation Fund Total

THE Sir Robert and Lady Kelly Foundation Fund, proceeds of which will purchase and install a therapeutic bath in the Rosewell Home for the Handicapped, closed last week at a total of £3,076 15s. 2d.

Although the Fund is now officially closed, late donations will be passed on to the Home.

The Celtic Football Club donation of £750 took the total over £3,000.

All other donations received during the week are acknowledged below.

SIR ROBERT AND LADY KELLY FOUNDATION FUND

Balance b/f	£2176 15 2
The Customers of Messrs. P. and H. Scott, 6 Prestonhill Rd., Rosewell	18 10 0
Whitfiel St. Mary's Celtic Supporters Club	7 0 0
Union of Catholic Mothers, St. Luke's, Mayfield, by Dalkeith	1 0 0
The Celtic Car Club	20 0 0
M. J. B. Rogerson, Edinburgh	3 0 0
Anonymous, Glasgow	2 0 0
Shieldmuir Celtic Supporters Club	30 0 0
Mrs. B. Hester, Leuchars, Fifeshire	1 0 0
Blackburn and District Branch, Celtic Supporters Association	6 0 0
Daily Express Br., Celtic Supporters Association	10 0 0
Sarazen Branch, Celtic Supporters Association	7 0 0
Airdrie Branch, Celtic Supporters Association	6 0 0
Luton Branch Celtic Supporters Club	10 0 0
M. V. McCluskie, Newlands	5 5 0
Anonymous	1 0 0
Calderbank Celtic Supporters Club	10 0 0
Glenties Celtic Supporters Club	10 0 0
Mary and Mick Connelly, Maryhill Celtic Supporters Club	10 0 0
Dr. A. B. Gilfedder	2 2 0
Celtic Football Club	750 0 0
	£3078 15 2

Souvenir programmes, in Appreciation of Our Chairman, are still available from the 'View' or from the Celtic Supporters Association, price 1/-.

Proceeds from programmes will still be donated to the Rosewell Home.

There's a jump of two years between featured *Celtic Views* here, but that's not to say that the Bhoys had been lax in their duties in the intervening games.

In the 1967–68 season, the championship was retained, as were the League Cup and Glasgow Cup, thanks to thumping 5-3 and 8-0 victories over Dundee and Clyde respectively. The Scottish Cup was the only domestic trophy to escape the clutches of the Celts, but they were to make up for that lapse big-style in 1968–69. Indeed, by the time the Bhoys lined up against Rangers in the Scottish Cup final that season, the championship and the League Cup were already in a big green and white bag. In fact, all three competitions were wrapped up in little more than three weeks during April as the team went into overdrive.

First up was the League Cup on 5 April with a 6-2 win over Hibernian, and the championship was finally tied up at Kilmarnock on 21 April, although it had long been a foregone conclusion that Celtic were on course for four in a row.

Next up was the Scottish Cup. There was no doubt that Rangers would do all in their power not only to stop Celtic achieving their second Treble in two years, but also to end a three-year trophy drought south of the Clyde. As early as the second minute, though, there wasn't very much doubt about which route the cup would be taking from Hampden – north!

Billy McNeill opened the scoring while Bobby Lennox and young George Connelly also hit before the break. Stevie Chalmers added another in the second half as Rangers tasted defeat in a Scottish Cup final for the first time in forty years.

The *View* said: 'We do not intend to repeat the record of "firsts" that Celtic have achieved. But the feat to which we now refer is unprecedented or, if you like, unique. Never before have a Scottish club won all three major trophies within a month. This month Celtic have annexed the League Cup, the First Division championship and the Scottish Cup.

'It is but fair to point out that this is the first time the League Cup final had been played in April – the usual October match was postponed because of the damage caused to Hampden Park through fire. Nevertheless, because of the extra strain involved Celtic's is a magnificent

Anagrams of Celtic

OUR anagram feature of this issue gives the following twelve words, the rearrangement of the letters of which provides the surnames of Celtic players:—

CRENALM
NYLONCEL
NOONYCLL
RAMURY
DELDLAW
TNEENTB
VUMELY
DIMBCRE
CLEARFON
TENNER
PLOTEMENT
CLAWELA

This sentence of anagrams forms a statement of fact about Celtic:—

YAPREL SPOMINS SI DOSTEL CISTECL ENORIN.

week's "Celtic Boy" is John McColl, 17 Birniehill Bathgate. Aged 9, he goes to St. Mary's Primary athgate. His favourite player is Jim Craig. John ar attender at all Celtic's games.

(CALIFORNIA)

"CELTIC BOY"

Tommy Squires, 3 Dubton Street, Easterhouse, aged 9 years, is this week's "Celtic Boy." Tommy is a pupil of Blairtummock School and his favourite player is Billy McNeill.

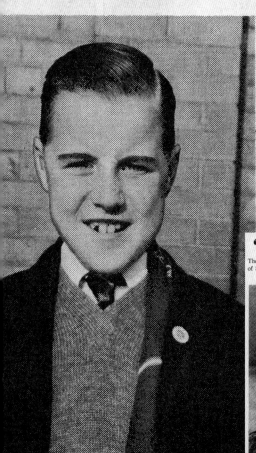

'CELTIC BOY'

The Celtic Boy this week is 10 year old John Buchanan, of 83 Houshillmuir Road, Pollok. He goes to St. Robert's School and his favourite player is Billy McNeill.

ornia.
St.
iday

"CELTIC BOY"

e " Celtic Boy " this week is 10-year-old Neil Kelly, 62 Lam scent, Cranhill, Glasgow. His favourite player is Steve Chalm whom he'll meet at Celtic's first Saturday home game.

Celtic Boys' with their star players,
of Dumbarton and James Quinn of
ers of Ronnie Simpson and Jim Craig.

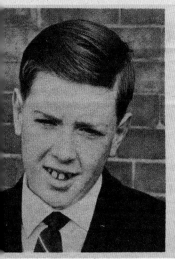

"CELTIC BOY"

The "Celtic Boy" ... week is Iain McNeill, ... Earsary, Castlebay, Isle of Bar... Iain is 12 years old and is ... pupil of Castlebay Juni... Secondary. His selection prove... the highlight of Iain's first visi... to watch his favourite team i... action. Until now he has had to content himself with reading about Celtic and watching his favourites on television.

Indeed, television has only recently been introduced into the McNeill household in common with most homes on the island. Iain told us that he watched the European Cup final last year along with about 100 other islanders on a television set installed in a village hall.

Since Iain cannot attend the game next week he was pictured with his favourite player, Bobby Lennox, before the game with Dundee.

THIS week's Celtic Boy is nine-year-old RICHARD GORDON.

Richard, of 116 St. Andrew's Drive, Pollokshields, attends Our Lady of the Rosary School, Glasgow.

His favourite player is Dixie Deans whom he hopes to meet shortly.

Hero Harry

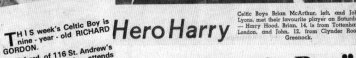

Celtic Boys Brian McArthur, left, and John Lyons, met their favourite player on Saturday — Harry Hood. Brian, 14, is from Tottenham London, and John, 12, from Clynder Road Greenock.

Celtic boys

In the late sixties and early seventies it was every schoolbhoy's dream – actually playing for the club could wait until you made your scoring debut on your sixteenth birthday… But there was the chance before that of being the *View*'s 'Celtic Boy' – plucked from the gathering crowd outside Paradise, having your pic in the paper and then returning at the next home game to meet your favourite Celt. Many were called, few were chosen and the rest of us could but dream…

"Celtic Boy"

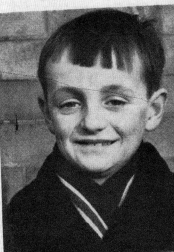

This week's "Celtic Boy" is Brian Crampshee, 44 Meolar Road, Abron Hill, Cumbernauld. Brian is 9 and attends Sacred Hearts School. His favourite player is John Hughes, whom he will have the opportunity to meet at Celtic Park in the near future.

"CELTIC BOY"

...he Celtic Boy this week is 7-year-old Daniel Crainie, o... and Fauld, Kilsyth. ...pil of St. Patrick's School, will have the ...George Connelly, in

"CELTIC BOY"

This week's "Celtic Boy" is Alex Carmichael, 249 Pullman Avenue, Rochester, New York. Alex is a pupil of Sacred Heart School, New York. Jimmy Johnstone is his favourite player and a meeting has been arranged before his return to America.

"Celtic Boys" Thomas Sweeney and Thomas Polland were ... their favourite player, Jimmy Johnstone, before the recent lea... Airdrie at Celtic Park.

THE CELTIC VIEW

No. 233   WEDNESDAY, APRIL 22, 1970   Price 6d

Saints pay tribute to Scotland's European heroes

COUNTING THE COST OF VICTORY

By John McPhail

CELTIC marched magnificently into the European Cup final last week — but their victory was not won cheaply.

With the final against Feyenoord only two weeks away the fight is on to clear up the injury list.

Skipper **BILLY McNEILL** is causing most concern. He told me :

" I still feel pain in my ankle but Bob Rooney has worked wonders and with extra treatment I expect to be back in action soon."

BOBBY MURDOCH has a groin strain and **JIMMY JOHNSTONE** strained ligaments. **WILLIE WALLACE** is still suffering from the strained ankle tendons that kept him out of the Leeds game.

Physiotherapist Rooney said : " They are all quite serious — but with intensive treatment and massage, I hope to get them fit for at least a game or two before the final."

ACCLAIM

Celtic will arrange two or three friendly games in the coming weeks, for Manager Jock Stein intends to keep his players at peak fitness for the vital match in Milan.

But the nagging injury worries cannot dim the magnificence of Celtic's triumph over Leeds, a victory even the English sportswriters had to acclaim.

This was the greatest display I have ever seen from players in Celtic jerseys and the tremendous fight back after Leeds had gone ahead with that shock Billy Bremner goal showed the wonderful courage, team spirit and technical superiority of this majestic side.

They were inspired by the courage and ability of the injured McNeill who strode through the match crushing all aggression from the Leeds attack.

George Connelly gave a fine display of cool, composed midfield play on a par with his display at Leeds.

Then there was the morale-blasting ball wizardry of Jimmy Johnstone who shattered Leeds with his own particular brand of genius which must be unchallenged anywhere in the world today.

But they were all magnificent men in green and white jerseys, masterminded by the game's shrewdest tactician and backed by the greatest and most inspiring set of supporters in the world.

Until Wednesday even Hampden had never heard noise of such frightening intensity and no team could fail to be inspired by it.

RECORD

Celtic wrapped up their league programme on Saturday with a narrow win over St. Mirren. Young star Vic Davidson got his name on the score-sheet again.

The pre-match tribute from the Love Street club and fans was much appreciated and bears out Celtic's belief that, when they play in Europe they are playing for Scotland as much as for themselves.

Celtic's 12 point league win is a record for the club.

New cap David is a big hit

CONGRATULATIONS go to young David Hay who showed up very well in his first international on Saturday.

David played a big part in getting Scotland off to a flying start in the British Championship with a 1-0 win over Ireland.

Joined

This has been a wonderful season for the youngster who has really broken through into the big time and has made himself an invaluable member of Celtic's home and European campaigns.

David will feel more at home for the remaining two games. He has been joined in the Scotland pool by team-mates Tommy Gemmell, Billy McNeill, Jimmy Johnstone, Bobby Lennox and John Hughes.

All of them, of course, are old campaigners in the international field, but the new boy proved at Windsor Park on Saturday that he has all the qualifications for a long and successful career in a Scotland jersey.

McNeill and Johnstone, of course, are still nursing injuries and on Monday Gemmell was injured in a car crash.

Another twelve months had passed and Rangers' trophy drought had now reached four years, while sales of silver polish up at Parkhead Cross had reached an all-time high.

Again, it was just the Scottish Cup that slipped from Celtic's grasp as they succumbed 3-1 to Aberdeen in the final, but the League Cup and the championship each winged their way to Paradise for the fifth consecutive year. The season was far from over, though, despite this *View* featuring St Mirren applauding Celtic on to the pitch for the final domestic game. The main reason for the Love Street tribute was that Celtic still had one more game to play, and it was probably more for overcoming that final hurdle than reaching the European Cup final itself that St Mirren formed that guard of honour.

That hurdle constituted Don Revie's Leeds United side and Celtic found themselves not only combating the redoubtable quality of the Elland Road outfit, but also the indiscernible rationale of the Fleet Street squad, as the English press had gone to town in writing off Celtic.

A 1-0 win thanks to a George Connelly goal in only forty-five seconds, with another by the youngster chalked off, gave Celtic the upper hand down in Yorkshire and a UEFA record crowd of 136,505 packed Hampden for the second leg. Billy Bremner equalised the tie with a stunning shot, but John Hughes and Bobby Murdoch made Hampden erupt as it never had done

before and the Bhoys were in their second European Cup final in three years

The club newspaper had by now gone up in price to a tanner (6d) and doubled to a whopping eight pages, and in his *View* homage, former Celt John McPhail classed the Leeds game as the greatest display he had ever seen from Celtic. He went on to say: 'There was the morale-blasting ball wizardry of Jimmy Johnstone, who shattered Leeds with his own particular brand of genius which must be unchallenged anywhere in the world today.

'But they were all magnificent men in green and white jerseys, masterminded by the game's shrewdest tactician and backed by the greatest and most inspiring set of supporters in the world. Until Wednesday, even Hampden had never heard noise of such frightening intensity and no team could fail to be inspired by it.'

THE CELTIC VIEW

No. 235   WEDNESDAY, MAY 6, 1970   Price 6d

CELTIC'S EUROPE D-DAY

THIS is the Cup. This is the Day. Milan is the Place. The place where all roads lead . . . where all eyes focus . . . and where the hopes of all Celtic fans lie.

For the European Cup is more than a trophy, it is a mantle of greatness.

Celtic have won it before — in 1967. That was a victory for Celtic, Scotland, and football.

Tonight thousands of fans throughout the world are hoping for a repeat, and to join those in Milan in toasting CELTIC — CHAMPIONS OF EUROPE.

From the men who lead the Club . . .

■ CHAIRMAN
SIR ROBERT KELLY

"THREE years ago, on the eve of our Lisbon triumph, I wrote in the View that the club's unprecedented successes in football's top flights gave me special pleasure on three main grounds.

These were: first, that in Celtic's true tradition our victories were achieved by playing attacking and entertaining football; second, that they were won by a pool of players whose backbone, as always, was the young men brought to Celtic Park in his formative years wanting to be a Celt and feeling honoured to wear the club's colours; and, finally, that we were not only the first British side to reach the final of Europe's foremost competition but were being represented there by an all-Scottish eleven.

Now as we stand on the threshold of fresh European laurels I take great pride and satisfaction in reflecting that these three considerations are no less applicable than they were in Lisbon.

PROVED

Once again our team is comprised almost exclusively of players reared in the Parkhead atmosphere. Talent which has fulfilled its early promise under the guidance and influence of a manager and staff who themselves have worn with distinction the famous green and white.

And yet again we have proved ourselves in this most exacting of tournaments with a playing staff that is entirely Scottish, a remarkable feat when one considers the international flavour of teams who have previously made their mark in Europe.

It is generally accepted that a side which reaches the final of a European competition represents country as well as club. I suggest that by this or any other reckoning no club is more fitted than Celtic to carry into the San Siro stadium the hopes and aspirations of Scotland as well as Celtic.

That this honour should be ours yet again is no less heart-warming for my fellow directors than myself. May our pleasure and pride be enhanced by a game worthy of this great football occasion and a result no less satisfying than that achieved in Lisbon."

■ MANAGER
JOCK STEIN

"CELTIC won the European Cup three years ago in the first season that the club had qualified to play in the competition.

We broke the barrier to become the first British side to win the trophy and we were delighted when Manchester United emulated our efforts the following season.

Tonight we have the opportunity to become the first British side to win the trophy for a second time.

However, all the talk that Celtic are considered hot favourites to win the match at San Siro has no meaning for the Celtic players or myself.

Feyenoord are a very good team indeed. They must be to have qualified for the final of the European Cup.

CONSISTENT

I watched Holland's champions in action ten days ago and saw nothing to indicate that they could be easily beaten by anyone.

Nor do we forget that Inter Milan were very much the favourites when we clashed in 1967.

Everyone knows what happened in that game and it should be remembered that the Dutchmen are no less hungry for success than Celtic.

Over the past couple of months the team have probably played their best and most consistent football of the whole season.

This was amply shown in the two titanic struggles with Leeds United to qualify for tonight's game.

PLANNING

Since that memorable second leg semi-final match at Hampden we have been able to snatch a short break in which we have played a couple of game with the strain off.

Our real planning for tonight however started at the week-end when we got down to business at Troon before setting out for Milan.

All the players are in the best possible physical condition and are fully aware that only the best Celtic football at the greatest speed will be good enough to win Europe's top accolade — Champions of champions — for the second time."

■ CAPTAIN
BILLY McNEILL

"NINE years ago, with the taste of defeat by Dunfermline in the Scottish Cup Final still lingering, if some one had told me I would win a European Cup medal only six years later I would have advised them to put their crystal ball in for urgent repairs.

If they had added that I would be in line for another "go" at the Big One three years after that I would have been the one to require treatment . . . for hysteries.

Yet here we are with the countdown in its final stages for the second part of a dream.

Here I must pay tribute to the fans for their truly magnificent support.

I feel I must pick out the last two legs which demonstrated the loyalty, faith and true dedication of our wonderful supporters.

When we trooped out that night at Elland Road the cheer from the green-and-white clad fans was FANtastic.

The only thing I can say about the return match at Hampden is that I have never heard anything like that in all my football career.

UTMOST

Now I am looking forward to hearing yet another roar of acclamation at the San Siro stadium when, once more bursting with pride, I hope to hold aloft the Cup this game in our Continent is all about.

With your help we can do it. All the hard grind of training and straining for this match has been done. The Boss has laid his plans and the rest of the lads and myself will do our utmost to make them come true.

Since the arrival of Mr Stein at Parkhead we have won our share of cups and medals but for me the best feeling of all was at Lisbon when we achieved our goal and became the first British team to win this trophy.

I will never forget that aftermath when I had literally to run the gauntlet of fans to get and bring back the cup.

It was sheer bedlam but I will force myself to tackle it again . . . just to get my hands on that Cup."

A new name appeared in the *View* for the first time, although it would be another thirty-seven years before it cropped up again. The name was Wim Jansen and he was a member of the Feyenoord team Celtic would meet in the final of the European Cup.

Celtic had reached the final after disposing of Swiss side Basel, Benfica of Portugal, Italians Fiorentina and, of course, English champions Leeds United. The Rotterdam side had advanced through seeing off KR Reykjavik of Iceland, AC Milan, Vorwarts Berlin and Legia Warsaw, and it was fair to say that Celtic were the favourites to lift the cup against the unfancied Dutch.

Jansen was only mentioned in the caption for the team photo and as one of the eleven full internationals Feyenoord had at their disposal, but special mention was given to skipper Rinus Israel and striker Ove Kindvall. It's just a pity that the Celtic team, already ensconced in Milan, couldn't check out the *View*, as these were the two men who did the damage that night in the San Siro.

Tommy Gemmell had repeated his feat of scoring in the European Cup final when he fired Celtic ahead just on the half-hour mark, but a couple of minutes later Israel had levelled matters. The game dragged on into extra-time before Kindvall hit the winner four minutes from the end.

On the face of it, the scoreline looked tight, coming as it did after two hours of football, but this off-form Celtic side had come up against a team from a country which was in the ascendancy on the football pitch. Ajax had reached the previous European Cup final and the Amsterdam side would go on to win the next three as Johan Cruyff and co stamped their undoubted quality on European and world football.

There is an argument that Celtic were guilty of believing the hyperbole, of 'winning the final before the final', but they totally underestimated Feyenoord and paid the price. Feyenoord did to Celtic what Celtic had done to Inter Milan three years previously, when the underdogs snaffled the bone from the top dogs.

LEEDS UNITED (England)

Semi - Final

1st Leg (April 1)

LEEDS UTD.   0
CELTIC   1

SCORER: CONNELLY

LEEDS UNITED—Sprake; Reaney and Cooper; Bremner, Charlton and Madeley; Lorimer and Clarke; Jones; Giles and Gray. Bates substituted for Bremner after 64 minutes.

CELTIC—Williams; Hay and Gemmell; Murdoch, McNeill and Brogan; Johnstone and Connelly; Wallace; Auld and Lennox. Hughes substituted for Connelly after 80 minutes.

Referee—Mr M. Kitabdjian (France).

2nd Leg (April 15)

CELTIC   2
LEEDS UTD.   1

SCORERS: HUGHES, MURDOCH

CELTIC—Williams; Hay and Gemmell; Murdoch, McNeill and Brogan; Johnstone and Connelly; Hughes; Auld and Lennox. Substitutes, Fallon, Craig, Hood, Callaghan and Macari.

LEEDS UNITED—Sprake; Madely and Cooper; Bremner, Charlton and Hunter; Lorimer and Clarke; Jones; Giles and Gray. (Harvey and Bates substituted for Sprake and Jones).

Referee—Mr G. Schulenburg (West Germany).

CELTIC QUALIFY ON AGGREGATE 3-1.

THIS was the goal that shattered a myth . . . of Leeds and English invincibility. After only a minute of the Elland Road game Celtic's "utility" star George Connelly hammered the ball past keeper Sprake. As Leeds supporters looked on in disbelief, 10,000 Celtic fans roared in delight.

THE CELTIC VIEW

No. 261   THURSDAY, JANUARY 7, 1971   Price 6d

'This terrible tragedy must help to curb the bigotry and bitterness of Old Firm matches. When human life is at stake this kind of hatred seems sordid and little. Fans of both sides will never forget this disaster.'

— JOCK STEIN

BLACK SATURDAY

VIEW POINT

A glimmer of hope for a better future

THE Ibrox disaster has stunned the football world. It seems somehow impossible that a tragedy on this scale could strike a stadium we know almost as well as our own.

There is little doubt how the average Celtic supporter feels. We have had many calls from fans asking us to express their sympathy to the victims' relatives.

This concern is shared by the Supporters' Association who are planning joint fund raising activities along with their Rangers' counterparts.

Weight

We wish them every success. We are confident that our supporters' generosity, so magnificently proved in the past, will not fail this time.

But all the money in the world will not bring back loved ones and all the sympathy in the world can only lighten by a fraction the weight of grief.

Yet, somewhere at the end of a very long, dark tunnel there is a tiny gleam of light. The light of hope.

It finds expression in the words of Jock Stein when he says that bigotry and bitterness seem sordid and little when human life is at stake.

Important

In the past few years it has become obvious to more and more supporters of both teams that what they have in common is infinitely greater and more important than what divides them.

Unhappily there are still some who cannot or will not accept this. But even they must see in the light of this appalling tragedy how futile, barren and petty their ancient feuds are.

There were no Billys or Dans lying still under these shrouds at Ibrox on Saturday. Only dead people, with families and friends.

If only we can hold on to that simple fact then perhaps something of value might emerge from this, the most heartbreaking day our Scottish game has ever known.

The Old Firm match that didn't matter

By JOHN McPHAIL

THE New Year clash between Celtic and Rangers should be one of the high spots of the season. On Saturday it was simply an irrelevance.

When so many people have been killed or injured even an Old Firm match can suddenly seem very unimportant.

On Sunday an air of gloom still hung heavily over Parkhead. Especially affected were the Celtic officials who helped with the injured and dying after the barriers collapsed.

Manager Jock Stein, assistant manager Sean Fallon, trainer Neil Mochan, physiotherapist Bob Rooney and the club doctor were among those who went to give what aid they could.

Jock Stein, still visibly shocked, did not want to discuss the match but he had this to say of the disaster: "On behalf of Celtic Football Club I would like to convey my deepest sympathy to relatives of those who lost their lives.

"A tragedy of this type was the furthest thing from all our thoughts. The game had been played out in the most sporting manner — and the good behaviour was reflected on the terracings. The voluntary workers, ambulancemen, nurses and the emergency team of doctors who did such tremendous work in the fog helping the injured and the dying deserve the highest praise.

"The Glasgow police, too, played a magnificent part, as they always do on those terrible occasions. Their competence, calm and strength prevented an even greater disaster and saved many lives.

"This was a black, black day in the history of Scottish football."

MARK

Mr Stein has always been just as much at home among ordinary fans as in the boardroom and this accident has left its mark on him.

His final comment was: "Surely this terrible tragedy must help to curb the bigotry and bitterness of Old Firm matches.

"When human life is at stake, as it was after the barriers crashed, then bigotry and bitterness seem sordid little things. Fans of both sides will never forget this disaster.

"The chances of the accident happening exactly as it did must have been very slim. If either side had been well ahead then fans would have been streaming away long before the end.

Celtic have given £10,000 to the Lord Provost's Disaster Fund and have promised full co-operation for any proposed game involving a Celtic-Rangers select.

JOCK STEIN . . . he helped the rescue work.

Supporters unite to help

CELTIC and Rangers Supporters' Associations have joined together to help the Fund.

After a meeting between both sets of officials at the Celtic Social Club in London Road, Secretary Hugh Delaney said plans included . . .

● The immediate setting up of collection boxes in pubs and social clubs.

● A dine - and - wine boxing night at the St. Mungo's Halls, Glasgow, on January 25.

The boxers will all be amateur except for one bout by two top Scots professionals. There will also be a cabaret.

● A special collection at both Celtic Park and Ibrox later this month.

The front page of this edition states that it was an Old Firm match that didn't matter and in many ways this was an edition of the *View* that didn't matter as, never before or since, has there been so little interest in the scoreline of a meeting between Glasgow's big two.

The New Year meeting went ahead on Saturday 2 January 1971, with 80,000 packed into the Ibrox terraces, and the game seemed to be heading to a 0-0 draw until Jimmy Johnstone put Celtic ahead with barely a minute remaining. That would have appeared to have been that, but Colin Stein equalised in time added on to finish what apparently was a very enjoyable ninety minutes for both sets of supporters.

It had been a good-natured contest both on and off the park with only two arrests, both for drunkenness, among the all-ticket crowd. The elation of the Celtic support at the Broomloan Road end when Celtic seemingly wrapped the game up was matched by relief from the opposite end when Stein tied the score… But Stein's late equaliser became an innocent bit player in the mystery that was to unfold as the crowd left the stadium to resume their traditional New Year celebrations.

Many continued to toast in the New Year unaware that they had just witnessed the match that was the precursor to the blackest day in Scottish football. The notorious

Stairway 13 at Ibrox had experienced fatalities before, but never like this. In the crush leaving the ground, sixty-six Rangers fans died and nearly 200 more were injured. It wasn't immediately clear what had happened, but early reports signified that a few people had died – only for the reported death toll to rise as the night unfolded. Initially it was thought that Rangers fans leaving after Celtic scored heard the roar greeting Stein's equaliser and tried to return to the terracing, but this has since been proved not to be the case.

In the dark days that followed, supporters from both sides of the Glasgow divide united in the grief and disbelief at what had happened and many ecumenical services were held throughout the country. As the *View* said: 'There were no Billys or Dans lying still under those shrouds at Ibrox on Saturday. Only dead people, with families and friends. If only we can hold on to that simple fact then perhaps something of value might emerge from this, the most heartbreaking day our Scottish game has ever known.'

Captain-for-the-day Tommy Gemmell and Rangers skipper John Greig.

THE CELTIC VIEW

No. 278   WEDNESDAY, 5th MAY, 1971   Price 2½p

After flag win No 6 it's all eyes on the Cup

SUCCESS — BY THE 100,000

Keep in touch - with the View...

WHEN the final whistle blew at Celtic's sunshine carnival on Saturday it signalled the end of one of the most remarkable weeks in the club's long history.

It was a week in which the first and second teams between them clinched two trophies and virtually tied up a third, scoring 24 goals in the process.

It also saw the magnificent and emotional farewell to the greatest eleven ever to wear the green and white.

But probably the most staggering fact of the week is that at a time when football is facing a crisis at the turnstile 100,000 people paid their money to watch Celtic. The breakdown goes like this:

Celtic Reserves	v	Rangers Reserves	...	...	...	...	10,000
St. Mirren	v	Celtic	...	...	...	...	20,000
Celtic Reserves	v	Falkirk Reserves	...	...	...	...	6,000
Celtic	v	Ayr United	...	...	...	...	22,000
Rangers Reserves	v	Celtic Reserves	...	...	...	...	7,000
Celtic	v	Clyde	...	...	...	...	35,000

What a vote of confidence for bright, attacking football. And there must be a lesson here for other clubs who have seen their gates go down and down.

But the game which will have the most lasting impression on the fans, of course, was the farewell to the Lisbon Lions.

From the moment Ronnie Simpson led the team out to the carrying off shoulder-high of free-transfer man Bertie Auld, it was an afternoon of magic, nostalgia and some very fine football.

But now it's back to the sterner stuff of the Scottish Cup Final. Manager Jock Stein told me:

"It was good to see the Lisbon team back but now we must concentrate on the game with Rangers.

"We have the players who can give us victory. Several of them have hit peak form when you would expect them to be shading off at this stage of the season.

COMPETE

"With wee Jimmy particularly in such dazzling form we will take some beating.

"The team will be on the Ayr United lines with Harry Hood fit again."

If Celtic do win Mr Stein will class this as in some ways the greatest season of the six in which Celtic have been champions.

He said: "Most important, we have seen some great young players come in to compete for places in the first team. The future looks bright indeed."

JIMMY JOHNSTONE . . . in dazzling form.   RONNIE SIMPSON . . . led out the team.

VIEW POINT

ONCE AGAIN Celtic are in the final of the Scottish Cup. This time the opponents are Rangers.

Obviously the result is important — to both clubs.

But the result off the pitch is equally important.

Celtic are justly proud of the behaviour of the vast majority of their fans in recent years.

Their conduct has rightly earned praise throughout Europe.

At Hampden on Saturday the club expects the best — ON AND OFF the pitch.

The rules for the fans are simple:

CO-OPERATE with the police at all times.

HELP drown out any obscene chants.

POINT out trouble-makers to the police.

Welcome to the new decimal *Celtic View*, which from 17 February had cost 2½p as opposed to 6d in 'real' money, although it was still classed as a tanner to most punters.

The 3 February issue cost 6d, the 10 February had both 6d and 2½p on the cover and by 17 February it was clear that the new-fangled decimalisation had completely swamped the *View*. That wasn't the only thing that was changing as the old South Stand, or the only stand at the time, was undergoing a major overhaul and by the end of the season had played a part in two of the major stories in the *View* featured here.

The main headline, though, refers to the number of fans through the turnstiles in one week, but the most staggering stat was probably the number of games played in that week:

Monday: The reserves, fresh from beating Rangers 7-1 to lift the league title the previous Thursday, played the Ibrox side again and won 4-1 in the first leg of the League Cup final.

Tuesday: The first team closed in on the title with a 2-2 away draw with St Mirren.

Wednesday: The reserves beat Falkirk 4-0 in the first leg of the Scottish Cup final.

Thursday: The first team clinched the championship with a 2-0 'home' win over Ayr United.

Friday: The reserves tied up the League Cup with a 6-1 victory over Rangers for a 10-2 aggregate score.

Saturday: The Lisbon Lions took their final bow as the first team beat Clyde 6-1 at Celtic Park.

The big news, though, was that the Celts had equalled the club's own six-in-a-row record set way back between 1905 and 1910. Of course, this side was to go on and reach nine in a row, although only one of these titles was clinched at home, and it happened to be this game against Ayr United which, because of the Celtic stand renovation, was played at Hampden! The building work also paved the way for one of the abiding images of the time – the Lisbon Lions clicking their way down the old enclosure steps to take their final bow.

By the way – Celtic also won that Scottish Cup mentioned on the front page after a replay, so there were no real changes on the country's silverware front.

THE CELTIC VIEW

No. 295   WEDNESDAY, OCTOBER 27, 1971   Price 3p

"The better team won on the day. This is a great result for Dave McParland and it should give the game in general a lift."

JOCK STEIN

NO EXCUSES

Now it's battle for the League

MANAGER Jock Stein rushes from his Hampden dug-out to congratulate Dave McParland, the Thistle manager at the end of the League Cup final.

It was a sporting gesture that was repeated by thousands of Celtic fans who stayed to the end to cheer both teams from the field.

For Dave it was the first taste of glory . . . something Celtic and their manager have long been used to.

THERE WILL BE NO witch-hunts at Parkhead following the League Cup Final defeat by Partick Thistle in spite of the signing of Denis Connaghan from St Mirren. Denis, who was a provisional Celt in 1964, will make his debut at East End Park, Dunfermline tonight when it is hoped the team will find the winning touch again.

Manager Jock Stein and the players are bitterly disappointed at Saturday's performance which let the fans down very badly. Of course the Celtic manager refused to take away from Thistle's great performance. " They played fast, effective football and kept catching us out deep in defence in the first half," said Mr Stein.

He added: " Thistle made chances and took them. We made even more in the first 15 minutes of the second half but squandered them all. The better team won on the day. This was a great result for Dave McParland and it should give the game in general a lift." The Celtic boss is determined to get the team back on the rails for tonight's vital clash at Dunfermline.

INJURIES

On Saturday he thought some of the players had the wrong attitude—just as they showed in the first European Cup game against the Danes.

Of course, injuries will affect tonight's line-up . . . Jimmy Johnstone, who required stitches in a leg wound after Saturday's game is out.

Billy McNeill will get treatment up to the last in a hope to have him back in the side and Bobby Lennox will be recalled.

VIEWPOINT

THE DEFEAT at Hampden was a bitter blow to the club . . . the players . . . and the fans.

But it was far from a disaster.

Manager Jock Stein has made it clear that the club is going through a period of transition. A new team is being built . . . new targets reached for.

One clear point emerged from Saturday's game—Celtic fans ARE the greatest.

Singing and cheering they stayed to the end. They clapped their team —and Thistle too—from the field.

Not the end of the world

Disappointed ? Yes. Angry ? No. They took this defeat like true champions—just as Celtic are.

For both the team and their fans the future is bright. It's far from the end of the world.

The headline says it all, but it's one that, luckily, neither the club nor the *View* have had recourse to experience to any great degree since their respective formations in 1888 and 1965...

And it's probably that lack of shock results which makes headlines like this reverberate all the more forcibly, as there was no doubt that this was the big kick in the teeth of Jock Stein's tenure at Celtic Park.

It was another League Cup final, Celtic's seventh in a row, and Partick Thistle, Glasgow's perennial bridesmaids, were to provide the opposition. The Maryhill side were the proverbial lambs to the slaughter and Celtic's name was seemingly on the cup once more but, as the saying goes, somebody forgot to tell Thistle to read the script. The final score was Partick Thistle 4, Celtic 1, and, as if that wasn't bad enough, the Jags were 4-0 up after only thirty-six minutes. Even when Kenny Dalglish pulled one back in the seventieth minute, there were those who thought the Celts could pull the game back, but it wasn't to be.

Four of that Thistle team – Ronnie Glavin, Alan Rough, Jimmy Bone and sub Johnny Gibson – would eventually join Celtic with varying degrees of success, but the only immediate change at Celtic Park was that keeper Denis Connaghan was drafted in from St Mirren, although Evan Williams would soon win his place back.

That week's *Celtic View* said: 'The defeat at Hampden was a bitter blow to the club... the players... and the fans. But it was far from a disaster. Manager Jock Stein has made it clear that the club is going through a period of transition. A new team is being built... new targets reached for. One clear point emerged from Saturday's game – Celtic fans are the greatest. Singing and cheering they stayed to the end. They clapped their team – and Thistle too – from the field. Disappointed? Yes. Angry? No. They took this defeat like true champions – just as Celtic are. For both team and their fans the future is bright. It's far from the end of the world.'

THE CELTIC VIEW

No. 315   WEDNESDAY, MARCH 15, 1972   Price 2p

Paradise for the fans...

A charity promise from Liz and Richard

THEY'RE CELTIC's newest fans . . . . and probably the most famous.

But already the Burtons are showing the flag. Or should it be scarf.

Richard and Liz were each presented with silk scarves at the fabulous party they threw for Celtic's fans in Hungary.

During it the Welsh actor promised to donate a cheque to charity equal to the amount spent on the function.

He also said that he and Liz would love to visit Scotland to see Celtic in action.

And that may not be too far away. For Chairman Desmond White has invited the famous couple to Celtic Park to show the club's appreciation of their kindness.

Filming schedules won't allow it before the end of the season. But they may manage it later in the year.

JIMMY AND DIXIE BACK

By JOHN McPHAIL

JIMMY JOHNSTONE and Dixie Deans turn out at Tannadice tonight in the reserve match against Dundee United.

A good game from both could mean a first team place for the Scottish Cup match against Hearts at Parkhead on Saturday.

Jimmy had a game in the reserves last week, and Dixie missed the Budapest tie due to a shoulder injury.

Both Jimmy and Dixie are fit again and will be giving all they've got at Tannadice to get back into first team business.

No selection for the Hearts game will be made until later in the week. Celtic will prepare at Seamill and manager Jock Stein will wait on fitness reports before picking his side.

The Celtic boss said, " Hearts are always hard to beat and we will have to be at our best to win."

Mr Stein was delighted with the Hungary game and the league match at Aberdeen.

He said, "The boys were magnificent against Ujpest. This was one of our greatest ever displays.

"I felt our fans were entitled to see the cup heroes in action at Pittodrie, and this point surely makes Celtic red hot favourites for our seventh consecutive league flag."

BOBBY SEITH
On The Spot — Page 3

A little bit of Tinseltown rubbed off on Celtic when they visited Budapest for the European Cup quarter-final first leg against Hungarian champions Ujpest Dozsa...

A lucky select band of Celtic followers, including *Celtic View* competition winners Joe Haffie, Patrick Murphy and George Donachie, partied the night away with Hollywood superstars Liz Taylor and Richard Burton as they celebrated the fortieth birthday of the actress. No fewer than 136 jet-set Celts joined in the celebration at the city's Intercontinental Hotel where the Welsh actor was staying while filming *Bluebeard* on location in Hungary. The *View* said: 'Before the party got underway a strict security net was thrown around the main reception hall and no one, other than Holiday Enterprises charter passengers, was allowed admission.'

The report went on: 'Earlier in the day Richard Burton had extended an invitation to Jock Stein and the players to join him after the game. The Celtic manager was unable to accept because the players and officials travelled back to Scotland immediately after the game.'

Celtic won the game 2-1, but that was despite the official party not exactly receiving the same level of hospitality afforded to the supporters by the Burtons...

The back page of the *View* noted: 'The bus carrying the Celtic team and officials to the Ujpest Dozsa stadium last Wednesday couldn't gain entry to the precincts of the ground. After being refused entry at a gate where sundry other vehicles were entering the stadium, the Celtic team bus was directed, by a circuitous route, to a gate on the other side of the ground. After an unavailing search for a key, a workman appeared, climbed the massive gates and proceeded to attack the iron barrier with a hacksaw. When it was obvious that he was getting nowhere fast, the Celtic players and officials left the bus and, entering through a side gate, walked the couple of hundred yards to the pavilion entrance. Whether the entry obstructions were by accident or design no one will ever know. Either way it had no adverse effect on the performance of the Celtic players.'

RESULTS

Wednesday, March 8
EUROPEN CUP (Quarter-final) 1st leg
Ujpest Dozsa 1 (Horvath)
Celtic 2 (Horvath o.g., Macari)

Ujpest Dozsa: Szentimbalyi; Nosko and Maurer; Juhasz, Ede Dunai and Horvath; Fazekas and Zambo; Bene; Antal Dunai and Toth.
Celtic: Williams; McGrain and Brogan; Murdoch, McNeill and Connelly; Hood and Hay; Dalglish; Macari and Lennox. Substitutes: Connaghan, Quinn, Callaghan, V. Davidson and Wilson.
Referee, H. Weyland (West Germany)

Saturday, March 11
SCOTTISH LEAGUE
Aberdeen 1 (Harper)
Celtic 1 (Lennox)

Aberdeen: Marshall; Boel and Hermiston; S. Murray, Young and G. Murray; Forrest and Robb; Harper; Willoughby and Graham. Twelfth man, Taylor.
Celtic: Williams; McGrain and Brogan; Murdoch, McNeill and Connelly; Hood and Hay; Dalglish; Macari and Lennox. Twelfth man, Callaghan, replaced Dalglish after 80 minutes.
Referee, Mr J. R. P. Gordon (Newport-on-Tay).

THE CELTIC VIEW

POOLS TIME

The Celtic Pool is back again with better prizes prizes than ever. See Page Six.

No. 327 WEDNESDAY, AUGUST 16, 1972 Price 3p

WHY I DID IT

Jock Stein explains that foray into the crowd at the Stirling game

'The wreckers are chanting about things that have nothing to do with football'

JOCK STEIN

I DON'T LIKE criticising Celtic fans. But I have to take odds with at least a section of them. What I did on Saturday was something I've felt like doing for quite a while.

It's my sincere wish that it will have a lasting effect, as I'm sure that the vast majority of our fans do. Celtic supporters have enjoyed a lot of good times during the past few years, and all of it was due to hard work—by the players, the backroom boys and the directors.

The fans, too, have played a major role and we don't want to see it all ruined now by the bad element who have recently emerged. Nor do we want to see the fans of long standing who followed us through the lean years discouraged from watching us play.

This bad element—or the wreckers as the View called them last week—are singing and chanting about things which have nothing to do with football.

Surely there are enough Celtic songs without introducing religion or politics or anything else.

OFFERS

These offensive songs and chants could damage Celtic's hard-won reputation built up by good football and sportsmanship.

Offers to play all over the world keep arriving at Celtic Park.

Last year we took part in the Bobby Moore testimonial. Next month we play in Bobby Charlton's benefit match.

This is an indication of our high standing in world football.

The club don't want to lose all this. Neither, I'm sure, do any of our real supporters.

Continued on Centre Pages.

FLASHBACK . . . . Manager Jock Stein climbs out of the crowd after delivering his half-time tongue lashing to the chanting section of fans at Annfield.

Following crowd trouble in the Drybrough Cup final, where Celtic lost 5-3 to Hibernian after extra-time, the *View* of 9 August 1972 carried a front-page leader entitled, 'War on the Wreckers'.

No punches were pulled as the club set out its manifesto for dealing with the hooligan element of the early seventies and the leader started off by saying: 'The wreckers have done it again. A great football spectacle was almost ruined because a bunch of cowardly thugs decided violence was the way to show displeasure at the way the game was going. And this is with the season proper not even started. Once again we are treated to the whole sickening spectacle – the frightened youngsters, the injured, the struggling figures being led away by the police.'

The *View* carried on: 'The club have said it time and time again but we will go on saying it until the hoodlums get the message.

- *We don't want you*
- *We don't want your so-called support*
- *We don't want your money'*

However, the following Saturday when Celtic travelled to Annfield for their League Cup sectional game with Stirling Albion, Jock Stein decided that the message hadn't been communicated strongly enough. While supporters at the uncovered end of the small ground dodged the attentions of a swarm of wasps, those under the shed at the other side soon felt the wrath of Jock Stein as the chants became too much for him. He vaulted over the perimeter fence at half-time and returned a bit of verbal to a small section whose chants he considered offensive.

The manager said in the *View*: 'The bad element – or the wreckers as the *View* called them last week – are singing and chanting about things which have nothing to do with football. Surely there are enough Celtic songs without introducing religion or politics or anything else.'

He added: 'But I have been heartened by the way most supporters at recent games have tried to drown out the chants and the way they have assisted the police. Now we want to get rid of this hard core of troublemakers. Then we'll all be able to play and watch the game – in the right atmosphere and in peace.' Celtic won the game 3-0.

CONTEST FOR YOUNG READERS

SIX PRIZES of one guinea will be awarded to the winners of this week's competition for young readers No. 327. The winners will be the senders of the first six letters opened which contain the correct answers to these questions :

1. On Saturday Celtic play Arbroath in a League Cup match. What are Arbroath's official colours ?
2. Who is the manager of the Gayfield Park club ?
3. When did Arbroath last play in the Scottish League First Division ?
4. Arbroath and Dumbarton won promotion last season. Which team finished the Second Division campaign in third place ?

THE CELTIC VIEW

Big pools pay-out

No. 392 WEDNESDAY, JANUARY 30, 1974 Price 3p

SUNDAY SOCCER SUCCESS

By JOHN McPHAIL

WHAT A fantastic start for Sunday football when 28,000 cheering soccer fans turned out on a cold January afternoon.

Crowds like this must make the soccer world sit up and ask: "Is Sunday football here to stay?"

The bosses of both teams were very happy after the match. Clydebank director, Charlie Steedman, one of our staunchest advocates of Sunday soccer said:

"This was wonderful. The crowd was magnificent and does not this highlight my argument about the three division leagues."

HEALTH

Celtic boss Jock Stein was also delighted with the attendance:

He said: "A tie like this against a Second Division club on a Saturday would hardly have brought out a 12,000 gate."

However, the Celtic boss was more cautious about a complete switchover to Sunday football. He added: "I would prefer to pick and choose, but this was very healthy indeed — in fact a splendid indication of just what could happen."

Fans roll up and bring success

One noticeable and very welcome point was the increased presence of women and children. There was a happy holiday atmosphere around.

Celtic certainly had plenty to be happy about — a big crowd, a good game and a passport to the next round of the Cup.

We will know today whether we meet Stirling Albion or Montrose.

But it wasn't just Celtic who got the benefit of the switch to Sunday. Everywhere the gates were up.

When nearly 6,000 people turn-out at Firhill to watch Ferranti Thistle the experiment can't be other than a success.

The situation even took a bizarre turn down at Palmerston Park, Dumfries, when Queen of the South were playing East Fife.

So many spectators turned up that the turnstiles couldn't cope. The lucky last 1,000 to arrive were let in free.

● Former Celtic manager Jimmy McGrory, the club's P.R.O., who was re-admitted to the Southern General Hospital last week was progressing satisfactorily when we phoned the hospital yesterday. Mr McGrory thanks all well-wishers.

SILENT SATURDAY

AND SWINGING SUNDAY

Parkhead near the usual Saturday match time—and not a fan in sight. But what a difference 24 hours can make as the crowds in their thousands arrived for that historic kick-off. They were in no doubt about the success of Sunday football.

DIXIE MAKES HISTORY

ALL the publicity about Sunday mustn't detract from the game itself. It was a real cracker.

Dixie Deans shot himself into the record books in just four minutes when he became the first man to score a goal in senior football on a Sunday.

He almost blasted away the all-time record of Jimmy McGrory who once scored three goals in three minutes.

In four incredible minutes early in the match Dixie scored two beauties. Only the sun blinding him prevented a third.

Then to round it off, he cracked a glorious ball against the bar with the keeper licked.

All told Dixie struck wood four times and other great shots narrowly missed.

Fine Bobby Lennox moves laid on the first two, Lennox got one himself and Deans completed his hat-trick before the interval.

The second-half was merely academic with further goals from Lennox and Davidson and amazing misses around the Clydebank net.

Davidson and Wilson substituted for McGrain and Dalglish in the second half.

I must pay tribute to Clydebank. They always attempted to play good football and even although outclassed never at any time resorted to dirty tactics.

Director Charlie Steedman said later: "We learned a lot from this game. This wonderful Celtic side are in a different class."

Once upon a time, football kicking off at 3 o'clock on a Saturday afternoon was sacrosanct.

Midweek was for European ties, League Cup commitments, replays and such, while Sundays were for ending up wherever your conscience led you – but in the early seventies it certainly wouldn't be a football stadium… That all changed, though, as 1974 dawned and the *View* of 23 January said: 'Celtic will play their cup game on Sunday… and make football history. For the match against Clydebank is the first senior game ever played at Celtic Park on the Sabbath.

'The SFA gave the go-ahead to Celtic earlier this week. A number of other Scottish clubs have also been granted permission to play on Sunday. Agreements for the match on Sunday are the same as for Saturday games. It's cash at the turnstiles – there are no tickets. This is a different arrangement from England – where the law forbids cash admissions on a Sunday.'

The switch proved to be a great success, especially for Dixie Deans, who not only became the first senior player to score a goal on a Sunday, but who also went on to score a hat-trick (he hit the woodwork four times, too). The Bankies were hit for six as the Celts produced a sterling Sunday service, but the 6-1 scoreline wasn't the only talking point after the game.

The 28,000 crowd delighted Jock Stein who told the *View*: 'A tie like this against a Second Division club on a Saturday would hardly have brought a 12,000 gate.' The *View* added: 'One noticeable and very welcome point was the increased presence of women and children. There was a happy holiday atmosphere around.'

There was still some Saturday action, though, as, just twenty-four hours before the cup-tie with Clydebank, a challenge match was played against Albion Rovers at Cliftonhill, but Jock Stein wasn't too impressed with his charges' display on a boggy pitch against his first senior team. Despite that, no fewer than three Celts on duty in Coatbridge – Tommy Callaghan, Paul Wilson and Vic Davidson – played in both games, with the latter finding the net in each game, including a brace in the 3-2 win over Albion Rovers.

NO Why ex-ref Jack Mowat thinks Sunday soccer is unlikely to succeed

YES Why the players' boss wants to give Sunday a chance

THE CELTIC VIEW

Boys' Club win both European tournaments

No. 403   WEDNESDAY, APRIL 17, 1974   Price 3p

The European Youth Tournament played in Glasgow and Motherwell last week-end proved a feast of football and attracted great attendances.

Organised by The Celtic Boys' Club and the Glasgow Area Union of Youth Clubs and sponsored by the Jeyes Group, the competition looks like becoming a regular annual event on the Youth Football calendar.

Apart altogether from the trophies and prestige at stake the youngsters in both age groups shared in the success of good sportsmanship which was evident throughout the tournament.

The games were played along League Cup lines at Saracen Park, Lesser Hampden, Roseberry Park and Fir Park, Motherwell and the finalists to emerge were: under-14— Celtic B.C. and Fir Park B.C.; under-17—Celtic B.C. and Manchester United.

In the finals at Celtic Park on Monday Celtic Boys' Club beat Fir Park Boys' Club by 5-0 to win the under-14 trophy and Celtic Boys' Club beat Manchester United by 1-0 to lift the under-17 award.
     (Full coverage with pictures in next week's View).

STAY AWAY!

Turkish referee Mr Dogan Babacan orders off another Atletico player. But even this didn't stop the brutal tackles.

Club's plea to fans for Madrid clash

CELTIC have never been more proud of their fans than after last week's disgraceful game with Atletico Madrid.

But for the second leg of the European Cup semi-final in Spain they don't want ANY supporters with them.

The Directors feel that the situation is too dangerous . . . . too explosive. They don't want the responsibility of having fans in Madrid.

Even the official party has been cut in size. Supporters who usually travel with the team won't be allowed to on this occasion.

APPEAL

Only the team, the officials and the accompanying Press will be aboard Celtic's plane when it leaves next Monday.

The club realise that they can't stop people from travelling . . . . but they appeal to their commonsense.

And with the game live on television and radio for once there is adequate coverage for fans in Scotland.

Of course, even the official party may not be travelling for the E.U.F.A. meet in Berne this week to discuss the disgusting scenes that took place during and after the semi-final at Parkhead.

The reports from Turkish referee Babacan and E.U.F.A. observer Mr A D. McMullen will be studied.

CHANCE

Celtic have handed over their report to the Scottish Football Association who have been in contact with E.U.F.A.

It states the good behaviour of their fans and players in a factual account of all the happenings.

Despite all this, Manager Jock Stein is working on the assumption that the game will go on.

He feels that if the team are given any chance to play football they can still get a result.

NEXT Wednesday's game from Madrid is being televised live.

The whole of the second half — along with radio coverage — will be broadcast by the B.B.C.

Commentator Archie McPherson is due to fly out with the Celtic party to Spain.

Transmission of the game should begin around 10 p.m.

Supporters to be proud of...

THE behaviour of the Celtic fans last week has won acclaim throughout Britain.

On television, on radio and in the Press they've been praised for showing restraint in the face of extreme provocation.

Officials of Glasgow's police force and civic leaders joined in the praise.

FINEST

After an emergency meeting last week the club directors had this to say about the fans . . . .

"We wish to compliment our supporters on their exemplary

VIEW POINT

behaviour despite severe provocation.

"Their conduct further enhanced the club's good name. We are indeed proud of them."

Praise indeed, but on this occasion fully deserved. Surely their finest hour.

But the fans must never forget the standards that they themselves have set — and that the club expects them to live up to.

It could easily have been described as the night that shamed football and it was a match that will never be forgotten by those who witnessed it, although, even to them, the events of 10 April 1974 are still scarcely believable.

The occasion was the European Cup semi-final, the club's fourth in eight years, and this was the first leg at Celtic Park when 70,000 clicked through the turnstiles intent on roaring the Celts on to the final. Atletico Madrid provided the opposition and reverted to tactics that belied the use of the word 'sport' to describe what happened.

They kicked, hacked, punched, spat and cheated their way to a 0-0 draw, as anyone in green and white, but particularly Jimmy Johnstone, was seen as fair game for the brutal and cynical aggression of the Atletico thugs. Make no doubt about it, these were thugs of the lowest order masquerading in football strips, who mugged Celtic and brought the European Cup into disrepute. There were brazen assaults both on and off the pitch as even the police had to intervene in an attempt to bring peace to this football match.

Three of the Spanish were sent off and it would be quicker to name those who weren't booked. In the aftermath, this *View* headline urged fans not to travel. Indeed, both Jimmy Johnstone and Jock Stein received death threats from Spanish paragons of fair play.

The *View* said: 'The behaviour of the Celtic fans last week has won acclaim throughout Britain. On television, on radio and in the Press they've been praised for showing restraint in the face of extreme provocation. Officials of Glasgow's police force and civic leaders joined in the praise.

'After an emergency meeting last week, the club directors had this to say about the fans… "We wish to compliment our supporters on their exemplary behaviour despite severe provocation. Their conduct further enhanced the club's good name. We are indeed proud of them." Praise indeed, but on this occasion fully deserved. Surely their finest hour? But the fans must never forget the standards that they themselves have set – and that the club expects them to live up to.'

The away tie was lost 2-0, but justice was seen to be done in a 4-0 final win for Bayern Munich over these footballing charlatans.

The game is stopped as Jimmy Johnstone lies on the ground injured after a brutal tackle.

THE CELTIC VIEW

No. 405   **WEDNESDAY, MAY 1, 1974**   Price 3p

IT'S NINE IN A ROW

NOW FOR THE CUP

By JOHN McPHAIL

MATT Lynch makes the presentation to Bobby, watched by vice-president Eddie Devine and president Peter Murray.

THE gloom and bitterness of the European Cup fiasco turned to joy on Saturday.

Celtic shot to their ninth successive League Championship with the 1-1 draw against Falkirk — and now have one more height to scale — the Scottish Cup Final this week.

It was not a great display at Falkirk, as manager Jock Stein accepts. He said: "No one has any idea of the strain and tension my players have endured.

REACTION

"The conditions from the time we landed in Madrid until we left were terrifying. The first match in Glasgow must not be forgotten.

"The boys were in no mental state for the second game. I thought there could be a bad reaction when they came out against Falkirk.

"I must say I am very happy about the result even though the boys did not play well.

"It will be very interesting to watch events in Europe this week and find out the final verdict."

Like all Celtic fans I do not blame the players for defeat in Madrid and I agree with the sorely abused Jimmy Johnstone who said:

"I felt if we had scored the fans would have invaded the pitch."

But when all is said and done Celtic have had another highly successful season.

The league title has been won — and now they meet Dundee United in the final of the Scottish Cup.

The coveted double is in their sights again but Celtic will approach this one with the right attitude.

If all the players are fit I expect the line-up to be along the lines of last week — and how we could do with a repeat of that Kenny Dalglish goal.

Bobby honoured by the fans who don't forget

BOBBY Murdoch was the Guest of Honour at the Celtic Supporters' Association Annual Rally in the Kelvin Hall in Glasgow, last Sunday night.

The presentation to Bobby of a portable cassette-tape recorder, a plaque and a framed coloured picture of him in a Celtic strip was made by Matt Lynch on behalf of the Association.

In thanking Celtic supporters in general, as well as the 3,000 assembled in the Hall Bobby said "This is probably the third greatest night in my career. The first was when I signed for Celtic and the second was the European Cup win in Lisbon."

Having thanked everybody connected with the club who had helped him during his time at Celtic Park, Bobby concluded by saying, "I've got to go back down south on Monday morning but I'll be back on Saturday to cheer the lads in the Scottish Cup Final at Hampden."

BOBBY and wife Kathleen with Second Division Championship medal.

A bedraggled, battered and drained Celtic returned from Madrid after the Atletico fiasco and their first port of call was Falkirk's old Brockville stadium, where a crowd of 13,500 awaited them.

Recovering from going behind in the third minute to earn a 1-1 draw at this unfashionable venue may not have been the ideal fillip to remedy the ills of a European dream fraudulently shattered at the penultimate hurdle, but there was a sting in the tail… It may be lost in the mists of time that Kenny Dalglish's nineteenth-minute drive nailed the coffin lid on Falkirk by relegating them, but, far more importantly for the *Celtic View*, history was made as Celtic clinched the title four games from the end of the season and the nine-in-a-row legend was born.

The Bhoys really were on cloud nine as they had just reached their ninth Scottish Cup final in ten years and had gone one better earlier in the season by playing in their tenth successive League Cup final. The big worldwide news, though, was the nine in a row and Jock Stein's clean sweep of

championship titles ever since he had returned to the club as manager.

It was around this time that increasingly raised voices stated their opinion that the league needed a shake-up and the new-fangled ground-breaking Premier Division would soon be inaugurated. More than one football pundit, though, hinted that the changes were introduced because it was Celtic who were so successful. For the record, the runners-up in each of Celtic's glorious titles were Rangers on six occasions, Aberdeen twice and Hibernian in this ninth season.

The *View* reported that there was also some good news for Celtic's press steward, Andy Cottingham from Garrowhill, who won a prize in a draw held to raise funds for St Ninian's in Knightswood. Andy had won two tickets for Celtic's game in Madrid, but had complied with the club's wishes that no supporters should travel to the Spanish capital. St Ninian's, however, came up with the ideal answer, though, when they presented a delighted Andy with £100 – quite a hefty sum in 1974.

NO SMILES FROM THE NINE TIMES CHAMPS

It's all over — and a strangely grim-looking Celtic leave the field. But the fans round about them seem happy enough.

THE CELTIC VIEW

No. 420   WEDNESDAY, OCTOBER 30, 1974   Price 4p

Records all the way

THAT splintering sound you heard on Saturday was records being smashed all over the place.

It was Celtic's eighth victory in the League Cup, one more than their closest rivals Rangers.

The nine goals made it the highest scoring final. Celtic had previously won eight-goal clashes with Rangers and Dundee.

And Dixie Deans' personal contribution sent the experts scurrying to the record books. This was his second hat-trick against Hibs in a cup final.

It was also his second hat-trick against them in two weeks. No wonder Willie Ormond was impressed.

HELLO AGAIN

By JOHN McPHAIL

YOU can't blame these happy Celtic players for keeping a tight grip on that League Cup.

It was the first time since 1969 that the trophy had been theirs. But how magnificently they won it back.

A week on Saturday the team delighted the fans by hitting Hibs for five at Parkhead. Not even the most rabid supporter would have forecast six goals in the Cup Final.

A lot has been made of the leaks in the Hibs defence — and certainly they were there. But how magnificently Celtic exploited them.

Change

There just wasn't a weakness anywhere. But if one player stood out for sheer skill it was surely Jimmy Johnstone. The wee man was magnificent and must surely be back at Hampden tonight against East Germany.

Not far behind was Dixie Deans — and what an astonishing

League Cup jinx ends

change of fortune he has had. Recently he was looking like a fixture in the second team.

Now he has hit two hat-tricks against the same team in the space of a week. And he has pushed himself into the Scottish pool.

Another player whose form is giving a lot of cause for satisfaction is Kenny Dalglish. Not so long ago he was really off the boil. Now he's back.

Celtic's display was a team victory, however, and there were no failures.

Like every Celtic fan at Hampden, Jock Stein was delighted with the team. He said : There was a bit of carelessness now and then but it was a fine, all-round performance which put the seal on our best ever start to the domestic football scene with two trophies won and equivalent joint leadership of the league."

DIXIE DEANS . . . a hat-trick of delight.

YOUR VIEW

We apologise to all our readers for the reduction in our pages. This has been caused by a shortage of newsprint, resulting from the road haulage dispute.

Scotland's favourite Supporters Bus!

The Celts had a love affair with the League Cup during this period and managed to reach fourteen successive finals from 1964–65 through to 1977–78.

Typically, the arrival of Jock Stein heralded five wins in a row, but a further four finals were lost before Celtic met Hibs in 1974. Joe Harper managed to score a hat-trick for the Easter Road side, but Dixie Deans did likewise for Celtic as the Bhoys won 6-3. The striker was called up to the Scotland squad by manager Willie Ormond.

As the *View* pointed out, it was Celtic's eighth victory in the League Cup, one more than Rangers, and the nine goals made it the highest scoring final – the Celts had previously beaten Rangers 7-1, Dundee 5-3 and Hibs 6-2 – plus it was Dixie's second hat-trick against Hibs in a Cup final, as he had scored a trio in the 6-1 Scottish Cup final in 1972.

By now the price of the *View* had gone from 3p up to 4p, but this particular edition had reverted back to four pages. The *View* said: 'We apologise to all our readers for the reduction in our pages. This has been caused by a shortage of newsprint, resulting from the road haulage dispute.'

Considering Celtic's violent experiences with Racing Club in 1968 and the heavily Argentinian-influenced Atletico Madrid just a few months earlier in 1974, a little piece of news coming out of Germany couldn't be ignored by the *Celtic View*'s long-running world football correspondent, Bob McDonald. In this week's issue Bob wrote: 'Independiente of Buenos Aires are club champions of South America. This is their third win in a row and the fifth since the competition started fifteen years ago. This is no mean achievement and it's understandable if Independiente are looking forward to the World Club Championship. The only trouble is they don't know who they will be playing.

Kevin meets Kenny

KENNY DALGLISH met another of his growing number of fans recently.
Kevin McGlynn, 12, of 23 Oakfield, Tarbert, Loch Fyne, rated Kenny his top player and was overjoyed at the chance of meeting his favourite.

Kevin attends Tarbert Secondary School and his dream is to some day line-up in the same team as Kenny.
Stick in at the soccer then, Kevin — you never know your luck !

'European Champions Bayern Munich are not keen to play and may yet withdraw. They remember only too clearly what happened to Celtic, Manchester United, Ajax and the rest. This would leave the way open for beaten finalists Atletico Madrid. And if ever teams deserved each other, it's these two. The idea of two sets of Argentinians kicking lumps out of each other is perhaps not too unpleasant for Celtic supporters but such a match would not do football any good.'

For the record, the butchers of Atletico did take part and beat Independiente 2-1 on aggregate.

THE CELTIC VIEW

No. 446   WEDNESDAY, MAY 7, 1975   Price 5p

BILLY . . . with the cup he knows so well

BILLY'S FINAL FLING

By John McPhail

......Y McNEILL, Celtic's captain for so many have been ....s years, ended a wonderful career when powered ad....udly held the Scottish Cup on high at paign. .....en.

So while ..isplay during the game epitomised the traditional spirit and skill of Celtic. Minutes after the final whistle Billy announced his retiral. It was sad—but what a wonderful way to go, as he himself acknowledged.

He said: "I wanted to bow out at the top and there's no better time than after a cup victory. I'm grateful to Celtic and to all our fans for these wonderful years."

The inspiration of the skipper, playing one of his best games ever, influenced the entire side.

Gone was the lethargy of recent lack lustre league matches. Here we saw the true Celts—fighting for every ball —and first to almost every ball.

Skill and determination were the hallmarks. They felt they owed the Celtic fans something —and how well they compensated for the loss of the league with this splendid display.

Manager Jock Stein was very happy about the victory. He said:

"I knew we would win— and win well, all things being equal. The players could not get on the park quick enough.

"For a side that has been recently criticised for lack of pace, they went tremendously fast for the ball.

"I was happy with the entire team and particularly Paul

'I wanted to bow out at the top and there's no time like a cup final'

Wilson after the death of his mother in mid-week. Paul's second goal virtually tied up the game."

This was great stuff and the fans loved it. Paul Wilson opened the scoring with a clever header from a fine Kenny Dalglish cross.

Airdrie shocked Celts with a goal two minutes from the interval, but hardly had the cheering of their fans died down when Wilson put Celtic ahead again with another header, this time from a corner.

A Pat McCluskey penalty when Bobby Lennox was dragged down in the box decided the issue but Celts could have gone further ahead with a little luck.

In a very good Celtic side my men of the match were Kenny Dalglish, Paul Wilson, Peter Lachford and Billy McNeill.

But who can forget the skill of full backs, McGrain and Lynch, and the power of Pat McCluskey?

Add to that the mobility of Steve Murray, the speed of Bobby Lennox and the astute skill of Harry Hood.

And what of Ronnie Glavin having his best game ever in a Celtic jersey?

Altogether, a very fine display—and it shall give us lots of confidence for the game against Rangers.

It won't be easy but I think Celtic will just do it.

THIS IS THE LAST OF THE WEEKLY VIEWS FOR THE SEASON BUT WE'LL BE BACK IN JUNE WITH AN ALL-ACTION MAGAZINE

Celtic may not have lifted the title in the 1974–75 season, but the League Cup and the short-lived Drybrough Cup were already in the bag by the time the Celts lined up against Airdrie in the Scottish Cup final.

Celtic fans had by now become used to contesting finals and silverware was very much the rule rather than the exception. Over the course of the past ten years there had been nine titles and no fewer than thirty-four finals contested in all competitions, so was this just another trip to Hampden for another cup final?

There was certainly a sense of familiarity in the air, with Hampden in the sun and the Celts emerging victorious once more as the Broomfield side were eventually put to the sword with a 3-1 scoreline. There was a difference, though, as this time, ten years almost to the day since he had headed a winning Cup final goal against Dunfermline to kick-start the glory years (not to mention getting the *Celtic View* off to a winning start), skipper Billy McNeill announced his retirement almost immediately after the game.

Lifting the Cup was his last act in over eighteen years as a Celtic player; eighteen years in which he had grown from a gangly schoolboy hopeful into the greatest captain Celtic Football Club has ever had. He told the *View*: 'I wanted to bow out at the top and there's no better time than after a Cup victory. I'm grateful to Celtic and to all our fans for these wonderful years.'

They were indeed wonderful and there was no doubt that he did bow out at the top, after winning nine championships, seven Scottish Cups, six League Cups and, of course, he was the first British player to lift the European Cup, when the Lisbon Lions were the pride of Paradise in 1967.

There were also touching words in the *View* from Jock Stein regarding Paul Wilson's input to the Cup win. The manager said: 'I was happy with the entire team and particularly Paul Wilson after the death of his mother in midweek. Paul's second goal virtually tied the game up.'

By the way, front-page names such as Pele and Evel Knievel may have been worth the 5p price, but the Pele piece was a book review and the American's stunt cycle show never came off.

Approximately 3,000 people packed the Kelvin Hall Arena on Sunday night to join with the Celtic Supporters' Association in paying tribute to two great Celtic buddies — Bobby Lennox and Jimmy Johnstone.

It was perhaps fitting too, that Billy McNeill performed his last public act as captain of the Celtic Football Club in presenting his two team-mates with watches on behalf of the Supporters' Association.

THE CELTIC VIEW

No. 527   WEDNESDAY MAY 11, 1977   Price 10p

THE CUP COMES HOME!

IT WAS down to business first thing on Sunday morning for manager Jock Stein.

The players had the day off after their Cup celebrations, but not the Celtic boss.

Despite his business-as-usual attitude that Hampden triumph was never far from his mind.

In fact, the Cup was right on his desk. Still bedecked in green and white ribbons.

It looked right at home too, Which isn't surprising really for it's the 25th time that the club has won it.

Already manager Jock Stein and his assistant Davie McParland are planning how to keep the silver trophy at Celtic Park.

Obviously it's a case of home, sweet home!

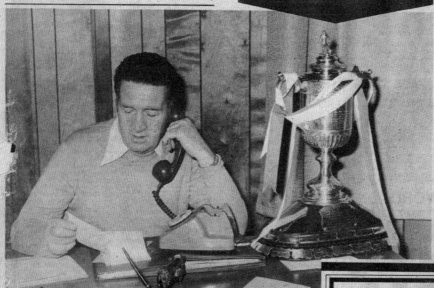

Manager Jock Stein wants to put an end to the speculation linking him with the Scottish Team manager position. He told the "View": "My future is with Celtic and that's where I'll be next season".

'DOUBLE' PLAN CAME UP

CELTIC Manager Jock Stein missed his first (and the club's last) Premier League game of the season at Motherwell last evening.

He underwent yesterday in Manchester what he described as a "minor operation" to a foot, but he hopes to be with his squad when they play Clyde at Shawfield on Saturday in a Glasgow Cup tie.

The boss of the Scottish champions put club before self in delaying the operation for some time because of Premier League and Scottish Cup pressures. But with the "double" secured on Saturday and tensions eased the way was clear to follow medical advice.

The Scottish Cup returned to Celtic Park . . . because for the umpteenth time, manager Stein called the shots correctly for his side BEFORE it went into action.

He freely admitted after the Hampden success against old rivals, Rangers, that it was "a pre-match blow to the team to lose through injury Ronnie Glavin, who has been such a regular scorer from midfield.

"It meant we had to change things a wee bit. We thought about Rangers' aerial power that has been such a factor against us in the past, and concluded that if we could blunt that we would be on our way to winning."

All who saw the Hampden action as stadium spectators or TV watchers know how brilliantly Celtic coped.

Manager Stein put it simply. "Roddy McDonald and Johannes Edvaldsson looked after that side. If anything went amiss, which was very seldom, Pat

Continued on back page

Another league and Scottish Cup double, the seventh of Jock Stein's managerial career at Celtic, topped a fine comeback season for the Bhoys.

Such had been the success rate of the past ten years or so that the previous season's best of just reaching the League Cup final was seen as a massive disappointment. A defeat to Aberdeen in November 1976 was the outcome, but the Celts rallied to end the season in whirlwind fashion. With five games remaining the league title was tied up in a 1-0 win at Easter Road, with Joe Craig netting the solitary goal, although for some strange reason Hibs chairman Tom Hart suddenly decided he was anti-TV and no cameras were allowed in for the highlights programmes that weekend. In fact, even the Celtic Cine Club were barred from Easter Road.

There was no such televisual barrier for the 1-0 Cup final victory over Rangers, but the TV coverage still prompted a back-page lead. It said: 'Celtic lifted the Scottish Cup for the 25th time in the club's history. But football wasn't the victor at Hampden. Television was clearly the winner. For live coverage resulted in the lowest Cup final crowd since the last war. But no one should have been surprised at the gaping, empty spaces on the Hampden terraces.

'Celtic chairman Desmond White forecast such a situation in the *View* in March. In an article, Sponsorship: It's Simply a Sell-out, he warned...

"Our cup final – our showpiece game – could become an embarrassment. Can we honestly expect fans to roll up to Hampden on what may be a wet, bleak afternoon to watch a match which they can enjoy in the comfort of their own home?"

'How right he was. On Saturday only 54,000 fans braved the elements to see the game. Despite a crowd limit of 85,000, how many would have turned up if the game had not been live on television? No one can be certain. One thing is certain, however. For the sake of an extra £12,000 fee, the SFA risk ruining the cup final as a spectator sport.'

A footnote to the Cup final was that Alfie Conn, in the space of four years, had won a Scottish Cup final medal for Rangers against Celtic and then for Celtic against Rangers.

> WALKING along London Road immediately after the victory, children were all over the place enjoying the hospitality of delighted adult supporters who were in the mood to celebrate no matter the cost. As one fan said: 'They are aff their heids in that pub, handin' away haufs like watter".
> **JAMES O'BRIEN, 28 Calderwood Road, Newlands, Glasgow.**

LISBON LIONS FOR THE BIG GALA — FILM NIGHT

TO MARK the Tenth Anniversary of Celtic's greatest football success. Celtic Films will be showing the Lisbon European Cup final on Sunday 22nd May in the Odeon Cinema, Victoria Road, Glasgow.

At the evening performance there will be a personal attendance of the Lisbon Lions team, also the present Celtic team and management.

This is a night that all Celtic fans will **NOT** want to miss.

Also being shown is the controversial film The Big Clubs.

The evening show will commence at 7.15 p.m.

Ticket prices — Stalls £1, Circle £1.25.

Tickets can be obtained from the Celtic View Office or postal bookings to "Celtic Films" — c/o Celtic View, 18 Kerrydale Street, Glasgow G40 3RW enclosing remittance and S.A.E.

Supporters clubs can obtain block bookings.

As Celtic Films expect a heavy demand for tickets for this show there will be an afternoon film show at 2.30 p.m. when the two films will be shown only. Price — Stalls 75p, Circle 75p.

THE CELTIC VIEW

Your New Year View

A Happy New Year . . . that's the seasonal greetings to all our readers from everyone at Celtic Park.

*

By the way, your New Year View will be on sale on Friday, January 6. It will be reduced to an eight-page edition due to holidays at our printers.

*

After that it's back to normal — a 12-page on sale every WEDNESDAY.

No. 549   THURSDAY, DECEMBER 29, 1977   Price 10p

TEAM MUST IMPROVE

It's vital we take chances

THE game with Dundee United last Saturday was a most disappointing encounter in everything except the fact that Celtic won both points.

However it was a better start to the second half of the season than our opening day game with the Tannadice team in August.

Celtic fans need no reminding that the game finished in a goalless draw that day and that both Pat Stanton and Alfie Conn came by injuries that were to result in cartilage operations.

Indeed Alfie Conn cut an ankle on Saturday and had to be substituted but it isn't too serious and he should be available for selection on Saturday.

Manager Stein talking about Saturday's game said — "We have played much better in games this season that we have failed to win but United played the game very cautiously throughout.

"Unfortunately we had too many players off form on the same day but had we taken one or two early chances it could have been so different.

"In the first twenty minutes or so I thought we played reasonably well and had we accepted a couple of early chances it would have been an entirely different match.

"However, instead of finding the net early and forcing United to be more attack-minded, we lost our early supremacy and struggled for a large part of the game.

"With another half of the league programme still to play we can be certain that there will be more upsets in the results so it is vital that we keep on winning.

"To do that of course we must rid ourselves of that old failing in front of goal. We have got to make sure that when chances present themselves we must take the majority of them instead of squandering most of them.

"John Dowie came into the team in a defensive role and he played well and possibly took more out of the game than anyone else in the Celtic team."

The Celtic manager hopes that the improved result against United will be continued in the week-end games against Ayr United at Somerset Park and Motherwell at home.

Both of these corresponding games were lost at the beginning of the season so it's essential that full points are taken to provide a springboard for a big push in the second stage of the league championship.

A FAMILY AFFAIR . . .

YOUNGSTERS Paul and William McStay sign on for Celtic . . . and continue a great family tradition.

For their father's uncles, Willie and Jimmy, were two of the club's greatest stars in the twenties and thirties.

Watching the lads sign are Sean Fallon, dad John, and Davie McParland.

Like their great uncles the boys have tasted the big time at an early age.

William right, was captain of the Scottish schoolboys side last year and Paul played for the Lanarkshire side. The boys attend the same school — Holy Cross, Hamilton.

Their uncle Willie was a regular in the Scottish side between 1920 and 28, while Jimmy went on to become manager of Celtic for a short spell.

Over the years, the *View* has always been first to inform the supporters when promising youngsters sign for the club.

Sometimes, as is the nature of the game, they are never heard of again, but every now and then the cream rises to the surface – and this was one of those occasions. Of course, these two young schoolboys could have commandeered some front-page copy because of their family connection with Celtic's past, or it could simply have been because they were two of the hottest

Manager Jock Stein congratulates the London Road Social Club team after they qualified for the final of the video quiz which is being organised by the members of Celtic Films.

properties at that level in Scottish football. Either way, this branch of the McStay clan would not only enhance the family's reputation, but in many ways eclipse the contribution made in the twenties and thirties by their predecessors.

The proud dad flanked by Sean Fallon and Davie McParland is John McStay and it was his uncles who first flew the McStay flag for the club. Willie McStay joined the club in 1912 and by the time he left in 1929 he had played 446 games and scored 39 goals. He was joined by younger brother Jimmy in 1920. Jimmy played until 1934 and scored eight goals in 472 games, before becoming manager during the World War II years and chief scout between 1951 and 1961. Having two such prominent Celts in their heritage would be more than enough for most

people, but this Larkhall family weren't prepared to rest on their laurels as thirteen-year-old Paul and sixteen-year-old Willie were about to prove.

It was, in fact, the younger sibling who would make his debut first, while Willie would follow him a year later. Willie, after signing this S Form in December 1977, played 90 times for Celtic between 1983 and 1987, but was to return as youth coach in 1994 before taking over the reserves in 2007. Paul made his debut in 1982 and was to finish second only to Billy McNeill in the all-time Celtic appearances charts with 72 goals in 677 appearances.

Younger brother Raymond also eventually signed for the club and was a stalwart in the reserves for a number of years, captaining the second-string while Paul skippered the first team.

THE CELTIC VIEW

No. 606   FRIDAY, MAY 25, 1979   Price 10p

CHAIRMAN HITS OUT AT TV RUMOUR

THE Celtic chairman blasted Scottish Television on Monday just hours before the Celtic match with Rangers at Parkhead which settled the destination of the championship.

Desmond White was furious about a quite unfounded Sunday newspaper report that the Old Firm game could be shown live if the match was a sell-out.

As a matter of fact, as late as Monday morning, Celtic hadn't ever been approached with regard to permission to film highlights of the match.

However Mr White issued the following statement which made the Celtic position crystal clear with regard to the live television of football.

"There was never any chance of the game being televised live. I received no approach from either STV or BBC for permission to transmit the game therefore I don't know how the story started.

"We were inundated with telephone calls asking if the match would be on television. But my responsibility is not to people who only want to watch football from their armchairs.

"I am only interested in the supporters who travel to grounds to watch football being played and I will always ensure that I look after their interests".

It's common knowledge now that a Scottish Television dispute prevented a showing of the highlights of the match late on Monday night.

This turned out to be a bonus for the fans who attended the match because they witnessed a spectacular game which will have a special place in the Scottish football history books.

WORLD HAILS THE CHAMPIONS

OFF to Majorca today went Celtic . . . to savour in relaxed holiday mood the winning of the 1979 Scottish Premier League championship, a feat achieved against the odds over their great rivals Rangers.

Even in the atmosphere of a holiday, manager Billy McNeill expects considerable benefit coming to club and team from this trip.

"I am a great believer in players going away together, for these occasions have the very pleasant result of 'jelling' things and establishing close contacts that are expressed later in players' work on the field".

It was on the trip to Portugal for a friendly during the weather-enforced break this winter that the Celtic team boss saw the first signs of togetherness that grew through the second half of the season and brought the magnificent climax with a 4—2 win over Rangers to take the title.

Maintaining that "family atmosphere", which the best of Celtic teams in the past possessed, is a priority after Monday night's triumph.

"It was a great night for everyone . . . great for the players, the fans and for myself," said the Celtic boss. "But let's not forget it was a great night, too, for the people associated with me . . . John Clark and the coaching staff.

"It was great for all of us to see the fruition of things in what amounted to a big season and a big challenge to us. There is no greater satisfaction than to see your side do things just right and get a good result.

"Obviously I am delighted for the players. They were asked for a response. They gave it. There has been response in other ways, too, from people on the staff.

"Returning to Celtic Park was a really big experience for John and myself. John hadn't been so long away as myself and coming back in a different role was a big test. He has come through it.

"The players too, have worked hard, working with each other, blending with each other and supporting each other.

Continued on back page

The league looked gone. In March the Celts were still six places off the pace, with no games being played between 23 December and 3 March because of the weather, but they clawed their way back into contention.

One of the postponed matches was the New Year game against Rangers and, as luck would have it, the clash took place as the final game of the season on a Monday night. Rangers only had to draw, Celtic had to win. Here is the *View* match report on what unfolded:

'Celtic got the win they required at Parkhead on Monday night against old rivals Rangers to clinch the Premier League title and a place in the European Cup next season. However, the manner of the Celtic win will live in the hearts of all Celtic supporters who witnessed it for the rest of their lives.

'Trailing from a goal scored by Rangers in virtually their first attack of the match, Celtic were faced with a mountainous task to get the two points they required to win the championship. That goal came very much into the preventable category and the Celtic defence were badly at fault as MacDonald scored from a Cooper pass. Despite almost continuous Celtic pressure, including a magnificent Roy Aitken header which came back off the crossbar, Celtic were unable to grab the equaliser and at half-time still trailed to that single goal.

'Twelve minutes into the second half the Celtic uphill task reached Everest-type proportions when Johnny

Doyle was ordered off following an incident involving Alex MacDonald. Quite undaunted, the 10-men Celts set about their work again and in the 66th minute, Roy Aitken scored the equaliser they so richly deserved from a Davie Provan free-kick. Even more incredibly they took the lead eight minutes later after a Roy Aitken shot was blocked, George McCluskey crashed the rebound into the net.

'The Celtic joy was short-lived, however, because just two minutes later they failed to clear a corner kick and Bobby Russell equalised with a first-time shot through a ruck of players which went into the net off Peter Latchford's right-hand post.

'Incredible though it seems, Celtic stormed back again and Peter McCloy brought off a fantastic save from a Roy Aitken header that looked a certain scorer. Then with only five minutes remaining Celtic raided on the right wing and George McCluskey's hard cross was touched by keeper McCloy on to the head of Colin Jackson and into the net to give Celtic the lead once again. Not satisfied at that, Celtic attacked again in the last minute and Murdo MacLeod scored with a screaming shot from about 20 yards to complete a night to remember.'

A dejected Colin Jackson having put the ball in his own goal to give Celtic a 3—2 lead.

PICK A CELT

G	Ronnie Simpson / Joe Kennoway
RB	Jim Craig / Bobby Hogg
LB	Willie O'Neill / Willie McGonagle
RH	Bobby Evans / John Gilchrist
CH	Bobby Quinn / Willie Corbett
CH	Joe Baillie / Bertie Peacock
OR	Frank Quinn / Tommy Donegan
IR	Bobby Collins / Willie Buchan
CF	Joe Carruth / Johnny McGrory
IL	Peter Scarff / Willie Fernie
OL	Jackie Millsop / Alex Byrne

Name ....

SUPPORTERS QUIZ

2nd Round

Glenties v St. Mungo's

THE Glenties Club from the Gorbals are through to the semi-final.

They beat St. Mungo's Supporters' Club in a high-scoring tie — 87½-80.

Glenties, who only won their first round tie by 2½, are the first team to reach the semi-finals.

St. Mungo's, who beat Broxburn in the first round, were represented by Tony Hefron, John McGlennan, Kevin Maguire and Andrew McGlennan.

The winner of the supporters' quiz will be presented with the Celtic View Shield — which they'll keep for a year.

Here are the questions this week's team faced — and the answers.

1. Neil Mochan's brother is coach to which English club? (5)
2. Name the boxer who was defeated by Benny Lynch in the final eliminator to fight Jackie Brown for the British and World Flyweight title? (0)
3. Who was the last Celtic forward to score four goals in an away Scottish Cup-tie? (5)
11. Celtic with Jock Stein at centre-half played an International XI in Belfast in the fifties. Name the player opposed to Jock Stein in this match. (5)
12. How much does it cost to enter for the World Cup competition? (5)
13. Name the reserve goal John Thomson in sease
14. The Strathcoma Cup is for by which sportsme

St. Mungo's . . . left to right, Tony Hefron, John McGlennan, Kevin Maguire, Andrew McGlennan.

GLENTIES IN SEMI

Spotlight on a Fan

Full name: **Brian Dennis Cox.**
Age: **22.**
Place of birth: **Glasgow.**
Occupation: Civil ...vant
...ou married? **No.**
...ou a member of ...y Celtic Supporters ...ub? **No.**
...urite other club: ...rde.
...urite player who ...esn't play for Celtic: ...rian McKenna ...lyde).
...urite away ground: ...mpden.
...tadium you have ...r visited: **Shawfield.**
...diest other fans: ...hemians.
...urite current player: ...ul McGugan.
...urite player (past): ...hn Thompson.
...liest memory: **Every ...e Celts beat ...ngers.**
...match: St Mirren v ...tic, Love Street, ...sley, 3rd May, ...86.
Favourite other spo... Synchronised swimming.

Best goal you have ...
Mo Johnston (C...
3rd in above me...

Best Celtic XI: Latc...
McGrain, McNe...
Connelly, Morri...
Murray, McSta...
Johnston, Dalg...
Nicholas.

Earliest memory: C...
PARTICK THISTL...
1971 League Cu...
Final.

and what the papers say

Ian Paul (Glasgow Herald). Celtic are the champions — and they did it in champion style, coming off the ropes not once, not twice, but three times to a victory every bit as memorable as anything achieved on the domestic scene by the Lisbon Lions or anybody else.

The bottomless courage, dynamic determination, and resolute reserves of stamina which have carried this Parkhead team from virtually nowhere to the title were displayed in glorious Technicolour.

Needing a victory to snatch the prize from Rangers, Celtic, a goal down at half-time, were reduced to ten men after Johnny Doyle was sent off ten minutes later; and despite hav-

No wonder thousands of Celtic supporters stayed behind to cheer their bedraggled but triumphant favourites. They barely had the breath to do so having seen their 10-man side score four goals, a feat which must be something of a record. They had also seen a performance by Roy Aitken which must rank among the finest by any Celtic player in a 90-minute spell.

Ian Archer (Scottish Daily Express). Celtic are Scottish champions for the 31st time. And the title came on a night as dramatic as memorable and downright unbelievable as in all their history. They clinched it in just half an hour of the kind of mayhem football you see once in a lifetime.

Doyle was sent off for kicking the Rangers' goalscorer.

Half an hour later it was all over and the time table came straight out of a fairy tale.

After 67 minutes from a Provan cross, Roy Aitken, Celtic's man of the match, equalised. After 75 minutes it was Aitken's pass which allowed McCluskey to carry the new champions into the lead. After 67 minutes Rangers hit back with a Russell cross shot. After 83 minutes Colin Jackson put into his own net from a McCluskey shot. After 90 minutes MacLeod, that other extraordinary talent, hit a 25 yard shot which tidied up for Celtic.

Alex Cameron (Daily Record). Celtic are Premier League champions after one of the most remarkable wins in

battled against the odds as they have never done before.

In 55 minutes Johnny Doyle was sent off for aiming a kick at Alex MacDonald who lay sprawled on the ground. It looked as though the aloof, cool-looking Rangers would grab command. It was what the Rangers fans in the 52,000 crowd must have expected.

But it turned out to be a prep osterous fallacy, as Celtic found energy and style even they didn't know existed. It was an inspired night for the Celts. Even their most partisan followers couldn't have predicted such a dramatic revival.

The match sizzled for 90 minutes. The Celts attacked Rangers as if their lives depended on it. The Ibrox team were kept in their own half for two-thirds of the match. Rang-

Celtic team who three months ago would never have forecast themselves as champions.

Hugh Taylor (Evening Times). Celtic are champions — really great champions. They proved that with a display of fantastic football unsurpassed by any of the heroes of the Parkhead past — a torrid, heart-stopping, courageous display that had everything that is superb in Scottish football.

Now the head-shaking, even among Celtic supporters, over a team reckoned anything but wonderful must stop.

Any side who play the way these young Celts did in beating Rangers 4—2 to win the Premier League in one of the most dramatic games Scottish football has known, must be ...

World Football

by Bob McDonald

ITALY

MARADONA? for Barcelona

...IN

... matches left, ...dad won 3—1 to ...in touching dis... their first ever

...e to bottom club ...ociedad won 3—1 ...r 32nd successive ...ch without defeat.

...drid, shrugging off ...pointment of their ...eat by Hamburg, ...ned Atletico Madrid ...ith Camacho and ...us two own goals ...Atletico net. Real ...their two final ...and hope that at ...op two points in ...atches. In Spain, ...does not count. ...y points for away ...y draws are used ...of a tie on points ...ed are also one ...an bonus points. If ...a tie on points and ...the results of the ...tween the two ...the issue, and ...ad have a clear ...winning 4—0 at ...rawing 2—1 in

Gijon (2—0 winners over Espanol) stay in third place, and Barcelona (2—1 winners over Rayo) move into fourth place, closer to a UEFA Cup spot.

The Barcelona fans are buzzing with the news that their club have agreed terms with Argentinos Juniors for the £3 million transfer of the world's No. 1 player, 19-year-old Diego Maradona. The Argentine FA are not keen to let Maradona leave, but the odds are that the young superstar will be wearing a Barcelona shirt next season.

GERMANY

WITH three matches left, Hamburg are in a good position to retain their title. With Bayern München's match against 1860 München postponed by a freak snowstorm, Hamburg took advantage, scrambling a 1—0 home win over Dusseldorf (goal by Milewski) to go back to the top again on goal average.

More good news for Hamburg fans is that they are hoping to sign ex-Bayern star ...

MOZZINI scores the title winning goal for Inter

INTER MILAN are Italian champions for the 12th time, but once again they made heavy weather of getting the clinching the point.

At home to Roma before 45,000 flag-waving fans, Inter had to come from behind twice, with full-back Mozzini's goal just two minutes from time giving them a 2—2 draw and the title.

Challenging Juventus kept themselves in second place ...

before 55,000 in the Westphalen Stadium in Dortmund, they lost 1—0 and now Hamburg have a vital advantage, having survived the trip to Stuttgart, a dangerous visit which Bayern have still to face.

PICK-A-TEAM

PICK-A-TEAM . . . that's the exciting contest for every Celtic fan. It's an easy-to-enter competition that is open to ALL the family.

And the fan who knows his football can . . .

WIN two complimentary tickets for one of Celtic's home league games.

WIN five pounds to cover match-day expenses.

And if the contest isn't won, the fiver bonus keeps accumulating into a big cash snowball.

All you have to do is . . .

PICK the Celtic squad of 13 players for the game a week on Saturday.

THE PICK-A-TEAM contest goes up by another £5 ... with the game against Rangers at Ibrox a week on Sat... the test. Why not have a try — there's no entry fee

PICK-A-TEAM CONTEST IS ...

was Paul's turn to collect three
acLeod picking up two and Davie

Placings	First Placings	Second Placings	Third Placings	Total
	2	1	2	10
	2	1		7
	2			6
	2		2	6

ints for a first, two for a second

CELTIC retained their League championship flag for the second successive year at Ibrox after failing to clinch the title against Dundee United at Celtic Park.

The details and teams were as follows:

Wednesday May 3
Celtic 2 (Gemmell, Wallace)

Dundee United 3 (Hainey, Gillespie, Graham)

CELTIC: Simpson; Craig and Gemmell; Murdoch, McNeill and Clark; Johnstone and Gallagher; Wallace, Lennox and Hughes. Substitute: Chalmers.

DUNDEE UNITED: Davie; Millar and Briggs; Neilson, Smith and Moore; Berg and Graham; Hainey; Gillespie and Persson.

Saturday May 6
Rangers 2 (Jardine, Hynd)

Celtic 2 (Johnstone 2)

RANGERS: Martin; Johansen and Provan; Jardine, McKinnon and Greig; Henderson annd A. Smith; Hynd; D. Smith and Johnston.

CELTIC: Simpson; Craig and Gemmell; Murdoch, McNeill and Clark; Johnstone and Wallace; Chalmers; Auld and Hughes. Substitute: O'Neill.

During the same week Celtic Reserves defeated Dundee United 2-0 and lost by the same margin to Hearts then travelled to Aberdeen and took a 3-1 lead in the first

" Never before in modern times have a Scottish club won all the competitions open to them. Now the league championship trophy remains in our boardroom and stands alongside the Scottish Cup, the League Cup and the Glasgow Cup.

"It was, of course, especially pleasing to win the title finally at Ibrox against the only team who have been challenging us for many weeks. It was also gratifying to see so good a match in such difficult conditions.

"So heavy was the rain in the hours before the kick-off that I wondered if the game would go on.

"What a mess the league authorities would have been in had the game been postponed.

"I make no apology for continuing to be critical of the set-up in Scotland. Winning the Scottish Cup or the League Cup is fine but winning the league championship is the most important of all for any club. Yet the one competition which gets knocked about in the mat

BENNY ROONEY ... ON THE SPOT

Benny Rooney, ex-Celt and now St. Johnstone skipper, met Jimmy Cairney after Saturday's game at Parkhead. Here's how their conversation went.

EUROPE IS MY TARGET

I SUPPOSE we could aptly describe Saturday's game as a "duel in the sun" and I'm happy with the result.

All the boys are pleased, not only with the point but with the way in which it confirms that our organisation there were no that our optimism confirms fluke. Personally I felt that a draw was just right. Celtic pressed hard in the last ten minutes when we were wilting a bit in the heat but over the whole game I think we played well enough to justify our point.

WERE there any aspects of the game that disappointed you?

Maybe a wee twinge of regret that after being in the lead twice we didn't manage to hold on for a win! I think Celtic's first goal might have been prevented and here I blame myself. Before Willie Wallace got possession to make the vital pass I allowed the ball to bounce. If I had taken it first time I might have put it out of play.

been on the receiving end for I've not yet played in a winning side against Celtic. The best I've achieved are three draws, two with St. Johnstone and the other when I played for Dundee United. But one of these days I'll put one over on the "old man" — maybe at Hampden in the League Cup final!

THE transformation in St. Johnstone's fortunes in the Celtic View.

thought. Mind you I've got half-a-dozen team-mates for company. We travel by train and it's an opportunity to discuss the game in depth. But th

Blasts from the past

Any publication stands or falls on its features and many of these stood gallantly for many years before falling to oblivion. Some may have been a vital part of your early footballing education, while others are barely remembered, but they have all been integral parts of the *View* down through the years.

Spotlight on a Fan

Full name: **James Lovell.**
Birthplace: **Glasgow.**
Occupation: **Chartered Structural Engineer (Retired).**
Married: **Widower.**
Children: **Married daughter.**
Are you a member of any Celtic Supporters Club: **No.**
Favourite team other than Celtic: **Notts County.**
Favourite Player who does not play for Celtic: **Kenny Dalglish.**
Favourite Away Ground: **None.**
Best Stadium visited: **Wembley.**
Friendliest Fans other than Celtic: **Plymouth Argyle.**
Favourite current Celtic player: **Danny McGrain.**
Favourite Celtic player of the past: **Patsy Gallagher.**
Happiest moment as a Celtic supporter: **Scottish Cup Final 1931, Motherwell 2, Celtic 2.**
Saddest moment as a Celtic supporter: **Death of John Thomson.**
Best match you have ever seen: **Scottish Cup Final 1925, Rangers 0, Celtic 2.**
Best goal you have ever seen: **Free kick goal by Willie (called Peter) McGonigle against**

Rangers at Paradise from 45 yards.
Best All Time Celtic XI (players you have seen): **John Thomson, Danny McGrain, Willie McStay, Peter McGonigle, Peter Wilson, Steve Chalmers, Jimmy Johnstone, Bertie Thomson, Patsy Gallagher, Tommy McInally, Jimmy McGrory.**
Earliest Memory of watching Celtic: **Partick Thistle versus Celts at Firhill, Tuesday game 1920, aged 10.**
Which player before my time regret not seeing playing: **Jimmy Quinn.**
Favourite sports programme on TV: **Horse racing.**
Favourite other sport: **Greyhound racing.**
Favourite sportsman who is not a footballer: **Henry Cooper.**

MATCH REPORT...

Team climbed a mountain to win title

Picture Special

CELTIC got the two points vital to their Premier League challenge in the game against Hearts last week but they made it difficult for themselves.

With a lot of well known players being released, one way or another, by the Tynecastle club they introduced some new faces to the match at Celtic Park and they made a fight of it.

Right from the start Celtic dominated the proceedings but for all their supremacy they couldn't put the ball in the net.

Davie Provan was in outstanding form in the Celtic side but despite all his wiles and endeavour the finishing touch was lacking in the Celtic team.

Certainly the dry hard pitch wasn't too conducive to good football but nevertheless Celtic should have been able to find a way past the backs to the wall Hearts defence.

It may not have been one of Celtic's better all-round performances but in this instance a win was vital to their league challenge and they got the desired result.

In the second half the Celtic uphill task reached Everest type proportions when Johnny Doyle was ordered off following an incident involving Alex MacDonald.

Quite undaunted the ten men Celts set about their work again and in the 66th minute Roy Aitken scored the equaliser they so richly deserved from a Davie Provan flick.

Even more incredibly

FINAL SPECIAL . . .

THE CUP COMES HOME

CELTIC finished the 1979-80 season on a high note . . . winners of the Scottish Cup. Of course, as manager Billy McNeill observed, it didn't completely obliterate the fact that the Premier League championship was lost but the Hampden success in the Cup against Rangers "compensated in some measure for the title disappointment."

The Celtic team boss had some words about "the unfair criticism of players. I think my players and indeed the Rangers players, considering all the circumstances, behaved in a manner fit for any Cup final.

"My players didn't do anything at Hampden that players from other clubs, not just in Scotland but throughout the world, would have done in similar circumstances.

"If displaying joy and happiness on winning a major trophy is a crime then I suppose my players are guilty of it. In no shape or form did any of my players behave in a manner likely to upset other than the most biased."

He emphasised that "it was a good Old Firm game. Obviously Cup finals are always tense and often drab because of it. Saturday's game wasn't drab. There was enough action around both goals to make it an exciting game."

He agreed that Celts took a little time to settle. "That was hardly surprising because we had to try out a new formation and a new style. Yet there never was a stage in the match when I felt we were going to lose. I was always confident.

"Goalkeeper Peter Latchford had few remarkable saves to make and we created the better chances. The play went very much the way we anticipated it would develop.

"Of course I'm delighted for the players. They showed a lot of pride in themselves and the club, getting themselves set to do a good job despite the league championship loss."

On the George McCluskey goal that won the Cup, manager McNeill had a viewpoint quite different from some commentators.

"With the benefit of TV we now can see George was most aware of what he was trying to do when he flicked at the goal shot of Danny McGrain.

(Continued on back page)

(Continued on back page)

JOY AGAIN FOR TWO GREAT CELTS

AS the Celtic players show the cup outside Hampden on Saturday it was an especially happy occasion for two of them in particular.

Danny McGrain, who has played throughout the seventies, was celebrating his first Scottish Cup win, as club captain and, Bobby Lennox, standing beside him, had just taken his Scottish Cup medals tally to five.

Other players in picture are Peter Latchford, Murdo MacLeod (behind cup), Mike Conroy and Roy Aitken.

VIEWPOINT
CLOUD OVER A GREAT GAME

SOME of the glitter was taken off Celtic's excellent Scottish Cup final victory on Saturday because of the shameful behaviour of a number of vicious hooligans masquerading under the name of football enthusiasts.

The Celtic Football Club never has and never will condone hooliganism and bad behaviour of any description at matches and everyone connected with the club was appalled by the disgraceful scenes after Saturdays match.

Celtic would also like to extend their congratulations and admiration for the work of the skeleton police presence in the stadium when the trouble flared into a series of running battles before the arrival of the mounted police and other reinforcements.

But the question should be asked:

Where was the police strength at the flashpoint of any such game — the end of the match?

When some Celtic players ran to the traditional Celtic end of the pitch to acknowledge the cheers of the supporters, a handful of youngsters, carried away in their exuberance, ran on to the park.

There were only about half a dozen policemen at that end of the park and as more youngsters poured onto the park they were powerless to stop the flow.

However, if that area had been manned by about 50 or 60 constables that 'invasion' would not have taken place.

Another vital factor in the whole sad affair was the fact that the fence gaps (provided for first aid access) were not manned and the majority of people who entered the playing area from both ends did so through these openings and not over the tops of the fences.

It should also be borne in mind that the youngsters who entered the field from the Celtic end were, quite wrongly, going towards the tunnel to watch the trophy presentation.

They were happy as they celebrated the victory but they did not charge towards the Rangers end as some newspapers have reported.

Then hundreds of Rangers fans spilled onto the park and charged the Celtic fans, throwing missiles and brutally attacking anyone they caught.

It's only fair to say that at that point the police on the field were powerless to stop the battles that followed because by then it was too late.

Indeed only the swift and fearless intervention of the mounted police put an end to a situation which would have assuredly have resulted in fatalities.

The police by their own admission have said that their forces had been redeployed before the end of the game. It would seem that the redeployment took place too soon.

In conclusion we would also like to salute the courage shown by the ambulance corps and the stewards who carried out the duties in most trying and frightening circumstances.

As Scottish football recently prepared itself for the 2007–08 season, there were moves afoot to alter the laws which ban alcohol consumption by supporters watching the game in any stadium in the country.

Prior to 1980, the laws were pretty lax and it was events in the immediate aftermath of the Scottish Cup final that year that prompted stiffer regulations. The final was, of course, contested by Celtic and Rangers and, as the victorious Celtic paraded the trophy, there was a break-in at the Rangers end followed by another at the opposite end. Millions and millions watched on live on TV as both sets of fans squared up to each other on the Hampden turf.

There had been a game of football before this, though, and with both teams tied 0-0 at the end of ninety minutes, extra-time was called for to decide the tie. The *View* report started: 'A huge shirt-sleeved crowd in excess of 70,000 attended the Scottish Cup final at Hampden on Saturday. The game was never

a football classic, but it had plenty of excitement and action around both goals and it took an extra 30 minutes to produce the only goal of the game.'

It carried on: 'The game continued to rage from end to end in extra-time with near things and good goalkeeping. Celtic's cup-winning goal came in the third minute of the second period of extra-time. Following a corner kick and two headed clearances from the Rangers defence, Danny McGrain's shot for goal was flicked by George McCluskey and Peter McCloy couldn't prevent the ball going into the net.'

The *View* also reported that in the Reserve League Cup semi-final first leg, the Celtic second string recorded what looked like a fairly safe 5-0 win over St Mirren on Monday 5 May, with the second leg being played on Thursday 8 May. The teams turned out at Love Street and the home team scored after ten minutes, but Danny Crainie equalised almost instantly. That leveller proved to be crucial as St Mirren were to go on and win the game 5-1, for Celtic to scrape through on a 6-5 aggregate.

THE
CELTIC
VIEW

No. 767
October 27,
1982
Price 12p

DRAMA AND THRILLS

... as Celts go for three in a row

THERE'S a great deal of drama and thrills in store for our fans over the next seven days. Top games in the League Cup, Premier League and the European Cup will all provide a footballing feast for our fans.

Our task in Europe is now clear. We must go out and play to score. This is the kind of football that suits us and we know we can beat Real Sociedad and continue our challenge in Europe.

Last Wednesday in Spain we played well but an unfortunate five minute spell when everything seemed to go wrong sees us fighting from behind a two goal deficit.

I was very disappointed for our players who played composed and profesionally — we really should have had a better result.

Next week's will be a game when the supporters can really do their bit by getting behind the players and help their game. I must take this chance to congratulate our fans who travelled to Spain. They behaved really well and we all felt for them when we saw where the Spanish intended putting them for the match.

On Saturday we travelled to Cappielow and became the first team to defeat Morton there this season in the League. Our 2-0 half-time lead was justified and we should have consolidated it in the early stages of the second half. Morton, however, fought their way into the game and drew close with one goal.

Tonight we face Dundee United at Celtic Park in the first leg of the League Cup semi-final. This will be a very demanding game which will provide a spectacular for the fans.

Dundee United have their injury worries, but ours are as bad. Dom Sullivan and Tommy Burns will not be ready. George McCluskey played twice for the reserves over the weekend and should come into consideration. Our injury worries have now stretched to the reserve side where John McGoldrick and Ronnie Coyle are now both injured. Brian Scott must now be the hardest working member of our staff.

On Saturday we continue our league campaign at home to Rangers in the first Old Firm clash of the season.

BILLY McNEILL

HE WAS ALWAYS THE BOSS

CELTIC legend Jimmy McGrory died last Wednesday at the age of 78.

Above we see him in one of his happiest moments holding the League Cup which Celtic had just won with him as manager.

He was always known as "The Boss" to all who played under him right up to the day he died.

He earned respect by respecting others and his footballing achievements earned him the status of legend even before he took over as Celtic manager.

On page 3 we look at the man who was undoubtedly BRITAIN'S GREATEST STRIKER.

Praise for the fans

CELTIC fans earned more praise from people in high places for their behaviour in San Sebastian last week.

At the end of the match the Spanish fans stood and clapped as the Scots left the Stadium.

Two high ranking British Government officials took time to prise the well behaved fans. Mr Edmund Barratt, the British Consul-General had much praise for them and Raymond Pringle, the Vice-Consul based in Bilbao who actually watched the match, said of them:

"They did a lot of good for Britain's sporting reputation. They were good humoured and did not cause any trouble. I was absolutely delighted with them."

It's all action at Cappielow. For more action shots see middle pages.

43

One of Celtic's greatest ever servants, Jimmy McGrory, passed away on 20 October 1982.

In all he scored 550 goals in top-class football as he wrote and re-wrote the record books. And as the tributes to him flowed in, the *View* said: 'Anyone who has put on a green and white scarf since the early twenties has a place in their heart for Jimmy McGrory. There is no doubt that he was a great player, a great goalscorer and a great Celt. For many Jimmy McGrory is the greatest Celt who ever lived. A goal a game for 15 years is a heading often used for articles concerning the greatest ever Scottish striker. With a total of 410 goals in 408 league matches he averaged a goal a game from 1922/23 to '37/38.'

Celtic chairman Desmond White wrote in that week's *View*: 'Since the death last week of Jimmy McGrory the football world and beyond have paid tribute to one of Celtic's greatest and most respected servants. On behalf of the club's directors I would associate myself with these richly deserved appreciations of Jimmy's unique gifts as a player and goal-scorer supreme, his subsequent contribution as manager of Celtic and, not least, his special qualities as a person.'

Celtic historian Pat Woods also wrote: 'No one could read the football press at the time of Jimmy McGrory's playing career and fail to be struck by Celtic's indebtedness to him, not only for his remarkable goalscoring record, but also for the inspirational value of his limitless enthusiasm and determination.

'No cause could be considered lost when McGrory was on the field, perhaps most notably exemplified in the first match of the 1931 Scottish Cup final against Motherwell (a match vividly described in McGrory's life story A Lifetime in Paradise, a book worthy of the man who was probably the most popular Celt of all time). He embodied the sport's finest philosophy – the game played vigorously, skilfully and competitively, but, above all, in the best traditions of sportsmanship.

'Willie Maley paid him perhaps the greatest tribute when, writing in the 1938/39 Celtic Handbook, after McGrory had taken up the Kilmarnock managership, he said that Jimmy McGrory had adorned the club with his presence leaving behind "memories of the very finest and of deeds in our colours that will never fade".'

Jimmy McGrory as a player. In Dublin with team mates in 1936.

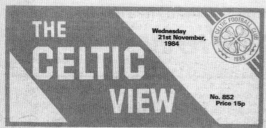

THE CELTIC VIEW

Wednesday 21st November, 1984

No. 852
Price 15p

UEFA decision on Rapid match

AN act of lunacy, by a couple of people purporting to be Celtic supporters, cost the club a £4,000 fine last week.

The bottle throwing actions by the lunatics responsible also robbed the Celtic team of the spotlight they were due for a quite magnificent display in turning a 3-1 deficit into an aggregate victory against Rapid Vienna at Celtic Park.

Celtic Football Club have been placed on "very thin ice" in European competition and the behaviour of all our fans will have to be above reproach in future

games.

It's only fair to point out, however, that the behaviour of the near 50,000 crowd at Celtic Park two weeks ago was exemplary with the exception of the couple of mindless morons who threw bottles onto the park.

If the people responsible happen to read this, we would be much obliged if they would stay away from Celtic Park in future.

The full findings of the Control and Disciplinary Committee of UEFA, as communicated to Celtic, were as follows:

- That two bottles were thrown onto the field of play by spectators in the 80th minute,
- That the allegation made by the club Rapid Vienna, according to which the player Weinhofer was struck by a bottle has not been confirmed, neither by the referee nor by the official delegate,
- That the team of Rapid Vienna has shown a particularly incorrect conduct during this match,
- That the player Reinhard Kienast was dismissed from the game for an act of violence against an opponent,
- That the coach of the team Rapid Vienna, Mr Otto Baric, and other officials have shown a particularly ungentlemanly conduct during the match,
- That, in addition, three players of the club Rapid Vienna were cautioned during the course of the match.

In consequence of the above, the Committee decided:

- To reject the protest entered by the club Rapid Vienna and to confirm the result of 3-0 in favour of Celtic FC,
- To impose a fine of 12,000 Swiss Francs on Celtic FC for the comportment of the spectators (in case of repetition),
- To impose a fine of 15,000 Swiss Francs on the club Rapid Vienna for the conduct of the team (in case of repetition),
- To suspend the player Reinhard Kienast (Rapid Vienna) for four UEFA club competition matches after his expulsion (already cautioned in a previous match of the current season),
- To suspend the coach of the club Rapid Vienna, Mr Otto Baric, for three UEFA competition matches,
- To censure the club Rapid Vienna for the comportment of the other team officials,
- To confirm the cautions administered to the players Zlatko, Kranjcar, Karl Ehn and Peter Brucic for foul play,

The protest fee will be withheld.

RAPID VIENNA HAVE APPEALED AGAINST THESE RULINGS. THE APPEAL WILL BE HEARD ON FRIDAY.

Rig Men Help Fund

DUNCAN DOCHERTY who works on the Morecambe Bay Gas Rig raised the incredible sum of £1400 from among this workmates for the Paul Rafferty Fund.

The money, in the form of sponsorship for Duncan completing the Inverclyde Marathon, will go towards the fund which helps at Yorkhill Hospital.

Duncan is seen with John McAuley of the Paul Rafferty fund among some other friends of the fund who won't need identified for Celtic supporters.

BP Scottish Youth Cup
SECOND ROUND DRAW

Holders Celtic have been drawn away to Clyde in the second round of the BP Scottish Youth cup for under 18 professional sides.

The complete draw is:

West and South Section: Ayr United v Stranraer, Queen of the South v Kilmarnock, St Mirren v Rangers, Motherwell v Queen's Park and **CLYDE v CELTIC.**

East and North Section: St. Johnstone v Brora Rangers, Aberdeen v Dundee and Dundee United v Hearts. Ties are to be played on or before December 31.

East and North Section: St. Johnstone 3, Fort William 1, Brora Rangers 4, Ross County 3.

Rangers, Celtic, St. Mirren, Aberdeen, Dundee United and Hearts all had byes in the second round.

The Rapid Vienna fiasco has gone down in the annals of Celtic history for all the wrong reasons, but that was far from anybody's mind after the first leg in Austria.

The competition in question was the European Cup-Winners' Cup of 1984–85 and, after beating Ghent of Belgium 3-1 on aggregate in the first round, the Vienna side awaited in the second. The Celts shipped three goals in Austria, but a Brian McClair goal gave them hope and that slim optimism was justified when the Bhoys triumphed 3-0 at Celtic Park. The crowd of 48,813 left the ground thinking that was that and looking forward to the draw after a supposed 4-3 aggregate win. It wasn't quite that straightforward, though, as it had been a pretty torrid night in the East End of Glasgow.

Reinhard Kienast was sent off for an off-the-ball assault on Tommy Burns, but the key moment came when a bottle and a few coins were thrown on to the pitch and, although none of them landed anywhere near him, Rudi Weinhofer collapsed as if felled by a sniper. Chaos ensued and Weinhofer was pictured swathed in enough bandages to cover Boris Karloff.

This front page shows that Celtic were fined £4,000 for the bottle incident, while Rapid received a heftier fine for the conduct of their team plus further suspensions for individual players. However, the *View* also adds as a footnote, rather ominously as it transpired, that the Austrian club would be appealing the decision.

The second leg was ordered to be replayed at least a hundred miles from Celtic Park and, on 12 December 1984, over 40,000 made the trip to Old Trafford, with local 'support' swelling the crowd to 51,500. The dream ended there, though, as Roy Aitken hit the woodwork and Rapid pounced on the rebound, raced to the other end of the park and scored the only goal of the night. More crowd trouble cost Celtic dearly and they were ordered to play their next European home match behind closed doors.

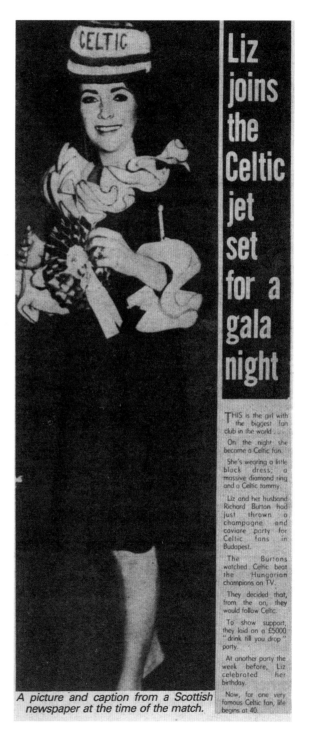

Liz joins the Celtic jet set for a gala night

THIS is the girl with the biggest fan club in the world . . .

On the night she became a Celtic fan.

She's wearing a little black dress; a massive diamond ring and a Celtic tammy.

Liz and her husband Richard Burton had just thrown a champagne and caviare party for Celtic fans in Budapest.

The Burtons watched Celtic beat the Hungarian champions on TV.

They decided that, from the on, they would follow Celtc.

To show support, they laid on a £5000 " drink till you drop " party.

At another party the week before, Liz celebrated her birthday.

Now, for one very famous Celtic fan, life begins at 40.

A picture and caption from a Scottish newspaper at the time of the match.

THE CELTIC VIEW

Wednesday 22nd May 1985

No. 877
Price 15p

WINNERS

CELTIC completed a double in six days last week and became Cup holders at two levels of Scottish senior football.

Paul Chalmers scored the only goal of the game in the second leg of the Scottish Second Eleven Cup Final at Easter Road on Monday.

This gave Celtic a 3-0 aggregate score and completed a double for the second string who had already been presented with the Premier Reserve League Champions Trophy.

HISTORY

On Saturday, the Reserves all sat together at Hampden and watched the first team win the 100th Scottish Cup Final with a 2-1 victory over Dundee United.

PAUL McGUGAN with the Scottish Second Eleven Cup.

This was Celtic's 43rd appearance in a Scottish Cup Final and the 27th time they have won it in their 97 year history.

For Danny McGrain it was his fifth winners medal. For Roy Aitken it was his third. Murdo MacLeod, Davie Provan, Tommy Burns and Frank McGarvey were collecting their second.

For the others it was their first and for many of them it came hard on the heels of last season's disappointment.

After coming second in the League twice and second in the two major Cup finals last season, this was Davie Hay's first trophy as Celtic manager.

Frank Connor's rush on to the park at the final whistle summed up the feeling of everyone associated with Celtic.

During an interview before the final Davie Hay said that Celtic supporters are winners, that they needed success and that they deserve success. They got it on Saturday.

From the kick-off of Celtic's Cup campaign this season at Hamilton on January 30 the support have made their presence felt, but never more so than during the last fifteen minutes of Saturday's final.

It was a great victory and the first of Celtic's trophies under Davie Hay. For the manager, the players and the fans it was a great day.

Looking back at the match on Monday morning, Davie Hay said: "It is a victory that will always be remembered because it is the one hundredth Scottish Cup Final, but even more pleasing for me is the manner in which we won, having come from a goal down.

"For years to come the biggest talking point from the final — apart from the fact that we won — will be the way the Celtic fans turned out on Saturday.

GREATEST

"I am continually saying that they are the greatest fans in the world. As a player I believed it and in all my travels I saw nothing to outdo them.

"I keep thinking that they have reached a peak and then they go one better, like they did on Saturday.

"If the team can improve like the support we will be right at the top for a long time."

The Celtic manager went on to say that he hopes to take the Scottish Cup to Canada with him next week to show it to all the Scottish exiles and Celtic fans living there.

We asked Davie what Saturday's victory meant to him personally. He said "It feels great. I have now been the manager of a winning Celtic team."

QUESTION

"Over the past two seasons we have come very close on several occasions, but fallen at the last hurdle. That must have put a question mark beside my ability, but now we've won a major trophy.

"This isn't the end, this is just the beginning!"

We also asked if he felt this victory had taken any pressure off him. He answered: "To be honest it has. I would not be telling the truth if I said that I hadn't felt pressure but we've all come through it with something to show. we must now keep up our effort and go on from here".

Closing, he added, "On the day it was the players who won the Cup. All 13 of them were superb. I'd like to congratulate and thank them".

TOUR DATES

HERE are the dates for Celtic's end of season tours. We know that wherever Celtic play a green and white scarf or two shows up.

An Under 20 team will play in a tournament in Groningen in Holland on May 25, 26 and 27.

A side will play in a six-a-side tournament in Bangor, Wales, on May 26.

Then a squad will be off to Canada to play in Toronto on June 5 and 6.

That winning feeling

■ DAVIE HAY'S expression tells the whole story of Saturday's victory when Celtic won the Scottish Cup for the 27th time.

YOUR SUMMER VIEW

TODAY'S is the last *Celtic View* of the current season but there will be a double sized summer edition in your newsagents on Wednesday June 26, priced 30p.

It will be full of facts, figures, memories and pictures of the season just finished, plus reports from Celtic's travels to Canada, Holland and Wales during the coming few weeks.

His father may have scored rather more important goals in rather more important finals, but, such is Celtic's fine tradition of promoting and encouraging youth coming through the ranks, it was typical that reserve player Paul Chalmers gets a name-check four lines into this leader, while those who did the business at Hampden have to wait until the sixth paragraph.

The youngster scored the only goal at Easter Road to give the second string a 3-0 aggregate score over Hibernian in the Second XI Cup final but, to be fair, the big news was the other half of this cup double. It was the hundredth Scottish Cup final, Celtic's forty-third appearance at the ultimate stage and the twenty-seventh time the trophy had returned to Celtic Park in the club's ninety-seven-year history. More importantly at this stage, though, it was Davie Hay's first trophy as Celtic manager after being so close but yet so far in four other competitions over the course of two seasons.

Celtic had defeated Hamilton Accies, Inverness Thistle (the old club, not ICT) and both Dundee and Motherwell after replays in the quarter- and semi-finals respectively. Dundee United had taken care of Hibernian, Queen of the South, St Mirren and Aberdeen as they looked forward to celebrating the hundredth Scottish Cup final with their first ever win. And when Stuart Beedie proved he had an eye for goal by opening the scoring nine minutes after the break it looked like their dreams might just come true.

Roared on by the majority of the 60,346 crowd, though, the Celts displayed all their redoubtable qualities for turning games around when all eyes are on the clock. As Roy Aitken was pushed forward by Davie Hay, Davie Provan sparked the revival by firing in a free-kick fourteen minutes from time (the first ever direct-from-a-free-kick goal in the history of the Cup). Then, with just six minutes to go, Frank McGarvey somehow managed to get his head on an Aitken cross and steer the ball into the back of the net at the Celtic End. Cue delirium as three-quarters of Hampden went ballistic.

The table for the SUNDAY POST CRIME COUNT 1984-85 finished like this:				
	FOULS	CAUTIONS	SENT OFF	TOTAL
Celtic	529	37	0	640
Dundee United	547	31	1	645
Dumbarton	536	45	0	671
Morton	543	39	3	675
Aberdeen	572	34	1	679
Hibernian	547	47	1	693
Dundee	587	45	1	727
St. Mirren	603	35	6	738
Hearts	592	49	1	744
Rangers	620	56	3	803

THE CELTIC VIEW

Wednesday September 18 1985

No. 884
Price 15p

Tributes to Jock Stein pour in

A loud and clear message

SCOTTISH football got a loud message from Celtic on Saturday and if it was to be put into words it might read "We are never going to lie down!"

As they took the lead over Aberdeen, then lost a goal only to establish themselves as leaders again inside the last five minutes, the scoreline does not do justice to Celtic's superiority over the defending champions.

Celtic were so much better in every department that even Aberdeen manager Alex Ferguson admitted that his team did not deserve the draw they looked likely to snatch towards the end.

The way in which Celtic refused to give in and worked for their late winner gave them the look of champions.

The mood of the day was illustrated by Paul McGugan who, having cut his forehead in a clash of heads with Eric Black, refused to leave the play and continued for half an hour with blood streaming down his face. Vaseline stopped the bleeding momentarily, but the tall defender refused to be cautious and the wound was soon opened again. After the match the wound was finally closed with two stitches.

Brian McClair, the double goalscorer, won most spectators' choice as man of the match, but it would be impossible to find a failure in the Celtic side.

A crowd of 39,000 filled Celtic Park for this meeting and gave the new segregation on the East Terracing its first test. The new arrangements passed with flying colours.

There were no exchanges of taunts and a remarkably reduced number of derogatory chants from the rival sets of fans separated by a no man's land and a high screen, through which they cannot see, on that terracing.

It would appear that this innovative idea is working and the risk of clashes of fans has been greatly reduced.

EUROPEAN ACTION

Tonight Celtic face Spanish Cup holders Atletico Madrid in the opening match of their European campaign this season. In view of the disappointing way the players were cheated of their semifinal place last season, a long run is necessary.

Although none of us will be in Spain tonight we are sure every Celtic fan is right behind Davie Hay and his team.

Saturday's match at Tannadice is all-ticket. At the time of writing there were still a few tickets available at 146 West Nile Street, Glasgow.

On the following Saturday, Celtic will travel to Dens Park, this match will NOT be a ticket game.

His face covered in blood, Paul McGugan refused to give in.

Jack McGinn (director of Celtic F.C.): "Coincidentally my association with Celtic started at the same time as Jock Stein was attending his first board meeting as manager in 1965.

"The Club had virtually agreed to start a club newspaper, of which I was to be editor, and I was at the meeting to have a layout for the first issue approved.

"On the front page was to be a team picture and Jock Stein said if we held the space for a couple of months we could put the Scottish Cup into the picture. He lived up to his word.

"In my dealings with him we had a good association with the occasional disagreements which are to be expected in any lengthy working relationship, but there was never any carry over or grudge borne.

"All that can be said has been said about Jock Stein over the past week, I would like to add that his success in football can be attributed to his total dedication and thoroughness in every aspect of the game."

● ● ●

Tom Devlin (chairman of Celtic F.C.): "I first met Jock Stein when he returned from Wales to sign for Celtic.

"He was primarily brought in to help in the development of the youngsters in our reserve side, but luckily, or unluckily, all our first team centre halfs were injured and from his first week, Jock took over that position for us.

"As a player he was not artistic, but he was very effective. Eventually he was offered the job as manager of Dumfermline and Robert Kelly advised him to take it. It is safe to say, however, that when he left us to take up that post we all knew that someday he would return in the capacity of manager.

"He came back much earlier than we all anticipated and became a Celtic legend.

"In all the years that we knew each other, I never had a cross word with Jock. His deeds at Celtic Park will never be forgotten."

SCOTTISH football paid tribute to Jock Stein with a minute's silence before every League match on Saturday. At Celtic Park, not a whisper was heard among the crowd of almost 40,000 during the minute when all thoughts were on the sudden loss of "The Big Man" who died after watching his Scottish national side draw 1-1 with Wales at Ninian Park, Cardiff last Tuesday evening.

Alongside we have some of the tributes to the former Celtic manager that have flooded into the Celtic View office.

In the middle pages we carry more and look back at a magnificent career.

Jim Torbett (founder of Celtic Boys' Club): "It was the 10th of November, 1966 when the late chairman of Celtic, Sir Robert Kelly and Jock Stein gave me permission to use the name of Celtic to form The Celtic Boys' Club.

"Jock Stein's interest and support from it's inception was immense, his help, guidance, advice and yes, sometimes his heavy hand is what kept us on the right lines.

"In 1967 he became the President of the Boys' Club. This was not to be an honorary position as the title suggested, He was very much part of the Club.

"In those early days our football was played on a Sunday at Glasgow Green, as often as not he would be seen at our games offering encouragement and support to the lads.

"He would never miss an opportunity to put the Boys' Club on show to give the youngsters the 'big time' feeling as pre-match entertainment before Celtic's big matches.

"He would be seen at dances selling raffle tickets for the Boys' Club funds. He would never miss a Boys' Club function. At one such function he described the Celtic B.C. as an asset that Celtic F.C. could not put a price on. How right he was. That asset lives on because of the 'Big Man's' foresight to encourage the small men at all levels of the game."

On 10 September 1985, while managing Scotland in a World Cup qualifier against Wales at Ninian Park in Cardiff, the legendary Jock Stein suffered a fatal heart attack.

In just over a dozen seasons as manager at Celtic he won ten championships, eight Scottish Cups, six League Cups and, of course, the European Cup. The *View* was bursting at the seams with tributes to the great man and here are a few from those who knew him best:

Lisbon Lion Stevie Chalmers told the *View*: 'I can still remember the day I signed for Celtic. Jock Stein, then the reserve team coach, came with the manager Jimmy McGrory to meet me at Green's Playhouse in Glasgow. I remember thinking how fit and healthy Mr Stein looked and I thought – that must be a good life to be in, and it has proved to be a good one for myself.

'Jock Stein lived for football and in the end he died for football. It is fitting that he was involved in football to the very end and I am sure he would be very happy about that. As a footballer I won every honour that was available, but perhaps the greatest honour in my career was working under Jock Stein.'

Club captain Danny McGrain said: 'Jock Stein was my first manager when I joined Celtic at the age of 17, a very impressionable age, and he moulded my future. He taught me habits that I have carried with me until today, habits that have helped get this far. My success in football is all thanks to him. It would take up more than two paragraphs, two pages or indeed two *Celtic View*s to say what he has done for me in 18 years of professional football.'

And former team-mate and evergreen Celt Neilly Mochan said: 'Jock Stein was always a realistic down-to-earth man. He didn't do himself justice when he often put down his own ability as a player. I saw him bring new qualities to the game and the same tactical flair that made a great manager was evident when he was a player.

'The record books don't tell the full story of the difference he made to Celtic. Before he came to Celtic, it had been a long time since the club had won any honour. Within a couple of years no one else was winning anything.

'He took very good players and knitted them together to make great teams. He was a great personal friend of mine, throughout our lives of working together, and when he moved away from Celtic Park he always kept up the relationship.'

AS Celtic travelled to Madrid on Monday for tonight's European Cup Winners' Cup tie against the local Atletico, the Spanish Press has prepared the public for Celtic's arrival.

As far back as the draw for this first round tie, the Spanish stated that in Celtic, Atletico had the most difficult opponents of the Spanish Clubs playing in Europe.

A direct translation from one Spanish story calls Celtic "None other than the great Glasgow Celtic."

THE **CELTIC** VIEW

Wednesday
2nd October
1985

No. 886
Price 15p

SUPPORT CELTIC — STAY AWAY

CELTIC have always had a close link with their fans and for many years the club and its supporters have shared great European moments. There have been great triumphs and sad defeats, but always there has been that great atmosphere provided by a full Celtic Park. This week, however, the Club must ask you to stay away.

Isolated and uncharacteristic incidents of hooliganism from Celtic supporters during last season's meetings with Rapid Vienna, have resulted in UEFA ordering the Club to play our first home European tie this season behind closed doors.

That match is being played at Celtic Park this afternoon when Atletico Madrid visit for the second leg of the European Cup-Winners Cup first round.

Nobody should come anywhere near Celtic Park today.

Every Celtic supporter is fully aware that spectators will not be allowed inside the stadium. The Union of European Football Associations rules are such that, for this game, Celtic have had to employ security to prevent anyone attempting to get near the stadium.

Television and radio coverage of today's match will be very limited, but it is reasonable to assume that you will be kept up to date with the half time and full time results.

Anyone who does try to come anywhere near Celtic Park will be wasting time and any travelling expenses. There is no way that what is happening inside Celtic Park can be communicated to anyone waiting outside.

Stewards and police will patrol the area surrounding Celtic Park to ensure that crowds are not able to assemble and there will be constant watches on the perimeter walls to prevent people gaining illegal entry.

Celtic fully appreciate that supporters will feel frustrated and disappointed at not being able to see this match, indeed the players will miss the comfort that a big Celtic crowd gives them, but the Club has no choice.

We have been made aware of the steps that UEFA are willing to take, the punishments are too great for any of us to take a chance.

This is certainly the first time Celtic have asked their supporters to stay away from Celtic Park, we all hope it is the last time it is necessary.

As the players take the field in the uneasy silence this afternoon, they will be aware that they take your support with them. Hopefully this will build on their fine result of two weeks ago and we will all be able to get together at Celtic Park for a special Celtic European night in the next round.

For today, the best way to support Celtic is to stay away.

A NEW INJURY WORRY

CELTIC'S victory at Dens Park on Saturday took them to the top of the Premier League and has given them a confidence booster for today's European tie.

Having acquitted themselves very well in Madrid and recording a 1-1 draw in the first leg, Celtic are going into the game as favourites, but with a down-to-earth attitude that they still have a job ahead of them.

Willie McStay had a game with the reserves on Saturday and having put injury behind him, is likely to find himself on the substitutes' bench tonight. Celtic have, however, picked up another injury worry.

Having had to leave the action on Saturday, midfielder Murdo MacLeod had stitches in a wound just above his ankle and immediately became doubtful for the European clash.

Peter Grant, who performed well in Madrid, received much critical aclaim for his part in Celtic's victory on Saturday. Other sources chose Roy Aitken as man of the match, some Danny McGrain, some Mo Johnston and others Tommy Burns. No doubt some of you could choose other Celts as star players. In all it was a magnificent performance and one worthy of European challengers.

We are sure we speak for all the absent fans from today's match when we pass on a message to the Celtic players — Although we are not there today, we are with you in spirit and — YOU'LL NEVER WALK ALONE.

As already indicated, after the Rapid Vienna debacle Celtic were ordered to play their next European home match behind closed doors and, as you would expect from a team of Celtic's calibre, there was no need to wait as they qualified for Europe right away.

Once more they were in the European Cup-Winners' Cup and, considering that supporters didn't want to miss a game and the financial penalties for the club, not to mention the further qualification hopes of the team, the best possible scenario would be to come out of the hat with the likes of Limassol of Cyprus or Fram Reykjavik from Iceland, before going on to meet the big guns. Of course, probably the worst possible scenario on all the above counts ensued as Spanish giants Atletico Madrid were paired with the Celts.

It was a triple whammy as Celtic Park would have been bursting at the seams, so the punters were missing the opportunity of taking in a possible classic was the reasonable possibility of an early first-round knock-out and no European football as such for the supporters.

The biggest drawback was yet to come, though – the Celts fought gallantly in the Vincente Calderon Stadium as Pat Bonner saved a Rubio penalty in the seventy-sixth minute to keep the score at 1-1… An away draw had been earned in front of 55,000 partisan Spaniards and the ball was in Celtic's court. The only thing was that it would be an empty court.

All other shortcomings were put fully and firmly in the shade by the fact that Celtic's famed twelfth man – the 60,000 souls who could strike fear into the most skilful of teams and suck the ball into the opposition net – would be missing and Celtic were to pay the price. In front of only a few pressmen and officials, and with reserves acting as ballboys, on a Wednesday afternoon the Celts lost 2-1 in the ghostly and eerie atmosphere of an empty Paradise. This front page makes the club's wishes clear and, considering what happened on the previous occasion when Atletico visited Celtic Park, maybe it's just as well that the game was played behind closed doors!

FAN CLUB CORNER

ANDREW Easton of Shotts has been chosen by Brian McClair as the winner in our latest competition.

Brian will be writing a personal message to Andrew after today's match.

We've had a bit of a hold up with our Fan Club kits this season, hopefully they'll all be in the post within two weeks.

See you next week, Ray.

Happy Birthday to the following Members

Monday 30 September
099, William McEree, Linwood (14); 765 Kevin McEnroe, Glasgow (2); 1079 Billy McFaul, Eire (21).

THE CELTIC VIEW

Wednesday 7th May 1986

No. 917
Price 15p

High Scoring Celtic Take The Crown of ...

CHAMPIONS

CELTIC lifted the greatest prize in Scottish football this season, not in two games played in Paisley and Dundee on Saturday, but with the points and goals amassed in 36 league matches over the season from which they emerged with 20 victories, ten draws and were only defeated six times.

The Scottish Sport Press have tagged this achievement as a "miracle," but no matter how highly Celtic supporters regard their heroes on the field, they are mortal and mortals do not work miracles. They can, however, work hard for attainable prizes and in the end they stretched to their limit and lifted the biggest one on offer.

It is not a miracle that Celtic haven't lost a league match since January 4, 17 games ago. It is not a miracle that they won every one of their last eight matches. It is not a miracle that they scored 12 goals in their last five league matches. It is not a miracle that in Mo Johnston and Brian McClair they have two of the deadliest strikers in the business, two men who between them netted 37 league goals during this season's campaign. These are all facts and in that are major factors in Celtic's 34th Championship victory.

The league set up is such that the most consistent side over the course of 36 games always comes out on top. The fact that Celtic's goal-scoring finally clinched it points to a quality which makes football exciting for all of us who flock to grounds around the

by Celtic View Editor Danny McCahon

country every weekend to watch the game.

After a season during which Celtic showed some very indifferent form at times, it was particularly pleasing for many fans to see them finish in true Celtic fashion — on the attack and looking like winners.

One fan in the stand at Love Street, watching as Celtic romped to their 5-0 victory and with a small radio pressed against one ear in the hope of news of a Dundee victory over Hearts, suddenly pushed the radio into his pocket and said "who cares what happens at Dens Park? This is brilliant."

It did matter what happened at Dens and in

waiting for news from that far-off stadium, the Celtic fans demonstrated the effect they can have on the team.

Knowing that Celtic had done enough and with the news of no scoring in the match at Dundee, the crowd went uncharacteristically quiet for a long spell during the second half. This feeling of strained anticipation seemed to spread from the terracing to the field of play and without performing badly the team had their least constructive spell of the match.

This Celtic support gives us all an extra prize to look forward to — the chance to stand among the best atmosphere in

sport when Celtic host action in the European Cup next season.

For a manager with Davie Hay's ambition the European Cup competition, the Champions' Cup as it is known on the continent, is a perfect stage, and he deserves it. At a time when things weren't going smoothly for Celtic he stood up to be counted by dispensing with the services of his assistant manager and going it alone.

His honour is unquestionable even when he has been the target of harsh and unconstructive criticism, he has spurned the temptation to hit back. A lot of that criticism must now be seen to be unjustified. If the manager is the man with whom the buck stops after poor performances, surely glory

should rest on him following success.

Always a realist, Hay quickly turned to practical matters following the jubilation of Saturday and in anticipation of next season's venture into Europe he hinted of possible big name defence signings before the campaign begins.

All that remains for Celtic this season is a trip to Ibrox on Friday night for the final of the Glasgow Cup. It would be nice to have another trophy to display in next season's team poster.

The Champions of Scotland salute their ever faithful fans, who have had a champion season themselves. More celebration pictures and the last five goals of the league season are on the middle pages.

In early editions of the _Celtic View_ the front pages were never giveaways as to who exactly had won the title the previous weekend.

More recently there had been the 21 May 1979 'ten-men-won-the-league' front page, which proclaimed 'World Hails The Champions', but this most recent celebratory end-of-season ball really tells it like it is and does what it says on the tin. It doesn't get any better or any clearer than this.

There's something about snatching victory from the jaws of oblivion to make the triumph all that sweeter and 3 May 1986 was certainly up there with the comeback job performed in the face of adversity back in 1979. At the end of 1985, the Celts sat in fourth place in the league, while Hearts were top, four points ahead in those two-points-for-a-win days.

By the end of February, Hearts were two points further ahead as Dundee United and Aberdeen also lengthened the gap between themselves and the still fourth-placed Celts. The fact that Celtic were then to draw with both Dundee United and Rangers in consecutive games didn't help matters, but from the end of March, with eight games left, the Celts went on a winning spree.

It all boiled down to the last day of the season with both Celtic and Hearts playing away from home. Hearts sat on top with 50 points and a goal difference of +28; the Celts had 48 points and goal difference of +24. Hearts only needed to draw and the championship would be theirs for the first time in twenty-six years. Celtic had to hope that Hearts would lose at Dundee, but if Dundee won 1-0 the Celts would have to win by three clear goals against St Mirren at Love Street.

The Celts went about their business like a team possessed in Paisley and by the thirty-eighth minute were 4-0 up. The problem was that they could have won 45-0 and it would have been no good if Hearts drew at Dens Park. Brian McClair added another at Love Street, but with thousands of ears glued to the radio report from Dundee, the biggest cheer of the day so far went up when Celtic-daft Albert Kidd came on as a sub and scored for Dundee. He was to repeat the feat as Hearts went down 2-0 and Celtic won 5-0 to finish on a goal difference of +29 to Hearts' +26. Even better, when news of Kidd's first goal was broadcast there was a massive cheer at Ibrox, because they thought it was Walter Kidd scoring for Hearts!

GROUND SEASON TICKETS

FANS have already responded to the news that Celtic are considering the possibility of introducing a ground season ticket for next season and in order to judge whether numbers are sufficient to support the scheme, we are now asking supporters who would like to have such a ticket, to write to: **Celtic Football Club, 28 Bath Street, Glasgow G2 1HE.**

Letters already received at the Celtic View Office will be passed on to the secretary's office.

LOOK AGAIN!

NO you're not seeing double. That's Maurice Johnston on the left and 'lookalike' David Donnelly from Baillieston on the right. The picture was taken during a surprise birthday celebration for Mo.

THE CELTIC VIEW

Wednesday 17th June 1987

No. 960 Price 30p

BILLY'S BACK

Paradise found for 'Caesar'

TODAY in your special edition of the *Summer View*, new Celtic manager Billy McNeill will spell out his hopes and ambitions for the club.

Billy returned to Paradise on May 28th following the departure of David Hay. The former captain who led Celtic to an unprecedented run of nine championship wins in a row, said he was "bewildered, but it's great to be back."

Celtic Chairman Jack McGinn said how reluctant the board was to make a decision to change. But, in the end, the decision to recall Billy McNeill was unanimous.

He told the *View*: "Telling David Hay of the board's decision was the hardest thing I've ever had to do. He's such a good man and we wish him well for the future. He knows he will always be welcome at the Park."

Billy McNeill was manager of the club from 1978 until 1983 when he left to join Manchester City. He stayed at Maine Road until September of last year when he took over at Aston Villa, where he was in charge until the end of the season.

Billy's been busy since his appointment talking to out of contract players and looking for new signings. But today, in the *View*, he looks forward to his dream for Paradise.

Billy McNeill pictured with skipper Roy Aitken and new signing Mick McCarthy.

He is one of the club's most honoured players and certainly its greatest ever captain, so when it was announced that Billy McNeill would be returning for a second spell as manager there was widespread and unconfined joy among the Celtic faithful.

Cesar had managed both Manchester City and Aston Villa during his sojourn down south, but as Celtic prepared for its centenary year there was only one man to call. Big Billy told the *View*: 'This is where my heart has always been and it goes without saying that the first result I looked for when I was down south was Celtic's.

'I feel that my four years in England have made me a better manager, and I have very definite views about where Celtic should be in football and that's at the top. All my greatest moments in the game were with Celtic and I'm confident that we can recapture this in the coming years.

'To say that I am happy to be back doesn't begin to describe how I feel. I am as excited now as I was 30 years ago when I signed as a young player. To me Celtic are the best.

This is my club and I can say that after being with two major English outfits. Believe me, they do not compare with Celtic.

'I cannot stress too much that I've had to live without this club for four years and this has heightened my ambitions for Celtic and has strengthened my determination to win success at the highest level. It is a great honour for me to lead Celtic into 1988 and the centenary year. Up until a couple of weeks ago I thought I would be playing no part in what will be a historic 12 months. But it's up to all of us on the playing side to ensure that our faithful fans have something to cheer.'

That summer *View* also featured the renovation work going on in the South Stand and former *View* editor Jack McGinn, who was now club chairman, said: '1988 is going to be quite a year for us all and the erection of this extension is part of our plan for the future. We always want to give our fans a team they can be proud of and that will remain our number one priority. But it's also vital that we constantly upgrade the park and that is something we have been doing now for many years. Last year saw the transformation of the Celtic End – this year it's the stand.'

SUPPORTERS ASSOCIATION
by George Delaney

ON behalf of the Association I extend best wishes and every success to Billy McNeill.

Billy always has and always will hold a special place in the hearts and minds of Celtic fans the world over.

The expectations of all our supporters are in Billy's hands, and, as always, the Manager of Celtic will get the full backing of the Association.

It is up to every one to give the manager the support he will need. With this backing I am sure we will get back to our winning ways.

Having said that, I would also like to thank David Hay publicly for his help and co-operation during his spell as Manager. David will always have the respect and admiration of our fans.

How to buy your season ticket for 87-88 CELTIC PEG PRICES *See page 6*

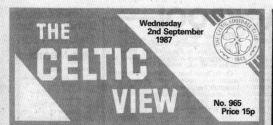

THE CELTIC VIEW

Wednesday
2nd September
1987

No. 965
Price 15p

Allan McKnight jubilant after Old Firm triumph.

Billy's happy habit

by Kevin McKenna

CELTIC manager Billy McNeill declared himself very satisfied with the weekend 1-0 victory v Rangers.

"In all the time I've been involved in these games that first half hour was the best football I've seen either side play."

And his praise will be echoed by Celtic's huge support who are currently enjoying a Celtic renaissance as the side continue to play very attractive football.

But what pleased the Celtic manager even more was the performance of Celtic's much maligned defence and especially the brave performance of young Allan McKnight in goal." You've got to remember that this lad

is making his Premier League debut and any mistakes he may have made would have been magnified in the glare that surrounds this fixture. But he was helped by the defenders around him, of whom only Roy Aitken could be called experienced.

The Belfast born keeper will not have too much time to dwell on

the praise being heaped on him at present. He was involved in last night's torrid encounter at Pittodrie and will face Dundee Utd., at Tannadice on Saturday as Pat Bonner recovers from injury. Seldom can anyone have had such a baptism of fire.

Referring to the sending off of Graeme Souness the manager stated that it seemed to have a galvanising effect on Rangers: "We had more problems afterwards than previously," he said, "But despite that we may still have scores a couple of goals."

Rangers seem to be shaping up as McNeill's most favourite opponents. In his time as Celtic manager up until 1983 and including Saturday he has tasted defeat against his old rivals on only four occasions. Meanwhile Celtic under his stewardship have yielded an astonishing 12 victories.

"If we show form like we did on Saturday we have nobody to fear," he enthused.

McGhee almost makes it two.

THIS WEEK
Andy Walker talks to *The View* P.3
All the action from the Old Firm clash P.4

NEXT WEEK
A great competition only for readers of the *Celtic View*
Order your copy now — only 15p

A comfortable 5-1 romp over Dumbarton in the League Cup may not be the best barometer of your team's capabilities just a few days before a game against your biggest rivals, but that didn't stop chants of 'Bring on the Rangers' ringing around Boghead.

That was Celtic's preparation just three days ahead of the first big derby clash of the centenary season, which also just happened to be Billy McNeill's first since his return. As it turned out, though, the fans' optimism proved to be spot-on as Big Billy drew first blood with Graeme Souness in what was to be a monumental season-long battle for supremacy.

The big talking point, though, was the all-out studded attack on Billy Stark's bootless foot by Rangers player-manager Souness, which resulted in a red card for the perpetrator. The *View* said of the 1-0 win: 'Billy Stark demonstrated once again on Saturday just why he could turn out to be manager Billy McNeill's most astute signing. "Stop-gap," "temporary" and "cost-cutting" were some of the adjectives in evidence at the time when the Celtic boss swooped to sign Stark in the close season at £75,000. His fifth-minute goal was superb. Walker's dummy from a McGhee cross paralysed three Rangers defenders and left Stark to plant a smooth left-foot shot behind Woods.'

The report carried on: 'Souness' second-half sending off after his wild lunge at Stark signalled the game's most untidy period as the game became peppered with fouls. A worrying aspect in the latter stages of the game were the inflammatory gestures to the Celtic fans by Rangers defender Graham Roberts who had an otherwise outstanding match at the heart of a beleaguered Rangers defence.

'Unfortunately the after-match recriminations surrounding the Rangers captain's dismissal tended to overshadow the fact that Celtic had played football of a high quality in a match impeccably refereed by David Syme.'

The manager added: 'I thought we played magnificently. You must also take into account that we had five players out there today who had never experienced an Old Firm match. And what can you say about the big laddie [Allen] McKnight? He handled the game oh so well. Some of our football was a joy to behold. But although I'm delighted with this win we won't be going overboard. We have a hard programme ahead of us.'

THE CELTIC VIEW

Wednesday 23rd March 1988

No. 993 Price 15p

VIEWPOINT

LAST week's postponed Aberdeen v Celtic match has now been re-scheduled for Wednesday March 30th by the Scottish League.

Celtic had proposed playing the match on either Easter Monday or Wednesday April 20th.

But these alternative dates were not suitable to Aberdeen. Their reasons for refusing these dates were that there is the possibility that TV will carry highlights of the game that night.

The club evidently felt they had a duty to their sponsors to utilise this opportunity of television coverage.

With regard to last Tuesday's postponement — this decision was made solely by the referee.

Celtic were bitterly disappointed at this decision and have the greatest sympathy for all their fans who travelled at such great personal cost only to discover that the game had been cancelled.

This has resulted in a slight alteration of plans for the official opening of the Celtic exhibition in the People's Palace.

The Lord Provost has kindly re-arranged his schedule to officially open the exhibition on the afternoon of Wednesday, March 30th.

The exhibition will be open to the public on Thursday March 31st.

SUNDAY BEST

by Kevin McKenna

"I thoroughly enjoyed it," was the McNeill verdict on his side's 2-1 victory over Rangers on Sunay.

The Celtic boss was talking the day after his side had taken a huge step towards their 35th league title with the Ibrox win. And he added: "What made the victory particularly memorable for me is the fact that Rangers played very well but we were still able to defeat them in their own territory.

"That's the best Rangers have played against us this season but it still wasn't enough. They did seem to be a big occasion club.

McNeill alluded to this when he praised his players: "They have consistently come up with the goods when it mattered most. This is to their eternal credit. Their attitude and preparation for crucial matches this season has been exemplary."

The Celtic manager though had to withdraw Paul McStay from the Scotland squad for tonight's match against Malta. The midfielder took a nasty knock on his shin which has become infected. The manager will monitor his progress this week.

have more actual possession than ourselves yet our defence was rarely in trouble.

"In the first half I felt much of our play was marked with signs of caution and nerves. But after weathering some slight turbulence at the beginning of the second half my players began to turn on the style."

Now Celtic have stretched their unbeaten record to 26 matches in league and cup. Much of this has been achieved because Celts are emerging

McStay's performance on Sunday was a major factor in Celtic taking a grip of the game — a point with which McNeill agreed: "Paul's football this season has been joyous to watch and his goal was something special too.

"That's the best shot he's ever hit with his left foot."

The Celtic boss also praised the contribution made by Anton Rogan when he appeared as a second half substitute for Joe Miller.

Now Celts take on Dundee United at Celtic Park on Saturday as they seek to tighten their stranglehold on this season's Premier League title.

And McNeill won't need to warn his players about United's ability. The Tayside outfit was the last team to beat Celtic when they triumphed 2-1 in Glasgow five months ago on October 24th.

But the Celtic manager aims to ensure that there is no repeat of that scoreline this Saturday: "It's no use achieving great results like last week's if we are unable to reproduce the same form in our next match. The Ibrox result is behind us. Now we must turn our sights to Dundee United."

▼ ▼ ▼ ▼

Would all Registered Celtic Supporters Clubs please note that they must uplift their allocation of Hibs tickets by Friday at Celtic Park.

Paul McStay

The scoreboard says it all!

Ticket sale

THERE will be a sale of tickets at this Saturday's match v Dundee United for the forthcoming away league game v Hibs on Saturday, April 2nd.

These tickets will be on sale at the London Road, Celtic end of the ground. Vouchers will be issued to permit one ticket per person.

There will be one significant difference though from previous ticket sales.

INSUFFICIENT

To allow people who have queued for a while prior to the United match to have a chance to eat and to enable them to have access to any part of the ground, we will start the sale at 12 noon.

Up until normal entry time of 1.30pm, fans will be allowed to leave the ground if they so desire.

From 1.30pm onwards though, the exit doors will be closed as usual.

Because of insufficient stand tickets for the Easter Road game there will be no public sale of these tickets.

From 1.30pm onwards, while tickets last, there will be an availability of one ticket per person at the front and back stand season ticket gates.

Celtic Story gala premiere

CELTIC are to hold a gala opening night of The Celtic Story stage musical.

The club in conjunction with Wildcat Theatre Group have arranged this gala premiere performance for Saturday April 30th at 7.30pm in Glasgow's Pavilion Theatre.

This special occasion will be attended by Celtic players and officials.

And to make it a night to remember the opening performance will be followed by a glittering buffet/reception in the new function suites at Celtic Park.

Tickets for the theatre/reception will be limited.

Only about 400 will be available to supporters. These tickets which are inclusive of theatre and buffet reception are priced at £25 and can only be purchased at the Commercial office in the Pools Building at Celtic Park.

All other tickets for this opening night are available at the normal price from the Pavilion Theatre Box Office in Renfield Street.

Meanwhile the demand for tickets for the two month run of the Celtic Story has astonished the Wildcat Theatre Group. Said a spokesperson for the group: "This is definitely our biggest project to date. And the response has literally run us off our feet. The interest from every area has been nothing short of remarkable.

Celtic Chairman Jack McGinn added: "The demand for this show has been phenomenal. And I would strongly advise individuals, clubs and parties who intend to watch the show to book as soon as possible to avoid disappointment."

Certainly the word among the more informed theatre-goers in the West of Scotland is that the show has all the makings of a classic.

One of the undoubted highlights in a season packed to the gunwales with them was the second visit of the season to Ibrox when the Celts returned with two very vital points.

And even today, as it was when leaving the ground immediately after the match, it's still debatable as to which Celtic goal was enjoyed more by the green and white masses in the Broomloan Road stand. There was Paul McStay's immaculate screamer from outside the box or Andy Walker's not-so-immaculate close-range body-check into the net – the fact that Jan Bartram scored a well-taken equaliser between these two Celtic goals is neither here nor there.

As Roy Aitken wrote in his captain's column: 'If it wasn't for the fact that I want to thank every Celtic supporter for that incredible show on Sunday I would be struggling to find the time to write this. But how could I fail to find the time for those marvellous fans

who seemed to be starting a bit of a party when I left the field at time-up on Sunday!'

He added: 'It was great, too, to see young Anton Rogan come on and do so well. The big man's such a laugh – nothing ever gets him down for long. So I had to laugh when he said that he didn't misdirect that header that led to our winner. He says he was aiming for the Celtic crest on Andy Walker's jersey!'

The *View* also stated: 'Sunday's victory at Ibrox now puts Celtic within ten games of a glorious double to mark the club's centenary year. Eight league games have to be negotiated before the Premier flag can fly once more over the Jungle. And a victory over Hearts in the Scottish Cup semi-final could see the Bhoys round off a momentous season with a Hampden gala day.

'Quite rightly Billy McNeill insists his players and staff approach one match at a time with single-minded determination. But even he has to concede that the supporters' thoughts are cast forward to triumphs that look more and more destined to become realities.'

THE CELTIC VIEW

Wednesday 27th April 1988

No. 998   Price 15p

Cup Final Ticket Sale

CELTIC will hold a public sale of Cup final tickets at Celtic Park this Sunday at 12 noon.

The ticket sale for the match against Dundee United will take place only at turnstyles at the London Road end of the ground.

The club would point out that there will be a limit of only one ticket per person and one ticket per season ticket holder.

Tickets can be obtained by going through the London Road turnstyles and exit will be through the turnstyles at the Janefield Street corner of the Celtic end.

There will be a limited amount of stand tickets on sale on Sunday.

Tickets for Hampden's family enclosure will be available from the Celtic Shop in Dundas Street from Monday.

Would fans please note that the car park at Celtic Park will not be available for use during Sunday's public sale.

Meanwhile the Celtic directors would like to record their appreciation of the Dundee players, management and directors for playing their part in what was a marvellous occasion at Celtic Park last Saturday.

PRICES BOOST FOR THE FANS

CELTIC are to reduce charges at all gates for the home game against Dunfermline a week on Saturday.

Announcing the move Chairman Jack McGinn said:

"We will have played 55 games by the time the season has finished and this is a token of our appreciation for the way the fans have supported us in our centenary season which has so far brought us the Premier League title."

Admission to any part of the stand will be £3.00. In addition to this admission to the ground will be £2.00 only and £1.00 for children and OAPs.

Speaking about the magnificent support on Saturday the team received, the chairman added:

"I would like to express my gratitude to all those fans who heeded last week's warning to arrive early for Saturday's game against Dundee.

"And I would like to express my regret to all those who missed the first few minutes of the game, owing to the huge crowd at the match."

CHAMPS AGAIN

RECORD breaking Celts with an impeccable sense of history have done it again.

Throughout its 100 year history the club has risen to the occasion with some dramatic victories when it mattered most.

And in this their centenary year it mattered most of all to have the Premier League flag flying over Celtic Park next season.

Saturday's 3-0 victory was enough to clinch Celtic's 35th title. And it meant so much to manager Billy McNeill. Written off by English pundits before the season began after his spell in the south — he returned and completely transformed the club in less than 9 months.

And as he savoured the sweet smell of success he said: "I'm so glad for those players — they are a superb

By Kevin McKenna

bunch of lads — its been a pleasure to work with them all season. Their attitude has been first class and they showed so much professional commitment allied to an abundance of skill."

"What pleases me most of all is the fact that in our first team pool we have eight players under the age of 23. Believe me, we have only just begun. If we can keep those players together for a few more years there is no saying what they can go on to achieve."

McNeill was also pleased for the fans: "If ever there was such a show of loyalty and passion by supporters anywhere in the world — our fans displayed it on Saturday."

And there was joy for assistant Tommy Craig. This is the first time he

has won anything in the game at any level — despite an acclaimed career on both sides of the border. And he found it difficult to contain his joy: "You don't know what this means to me," he said, "I cannot sufficiently convey in words how I feel at this time.

"There is such a marvellous atmosphere about this place — a real family feeling, which explains some of our performances throughout the season when the players played for each other and protected each other to overcome seemingly insurmountable odds. After the match on Saturday they all insisted on having everyone in the pictures including Neilly Mochan, Jimmy Steele and Brian Scott as well as Peter Grant and Lex Baillie who couldn't play."

But despite the euphoria at Celtic Park just now Craig insisted that the side is determined to gather four points from their remaining matches against Motherwell and Dunfermline. "We want to reach a points total of 72, which would be absolutely remarkable — given the amount of people who wrote us off before and during the season."

Celtic are the first team in the world to have won the league in their centenary year. This is their 35th success and if their goals against column remains at 23 the side will have created a club post-war defensive record in the league.

It may have been written in the stars, but that didn't stop countless thousands making their way to Celtic Park on 23 April 1988 just to make sure that the Bhoys actually did lift the championship in their centenary year.

The actual attendance against Dundee was given as the then official limit of 60,800, but the turnstile clickers at one end of the ground couldn't have been working that day as it seemed as if there were at least 30,000 more inside the ground as the trackside was utilised to cope with the throng.

The title should have been won the previous week, though, at Tynecastle, but a 2-1 defeat was all Celtic had to show for their troubles. Could they finally do it at Celtic Park in front of a capacity crowd? Chris Morris half-settled the nerves with the opener after only three minutes, but there was still a long way to go.

On seventy-five minutes, however, the party really started as Andy Walker grabbed the second of the day and the celebrations were such that many in the crowd actually missed Andy hitting Celtic's third immediately after the second – even the TV cameras nearly missed the goal!

And the *View* was on song with the intro to the match report. It went: 'It's a grand old team to play for – no one could deny that on Saturday judging by the expressions of sheer joy on the faces of the players who had just clinched the league title.

'And it's a grand old team to see – over 60,000 fans bedecked in green and white had a fine old party.

'And if you know the history – who but Celtic would have become the first team in the world to win their league championship in their centenary season!

'It's enough to make you heart go – oh Bhoy did the famous Paradise rock to the strains of triumphal celebrations following the post-match festivities. Surely in 100 years the grand old stadium hasn't seen scenes like it.

'Mothers and fathers, provoked by nostalgia, came along to see the team the whole country is talking about, and young children were hoisted above the throng to witness an occasion that will be told to many a grandchild in years to come.'

THE CELTIC VIEW

Wednesday 18th May 1988

No. 1001
Price 15p

Centenary 'Double'

Wildcat Single

THEATRE Group Wildcat are to bring out a new record.

The group, currently producing The Celtic Story at the Pavilion Theatre, have recorded two of the most popular songs from the hit musical. On the A-side is "We've come a long, long way."

And on the B-side is "Paradise." The single will be released at the end of May. They will be on sale at performances of the Celtic Story and at Celtic's club shops in Dundas St and Celtic Park.

The Summer View

THIS week's issue is the last Celtic View of the season. We will be back in a month's time though with a special centenary bumper edition.

This 20 page edition will be out on Wednesday, June 15th. The price will be 30p, the same as last summer's 16 page edition.

And starting in August will be the new look Celtic View with an extra 4 pages added. Full details will appear in the summer edition.

CELTIC fulfilled the dreams of all their fans by making it a centenary double on Saturday.

And despite the glorious successes of the club's 100 year history this year more than any other was one in which Celtic had to win something. And how the players responded to the call.

Saturday's Scottish Cup Final win over Dundee United gave Celtic their first double of championship and Scottish Cup since 1977 when Kenny Dalglish was captain. Its the first time manager Billy McNeill has won two trophies in one season as boss of Celtic. And in a year in which records have tumbled to these remarkable Celts it was also revealed that the side's latest success equals Rangers' record of league and cup doubles.

A euphoric Billy McNeill was lavish in his praise of the players' efforts: "They clung in there. The word defeat doesn't seem to have entered their vocabularies.

Even the lads who didn't play on Saturday all played their part and none more so than Pat Bonner.

"This squad has amazed me this season. They've had to accommodate so many interruptions and upsets and yet have refused to let these break their stride."

The Celtic boss' appraisal of his team's efforts are borne out by the statistics of an amazing season. In 55 competitive matches Celtic have lost only five and no side has scored more than two goals against them.

McNeill went on: "These players are a group of winners who will not settle for second best. Their great strength, apart from their all-round ability, is their superb team spirit. As, well as playing for each other on the park they are all friends off it as well."

But the manager has already set his sights on collecting more trophies next season and to this end he will call his players into Celtic Park this morning for a general chat about their objectives for next season: "I'll be congratulating them on their achievements this season but will also be posting an agenda for next season which I hope will lead to more success. Among other things, I'll be setting a date for them to report back for pre-season training. In the meantime though, I'll be encouraging them to relax and unwind. Its important that they get this extraordinary season out of their system and come back fully refreshed for next season."

And there was good news too for Celtic's two injury victims. Pat Bonner will train this week at Celtic Park and McNeill has no fears about him recovering in time to help the Republic of Ireland in this summer's European Championships. Mick McCarthy is due in hospital this week for an exploratory operation on his knee. Likewise though, there are no fears for his long-term fitness.

GO FOR TENNENT'S LAGER

NOTHING LESS WILL DO

Brazilians provide Centenary opposition in August

CELTIC are set to face a star-studded Brazilian outfit in a glamour, August centenary match.

Plans are well underway to bring Cruzeiro Belo Horizonte to Glasgow on Sunday, August 7th. Cruzeiro reached the latter stages of the recent South American championships and boast six current Brazilian internationalists.

They are coached by Carlos Alberto Silva one of Brazil's most famous international sons who doubles up by being boss of the current Brazilian national squad.

Speaking about the proposed plans Chairman Jack McGinn said: "Celtic gave some thought to several top European teams as possible opposition in our centenary match. But we felt that because we had already faced most of Europe's top sides in European duty or in friendlies, we should instead opt for the different type of glamour which top South American sides bring with them."

What makes this match even more intriguing is that Celtic have never met a Brazilian side before.

Explaining the decision to play the game on a Sunday the Celtic Chairman added: "We felt that by the Sunday most fans who would want to see this match would have completed their holidays. The Sunday fixture would give them a better chance of seeing the game."

The match is almost certain to be an all-ticket affair. Billy McNeill is also eagerly anticipating the match: "The prospect excites me. The fans love the Brazilians' style of soccer, and this side are one of the nation's best."

The centenary season double dream looked over just four minutes after the break against Dundee United in the Scottish Cup final when Kevin Gallagher put the Tannadice men ahead.

This was a season of eleventh-hour reversals of fortune for Celtic, though, when the opposition choked on the final dregs served up in the last-chance saloon and it was a season when no Celtic fans dared leave the game with a couple of minutes to go – they would miss all the action.

Frank McAvennie was Celtic's last-minute hero on this occasion and there were barely thirty seconds left on the clock when he smacked in the winner to cap a tremendous season all round.

The *View* said: 'On Saturday Dundee United were not trying to preserve their one-goal lead against 11 footballers, they were struggling against the weight of 100 years of history littered with similar scorelines that had so often seemed ridiculously fragile in the face of a Celtic side in full flow.

'At Hampden each one of the 1988 Celts were worthy carriers of the Celtic tradition. They had played reasonably well in the first half; certainly better than several others would have you believe. Except for a scare when Paul McStay kicked off his own line, Celtic had the upper hand.

'The Celts, though, found problems dealing with United's wind-assisted clearances into their penalty area at the start of the second half. This danger was underlined when Kevin Gallagher scored a superb opener for United as he shot high past Allen McKnight after outpacing Roy Aitken. But this was probably the best thing that could have happened to Celtic. They seemed to discover a higher gear and there was little United could do to stop the onslaught.'

It added: 'Stark, a 70th-minute substitute for Whyte, found Rogan, Saturday's man of the match, on the left and after he neatly turned Malpas his cross was headed into an empty net by McAvennie. Now the floodgates were open and Celtic poured everything into attack. McAvennie's winner 30 seconds from the end was no more than they deserved.'

It could be said that the whole of Scottish football, and Rangers more than most, were fighting a losing battle against a century of Celtic pride.

McAvennie nets the winner . . .

THE CELTIC VIEW

No. 1041   Wednesday 3rd May 1989   Price 22p

Fans make it day to remember

EVERYONE agreed that the Celtic v Liverpool match at the weekend was a very special occasion and was a dignified way for many Scots fans to pay their respects to the Hillsborough victims.

Owing to the circumstances, the game was arranged at far shorter notice than would normally have been the case. Celtic and Liverpool Football Clubs wish to thank everyone who made a contribution on Sunday and in the weeks leading up to it.

The fans deserve special praise for turning out in such vast numbers and for their moving tributes throughout the game. Police, stewards, caterers, advertisers (programme and trackside), the English and Scottish football authorities, indeed everyone who had anything to do with the match; we salute you all. Referee Bob Valentine and his linesmen also deserve thanks for their handling of the match and for donating their fees to the fund.

Return of the King. Kenny Dalglish salutes the fans after Sunday's emotion-packed game. (Below) Liverpool skipper Alan Hansen accepts a cheque for £25,000 for the Hillsborough appeal from Lord Provost Susan Baird on behalf of the people of Glasgow.

CELTIC supporters have once more been hailed as the greatest. And the praise come just days after five thousand remained behind in Aberdeen to chant for the team on a day when rivals Rangers lifted the title. This was followed on Sunday by over 50,000 turning out to show their support and solidarity for the people of Liverpool and the Liverpool fans in particular.

Liverpool Chairman John Smith said: "The Celtic supporters have shown once more that they can hold their heads high among the best of them. Anyone who has become disillusioned by football because of a series of events over the last few years should have been at Celtic Park on Sunday."

The Liverpool Chairman was speaking after watching his side beat Celtic 4-0 in Sunday's benefit game for the Hillsborough Disaster Appeal.

But the result was irrelevant when it became clear that the Disaster Appeal could be boosted by £500,000 from the profits of Sunday's game.

THOUGHTS

Liverpool boss Kenny Dalglish said: "They are the greatest. It wasn't just their money but their warmth and compassion which means so much to Liverpool at this time."

There was also a game of football to be played and while it obviously had to take second place to the thoughts of those who were bereaved at Hillsborough, nonetheless it was there to be won.

Celtic manager Billy McNeill, on this count, was far from happy: "The fans were great," he commented, "I only wish the team could have followed the lead given by them."

McNeill was angry at the defensive lapses that gifted Liverpool their first three goals. And friendly, or no friendly, he made sure they knew about his feelings before leaving the ground on Sunday.

But the Celtic boss was delighted to see Derek Whyte in action again — his first game in 13 weeks: "Derek came through with no ill effects but we will monitor him very closely before the cup final on May 20th. Obviously a fit Derek Whyte will be a big part of my plans."

And he was pleased with Mick McCarthy's contribution to the game against Aberdeen at Pittodrie: "Mick has shown us in the last few weeks just what a good central defender he is. He was also outstanding for the Republic of Ireland in their great win over Spain. That can only be good for Celtic as we look forward to the Cup final."

Stevie Fulton is also almost fit again after breaking his hand in the semi-final win over Hibs.

CENTRE PAGES ACTION FROM THE BIG GAME

The football world was shocked by the events of 15 April 1989, which resulted in ninety-six Liverpool fans losing their lives with hundreds of others injured in what would be universally known as the Hillsborough Disaster.

Celtic immediately offered to play a benefit game to help with the disaster fund and, as things turned out, Sunday 30 April would be the first time that Liverpool had taken to the pitch since that fateful day in Sheffield. Indeed, it was the first time they even remotely thought about playing football and a crowd of 60,437 with scarves raised aloft in a rousing rendition of 'You'll Never Walk Alone' greeted Alan Hansen and Roy Aitken as they led the teams from the tunnel.

Just twenty-four hours earlier the Celts drew 0-0 with Aberdeen at Pittodrie as Rangers claimed the title, but 5,000 supporters stayed behind in Aberdeen to chant for the team and, as the *View* pointed out, they also 'suggested an alternative target for the controversial poll tax'.

Alan Hansen said of Celtic: 'It says a great deal for them that they were able to play us at short notice at all. But the fact that they had played a tough game just a day previously makes their response magnificent.'

Liverpool won the game 4-0 and the *View* added: 'It was a day when the result didn't matter and when the fans were the real stars. They mingled with one another and sang each other's praises throughout the game.'

The small print on the front of the *View* said: 'Everyone agreed that the Celtic v Liverpool match at the weekend was a very special occasion and was a dignified way for many Scots fans to pay their respects to the Hillsborough victims.

'Owing to the circumstances, the game was arranged at far shorter notice than would normally have been the case. Celtic and Liverpool Football Clubs wish to thank everybody who made a contribution on Sunday and in the weeks leading up to it.

'The fans deserve special praise for turning out in such vast numbers and for their moving tributes throughout the game. Police, stewards, caterers, advertisers (programme and trackside), the English and Scottish football authorities, indeed everyone who had anything to do with the match; we salute you all.

'Referee Bob Valentine and his linesmen also deserve thanks for their handling of the match and for donating their fees to the fund.'

CUP FINAL COUNTDOWN

CELTS IN GREAT SHAPE FOR HAMPDEN

Mo's back — story and pictures, page 3

CELTIC are in excellent shape for Saturday's match of the decade Scottish Cup Final against Rangers.

Yesterday manager Billy McNeill reported a relaxed and confident mood in the Celtic camp as the finishing touches are applied to the team's pre-match preparations.

Said the Celtic boss: "The four-day trip to Portugal was ideal and worked in just the right way I wanted it to. The players are all rooting for each other and there's a terrific feeling of camaraderie among them.

They're relaxed and they're feeling good about themselves."

McNeill is delighted at the progress from injury shown by Derek Whyte and Joe Miller in recent games. Both are certain to start the game. The fact that both have suffered lengthy periods of injuries can work in Celtic's favour. For both will have the freshest legs on the park after such long lay-offs.

McNeill is delighted too with the recent form of Peter Grant: "Peter has shown in recent matches he's back to the player of last season. He is ready for the fray and feels happy with his form as he has every right to be."

Now the manager must wait before deciding about the fitness of Andy Walker. The striker's been out since an eye injury forced him out of a game a few weeks ago. McNeill though, is hopeful he'll be alongside Mark McGhee in the final.

Meanwhile Celtic have announced they're giving free transfers to three players.

Striker Charlie Christie and midfielders John

Continued on back page

SKOL CUP Draw

Rangers v. Arbroath or East Stirlingshire; Queen of the South v. St Johnstone; Airdrieonians v. Forfar Athletic; Albion Rovers v. Aberdeen; Heart of Midlothian v. Cowdenbeath or Montrose; East Fife or Queen's Park v. Morton; Dunfermline Athletic v. Raith Rovers; Kilmarnock v. Motherwell; Dundee v. Clyde; Dumbarton or Stenhousemuir v. Celtic; Dundee United v. Partick Thistle; Stranraer or Brechin City v. Falkirk; Clydebank v. Meadowbank Thistle; Stirling Albion or Berwick Rangers v. St Mirren; Hibernian v. Alloa; Ayr United v. Hamilton Academical.

Dates for ties – Tuesday, 15th or Wednesday, 16th August, 1989.

CELTIC Chairman Jack McGinn is the new treasurer of the Scottish Football Association.

It's the first time a Celtic official has held office at Park Gardens since the late Sir Robert Kelly in the late 60s.

The Celtic Chairman was voted in at an A.G.M. last Friday ahead of Jim Baxter, East Fife and John McBeth, Clyde.

Chris offered 3-year deal

CELTIC full back Chris Morris will play his 99th game for the club in Saturday's Scottish Cup final.

And yesterday boss Billy McNeill said: "I hope Chris goes on to play many more games for Celtic. He has been a superb player for us and I want him to be part of our future plans."

McNeill was replying to increased press speculation about Morris' future as he nears the end of a two year contract.

And McNeill added: "Chris asked us for a three year contract and we have been more than happy to offer him that. In my opinion he is being offered a very lucrative contract.

But I realise that in these days of freedom of contract players can through their weight around a bit more when it comes to new deals being discussed, and maybe that's not a bad thing. But there can be no doubt that I want Chris Morris to remain at Celtic Park where he can do well for himself on and off the park."

Morris was set to go into the record books with the record number of consecutive appearances for a Celtic player. But after having made 96 he missed out on four matches after an appendix operation.

His displays at right back have made him very popular with the fans and enabled him to become a regular in Jack Charlton's Republic of Ireland squad.

Following the highs of the centenary year, the 1988–89 proved to be a bit of a damp squib.

There was, of course, the Scottish Cup final to look forward to and the club seemed to have been quick off the mark in the transfer market. It was announced that Maurice Johnston was returning from Nantes. However, after being paraded in the hoops and professing that Celtic were his first and only love, that deal was completely turned on its head when he signed for Rangers.

In the calm before the storm, though, the *View* stated, when comparing Johnston's earlier departure to a 'distressing trend' since the overture to Lou Macari's going to Manchester United in 1973, that: 'A player's declaration of undying love for the immortal Hoops is simply a prelude to an inglorious exit.' So steady yourself for an unedifying statement of perpetual adoration for all things green and white that was simply a prelude to an inglorious entrance!

The former player said: 'When I joined Celtic in 1984 it was like an answer to prayers, and I don't say that lightly. At the time I fully intended to see out my career with Celtic if the club would have me for that length of time.

'I never fell out of love with Celtic, but certain events off the park had combined to convince me that I had to get away for a while if my career was to continue. I accept my share of the responsibility for some things that happened, but that could be put down to youthful high jinks rather than any serious behaviour lapses.

'And when I joined Nantes it had always been my intention to return to Celtic one day, although I'll admit that seemed unlikely at one stage given the circumstances surrounding my departure. No one can accuse me of being two-faced because I've always maintained that stance since then.

'I didn't want to leave Celtic and I don't intend to now. There was some fabricated rubbish about me wanting to join Manchester United. But it never entered my head to play for any other club. In fact, there is no other British club I could play for apart from Celtic.'

The maestro of mendacity added: 'I enjoyed playing against Rangers, but when I left I was unhappy about the fact that in games I'd played against them, Rangers were winning four matches to three. That's something I intend to remedy next season.' Aye right!

Mo returns, wiser and better...

THE CELTIC VIEW

No. 1044 — Wednesday, 24th May, 1989 — Price 22p

29th Cup win for incredible Celts

CUP-HAPPY CELTIC

CUP OK – Joe Miller's superb grounder flashes past Chris Woods for Saturday's Hampden winner.

HILLSBOROUGH PROGRAMMES

THE special souvenir programme produced to commemorate the recent Hillsborough Appeal match between Celtic and Liverpool was completely sold out just days after the event.

But such has been the continued demand for the programme that Celtic have ordered a reprint.

Copies of this are on sale at both Celtic Shops. Copies can also be ordered by post, price £1.50 inc. postage and packing. All proceeds of course, go to the Disaster Appeal.

This is the last edition of the Celtic View for this season. But we're back on the streets on June 21st with a special summer edition.

Order yours from your newsagent now.

CELTIC'S fifth win out of the last six Old Firm Scottish Cup finals can be the launching pad for even greater success next season.

That's the view of manager Billy McNeill after picking up his tenth Scottish Cup as both player and manager.

Said McNeill: "It was great to end the season on such a peak after what had gone before. I felt it was just reward for the players who at times had to battle against heavy odds throughout the season.

"It was significant that on one of the few occasions we had something resembling our strongest squad we were able to win so convincingly against a side many regard as the best in Scotland."

It's been a superb last five weeks for Celtic. Indeed, they have been as good as the first five weeks of the season were bad.

Winning the Scottish Cup against Rangers completed the healing process.

"Now we must ensure there is more, much more, of the same next season, both at home and in Europe."

McNeill has already hinted that his summer spending won't stop at Mo and it's clear that he sees the continental scene as one in which Celtic must make an impact: "In all my years at the club this is the most ambitious I have seen it. Great things are ahead."

The Celtic boss also praised the fans: "Their support was immense on Saturday, and it was good they gave us such superb backing without recourse to any sectarian or political songs."

He also revealed that one of the first people to congratulate him was old friend Des Connor

thousands of miles away in San Francisco.

"I don't know how he managed it, but he got through the Hampden switchboard from California and congratulated me. In that instant I once more realised how much winning this game means to the ordinary fan."

McNeill was also delighted about the inclusion of Peter Grant and Derek Whyte in the Scotland squad: "They're there on merit. They've played marvellously after having endured such long spells of injury," he said.

Meanwhile Chris Morris is still considering the offer of a lucrative new three year contract. But speculation that Mick McCarthy wants away have been dismissed by McNeill as "pure speculation".

WE MEET AGAIN – Billy McNeill with the cup he's won ten times as player and manager.

Celtic's whole season hinged on the afternoon of Saturday 20 May when the Bhoys took to a sun-drenched Hampden turf to take on Rangers in the Scottish Cup final.

This wasn't any old Scottish Cup final, though, as with the 'Souness Revolution' (© Scottish meeja) in full flow, the Ibrox side were seemingly hurtling towards a glorious treble as the title and the League Cup were already in the bag. In a mostly forgettable season, the Celts had already fallen to miserable 4-1 and 5-1 league defeats at Ibrox, but, as the *View* pointed out: 'You could sense things were going a bit crazy when the bookies began to offer 12/5 against Celtic wining the Cup.'

To say the relief when Joe Miller scored the winner was exhilarating would be a gross understatement, as everyone who saw it probably remembers their elated blowing-of-kisses celebration rather then the actual goal itself. The final whistle didn't just mean that the Celts would be lifting the Cup, it also signalled a mass groan from red, white and blue treble T-shirt sellers, unofficial or otherwise, as they battened down the hatches and shut up shop before heading off to the nearest dump.

The back page of the *View* featured a photo of the victorious Celts raising the cup aloft in the Hampden sun with an inset of the pic of the glorious support in full flow. Under a green banner headline of 'Let's Celebrate' and a subdeck of 'Sweet revenge for players and fans' to caption the images, the *View* stated: 'In one sweet second just before half-time, Joe Miller vanquished all nightmares of his penalty-kick miss against Rangers seven weeks ago. And Joe's clinical Cup winner also made the Celtic fans forget about the two heavy Ibrox defeats earlier in the season. It's taken several weeks, but in the end it was all worth waiting for.

'Said Joe: "This is the greatest day of my professional career. And now that I have tasted it, I aim to experience many more of the same." Judging by the looks on the faces of the Celtic players, he's not alone in that sentiment. And as for the delirious fans, they'll be back to savour it all over and over again.'

(Right) Celtic's wonder match-winner Joe Miller shows how much he enjoys that cup-winning feeling.

Billy McNeill, Tommy Craig and their wives celebrate with the Cup on Saturday night.

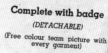

Another ad on

Just what were Celtic fans the target
market for in days of yore? Also includes
some with even more of a Celtic flavour,
featuring groovy anoraks… But did the
View really advertise Celtic 'cigarettes'?

THE CELTIC VIEW

Wednesday 20th June, 1990

No. 1086   Price 50p

HAYES IN THE HOOPS

DELIGHTED to pose in the green and white hoops for the first time — that's Celtic's £650,000 capture from Arsenal Martin Hayes on the day he signed.

The midfielder can't wait for the start of the 1990-91 season and the chance to demonstrate his ability to the Celtic supporters.

Martin Hayes' thoughts on his big money move and his targets with Celtic — Page Three.

TRANSFER MOVES HOLD-UP

WORLD CUP IS THE KEY

THE WORLD CUP in Italy has put on hold Celtic moves into the transfer market in recent weeks.

Three key club officials, chairman Jack McGinn, manager Billy McNeill and assistant Tommy Craig, are all in Italy in various capacities which prevented the signing of Martin Hayes from being followed up swiftly.

The conclusion of the World Cup together with the passing of June 30, the date on which players' contracts expire, should see Celtic renew efforts to add to the player pool.

The signing of Hayes delighted the manager, who had admired the Arsenal midfielder since his own days south of the border when boss of Manchester City and Aston Villa.

However, there was disappointment for him when another target, Scotland midfielder Gary McAllister, opted to join Leeds United.

Former Celt Charlie Nicholas, whose Aberdeen contract runs out at the end of the month, confirmed on Scottish Television that his present club had been approached by Mr McNeill with a view to a possible move.

He anticipated talks with the Celtic boss when Mr McNeill returns from Italy and could yet renew acquaintances with former Arsenal team-mate Hayes.

Other moves, to and from Celtic Park, seem sure to be completed before pre-season training begins in late July, swiftly followed by the trip to West Germany for practice matches against semi-professional opposition in early August.

As the twenty-first century came hurtling ever closer with each passing day, the *View* finally tripped over itself into the modern world by introducing colour to the proceedings.

And after twenty-five years of grainy black and white images of Celtic legends such as Jock Stein, Jimmy Johnstone, Kenny Dalglish and countless others, who did the *View* have in glorious grainy technicolour? Martin Hayes – that's who, the new signing from Arsenal. At one point in his Celtic career Hayes was accidentally locked in a team-mate's car in the Barrowfield car park (he traced 'HELP!' on the window condensation) and nobody at the training field even noticed he was missing. The story goes that when Billy McNeill departed as manager a year later the board told him he was getting a £650,000 golden handshake – he went home and Martin Hayes was sitting on his couch.

All kidding aside though, this summer special, still published on newsprint, paved the way for the new semi-glossy *View* that was introduced at the start of the 1990–91 season. It had full colour, although only on the outside and centre pages, its size had been upped to sixteen pages and it sold for the new price of 50p.

In this same issue that welcomed Martin Hayes, the *View* also said its goodbyes to two dyed-in-the-wool Celtic legends, as both Roy Aitken and Tommy Burns had departed during the season past. The *View* also hinted that Charlie Nicholas could be on his way back as his Aberdeen contract ran out at the end of that month, but it would be another year before that move would come off.

The most interesting thing in the *View*, though, was a letter which stated: 'Those Celtic supporters who have long advocated that the club go public must surely now realise the folly of that wish with the outrageous bid for Hibernian FC by Hearts.

'The money markets are not the slightest bit concerned about tradition and loyalty. The egotistical businessmen, who often front such organisations, see football only as a convenient means of personal propaganda.

'Like most Celtic supporters, I am not uncritical of the manner in which our club has been run in the past, but the solution must be to bring in people of ability and business experience, as had happened recently, not to leave our club in the hands of people who wish only to use it for personal glorification or financial gain. In any case, going public could not raise from shareholders the massive sums needed for players and the stadium.'

Hmm, enough food for thought to choke any malcontent. Wonder if Fergus McCann read this letter!

Pat Bonner's form certainly didn't go to the dogs but he has a playful opponent at East End Park.

No. 1128   WEDNESDAY 26th JUNE, 1991   PRICE 30p

CELTIC VIEW

SPECIAL ISSUE

LIAM'S DREAM IRISH START

BOSS'S No. 2 PLEDGE

THE identity of Liam Brady's no 2 at Celtic Park will be known before pre-season training begins on Monday July 8.

That was the firm message from the new boss as speculation abounded at the start of the week.

Tommy Craig and Frank Stapleton, who had both been strong contenders for the top job, were the candidates most widely backed.

However, former Celts Tommy Burns, Roy Aitken and Mick McCarthy have also been mentioned in despatches.

Though giving away nothing, Brady admitted that he would require assistance in familiarising himself with the Scottish scene.

The existing backroom team is more than capable of doing that and it may be that the manager's right hand man comes from outwith that category.

BY DONALD COWEY

LIAM BRADY'S term as Celtic manager seems sure to start on home ground ...

For the new boss confirmed that the club's proposed pre-season tour of Ireland will definitely go ahead.

Specific dates were still to be confirmed as Mr Brady outlined his plans for preparations but games against Shelbourne in his home town of Dublin, Cork City and Sligo Rovers had been proposed.

"We will play three or perhaps even four games in Ireland," stated the manager.

"Pre-season training begins on Monday July 8 and we will have a week to 10 days before going over to Ireland.

"After a week there we will head back for a game against Dundee on Monday August 5.

"There has been talk of a charity match for Save the Children but I have to speak to Steve Archibald about that.

"It will certainly be a hectic time — we have only just over four weeks' pre-season training before

the competitive action is underway, with lots of games.

"The Skol Cup comes up immediately and obviously it is my intention that we make a big impression in that competition, as in all the others."

The new boss admits to being a believer in the theory that there is too much club football in Britain and that it hinders the prospects of success at the highest level.

"If you look to the international side and success in the European club competitions, then you must play fewer games in

my opinion," he states.

"The success of the international side is very important for the well-being of football in general in any country.

"The fact that gates went up enormously in England last season after the national side reached the semi-finals of the World Cup demonstrates that the two go hand-in-hand.

"However, decisions on the size of divisions and the number of games which clubs must play are made by others.

"We have to get on with our jobs ... and I certainly hope that Celtic will be involved in an awful lot of games in the season ahead!

WELCOME ABOARD!

Chairman Jack McGinn welcomes a happy Liam Brady to Celtic Park and signals the beginning of a new era.

The popular Dubliner becomes only the seventh man to manage the Parkhead club and he is the first non-Celtic player to be offered the coveted post.

SOUVENIR COLOUR POSTER

TURN TO CENTRE PAGES

In the close-season of 1991 there was no *View* planned for 26 June and the final issue of 1990–91 on 15 May stated that a bumper summer edition would be out on 19 June.

However, a week after the final *View* of the season, it was announced that Billy McNeill had been sacked as manager and, by the time the summer *View* hit the streets, the front page was proclaiming that the managerial post was a 'decision too vital to rush' and the 'right choice must be made'. That *View*, as promised, hit the streets on Wednesday 19 June – and on Thursday 20 June the club announced that Liam Brady was the new Celtic manager.

Consequently, the printing presses went into overdrive and an eight-page special was produced for 26 June. It was the first time a special had ever been dedicated entirely to one person, new manager Liam Brady. Inside, the new man said: 'I felt a bit scared when I got home from the meeting with Mr McGinn and Mr Cassidy, during which I accepted the job, and heard it announced on the national television news. I was given a video charting the history of Celtic Football Club and, watching it, I became a bit scared again. That fear has disappeared and I am just looking forward to everything. I feel in control.'

He added: 'In so many cases, getting into football management means having to start at the bottom and working your way up. I felt that was not for me, but when the Manchester City post became available a few months ago it occurred to me that a job at that sort of level would appeal to me. Peter Reid was appointed almost immediately there but my mind had been set thinking. Then when I heard that the Celtic post was vacant I knew that I was definitely interested.'

The new man carried on: 'My playing ethic is quite simple – I like a skilful passing game, one where the people watching are going to be entertained. I think that fits very easily into Celtic's traditions. Watching the history of Celtic FC showed me that there were years when the teams played very attractive football, but did not win anything. I hope to put the two together and see no reason why that cannot be achieved in the first year.'

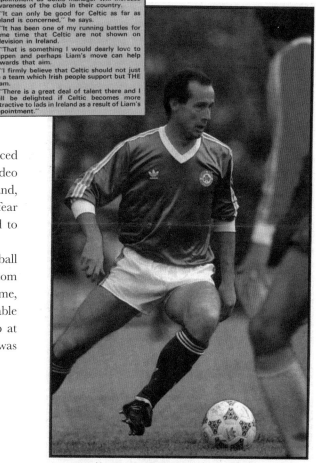

GOOD FOR CELTIC

PAT BONNER is confident that Liam Brady's appointment as Celtic manager will increase awareness of the club in their country.

"It can only be good for Celtic as far as Ireland is concerned," he says.

"It has been one of my running battles for some time that Celtic are not shown on television in Ireland.

"That is something I would dearly love to happen and perhaps Liam's move can help towards that aim.

"I firmly believe that Celtic should not just be a team which Irish people support but THE team.

"There is a great deal of talent there and I will be delighted if Celtic becomes more attractive to lads in Ireland as a result of Liam's appointment."

Liam Brady in the Republic of Ireland colours he graced for over a decade.

Celtic VIEW

No. 1225 JULY 14, 1993   **80p (R.O.I. £1.20)**

FOOTBALL'S OLDEST NEWSPAPER AND STILL No.1

JOE'S X FACTOR

HOOP HOOP HOORAY...Tommy Boyd and model Angela show off the new strip

● CELTIC are ready to hoop it up in the coming season – with a brand new look to the world-famous jerseys. Changes have been made to the collar, while the traditional green and white bands have been deepened.

● But the biggest change from last term is that old friends CR Smith have made a welcome return as club sponsors.

● The double glazing giants have signed a four-year deal which is worth up to £1.5 million.

Boss Gerard Eadie said: "We are Celtic people and the time was right to return. We hope this is the start of something big for both of us."

● Book your new kit – Page 15

Bhoys hoop it up!

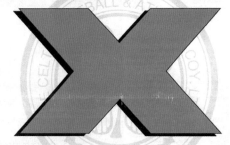

TICKET PRICES

ADMISSION prices for Celtic Park in the 1993/94 season will be as follows:
Ground – adult £7, child/OAP £4; The Jungle – £9; Front Stand – adult £10, child/OAP (Family Section only) £7; Upper Stand – £12.

Entry to reserve games will be £2 for adults and £1 for children and OAPs.

Season ticket prices are: Ground – adult £170, child/OAP £85; The Jungle – adult £200, child/OAP £125; Front Stand – adult £245, child/OAP (Family Section only) £170; Upper Stand – £295.

Children must be born on or after August 1, 1977 to qualify for reduced rates.

Those who apply for season tickets after July 20, using cheque or credit card, will not receive books in time for the Sheffield Wednesday game on July 31.

By DONALD COWEY

JOE JORDAN is ready to put the steel back into Celtic next season.

Liam Brady admits that his side lacked resilience last term and believes Jordan is the man to instill that X factor.

Lifelong Celtic fan Jordan won't compromise the club's long-established tradition of playing attractive, attacking football.

But he is firm in his belief that other qualities are vital if a side is to be successful.

Winners

He said: You've got to play football, but there has to be a resilience about the side too.

"You can have that through organisation. It's hard to explain how a team can develop the sort of qualities which are essential if players are to be winners.

"Individuals have to know their exact functions in the team and how to come through difficult spells.

"All great sides have times

Jordan to give Celts heart

when they're in trouble but it's their ability to survive them which separates them from the rest.

"It might be a 10-minute spell in a game, an entire game or even a run of games when the side is below-par and under pressure.

"Through good teamwork and a sound playing pattern, a side can come through difficult times unscathed.

"There's no magic wand, of course. It's a question of getting the message across on the

Turn to Page 2

ALL BHOYS TOGETHER...CR Smith boss Gerard Eadie (left) with Tom Boyd, chairman Kevin Kelly and Liam Brady

Italian job for Joe – See Page 2

By now the *View* was so glossy it was hopeless for keeping a fish supper in or any other sundry manner of things that people tended to use old newsprint for.

For the 80p asking price there was also full colour throughout all sixteen pages and the *View* even provides the opportunity to catalogue the changing face of women in football. In the summer of 2007, Celtic Football Club announced that, for the first time ever, the club would be running football teams for girls and women. Thankfully the pics used to promote the new initiative were a bit more PC and a little less 'saucy' than this 'ooh-er missus shot' from

the early nineties. Tom Boyd looks pretty pleased with himself though. The pic may not exactly be classed in the 'X-Factor' category it shares the front page with, but it's unlikely that a football club would take that tack today.

The launch of the new strip also heralded the return of CR Smith as sponsors with a £1.5 million four-year deal. The kit didn't meet with everybody's approval, though, as a correspondent to the *View* wrote: 'I have witnessed many significant events in Celtic's history, including the Janefield Street stampede and the Rapid Vienna fiasco, but this is the first time I've been compelled to express my thoughts in the *View*. The reason is Celtic's new strip.

'I'm astounded that such severe changes have been made to the famous hoops. It's been reported that fundamental changes to the Celtic top are difficult because of the design. So why change it? I've always bought the traditional Celtic tops irrespective of the sponsors, but this new wide hoop design has made me think twice. I'll be wearing an "old" top with extra pride from now on. If experiments must be made, surely they can be carried out on the away top.'

In fact, they most certainly had been and the three-tone crazy camouflage effort that looked like a throwback from the Korean War campaign was a fairly contemporary example of 'experiments'.

Celtic VIEW

NO. 1228 OCTOBER 27 1993   £1.00 (IRL £1.40)

COMPLETE FAN'S GUIDE TO LISBON

PAGES 8 and 9

NEW BOSS LOU'S EXCLUSIVE MESSAGE

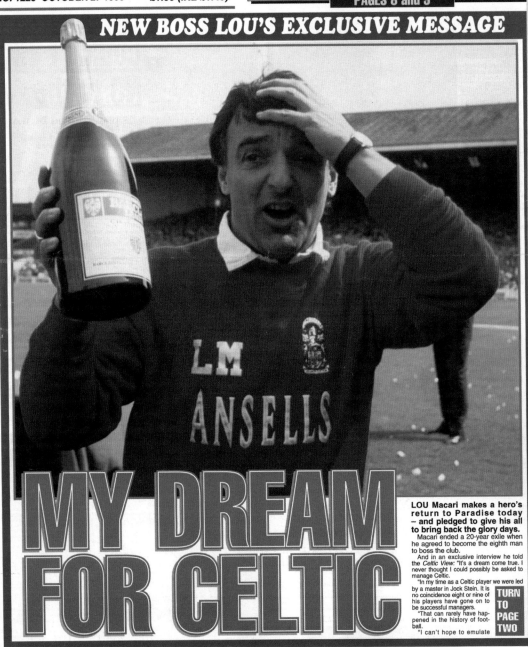

MY DREAM FOR CELTIC

LOU Macari makes a hero's return to Paradise today – and pledged to give his all to bring back the glory days.

Macari ended a 20-year exile when he agreed to become the eighth man to boss the club.

And in an exclusive interview he told the *Celtic View*: "It's a dream come true. I never thought I could possibly be asked to manage Celtic.

"In my time as a Celtic player we were led by a master in Jock Stein. It is no coincidence eight or nine of his players have gone on to be successful managers.

"That can rarely have happened in the history of football.

"I can't hope to emulate

TURN TO PAGE TWO

For a few weeks it was the worst kept secret in football, but as October 1993 came to an end it was officially announced that former Celt Lou Macari was the new Celtic manager.

Liam Brady had quit after a 6 October away defeat to St Johnstone and the new manager told the *View*: 'I can't hope to emulate Jock Stein overnight, but I can promise to work night and day to ensure improvement. You don't become world-beaters at the drop of a hat, but improvement breeds confidence and you build from there. The people at the club – like Frank Connor [reserve coach and interim manager] – know the set-up and players better than I do and I will rely on Frank on Saturday at Ibrox. Frank will be the man to get me through the early weeks and I hope a lot longer.'

In that week's edition, club chairman Kevin Kelly said: 'We are delighted to welcome Lou Macari today as the eighth manager in the proud history of Celtic Football Club. Lou's decision to accept the post vacated by Liam Brady is an enormous boost to everyone at the club. Lou Macari was our first and only choice – from outwith the club – as manager from the moment Liam told us he was leaving after the 2-1 defeat at McDiarmid Park. We made an immediate approach to Stoke City and, eventually, an amicable agreement was reached on compensation for Lou's services. We were then able to open talks with him.

'He obviously had commitments to be sorted out at Stoke City, but we were always confident that the lure of a return to the club where he gave almost seven fine years as a player would be too great to resist. I'm delighted to say that our confidence was justified. Lou Macari comes to us with a reputation as one of the finest young bosses in British football.'

He added: 'His success rate convinced us that Lou Macari was our man. Now the hard work begins for him as he leads Celtic into an exciting new era. He will bring with him fresh ideas and his appointment will excite the fans who deserve some success once again after a long lean spell. On behalf of everyone at the club, I wish Lou every success in the job.'

I'LL NICK BIG TAM'S RECORD!

RANGERS V CELTIC
Saturday, October 30
KICK-OFF 3.00pm
ALL-TICKET

Celtic VIEW

NO. 1245 MARCH 2 1994   £1.00 (IRL £1.40)

CAMBUSLANG:

PETROL STATION

CAR PARKING AREAS

TRAIN STATION

HOTEL

10 SCREEN CINEMA

OFFICE DEVELOPMENT

RETAIL, SHOP OUTLETS & COACH STATIONS

10 PIN BOWLING

CAR SHOWROOMS

10,000 SEATER INDOOR ARENA

CELTIC STADIUM ARENA **CAMBUSLANG**

STADIUM

THE DREAM COMES TRUE

SEE PAGES 8 and 9

KELLY: WE'LL STEP ASIDE

PAGES 2 and 3

HELP US DELIVER

DAVID SMITH ... "This package is superb for the club."

DEPUTY chairman David Smith today called upon Celtic fans to help him deliver ALL the promises made at Friday's momentous news conference.

And he urged the support not to be mislead into opposing the scheme.

The announcements on the imminent construction of a superstadium at Cambuslang, a short-term shares issue and the full public flotation of the club were the most far-reaching in our history.

But the club has been angered by reaction in the media, which has ranged in some places from the indifferent to the downright offensive.

Mr Smith said: "This package is superb for the club. I would now ask the fans to ask themselves a number of questions.

"**WOULD** you like a new stadium? **WOULD** you like someone else to pay for it? **WOULD** you like the manager to have money to strengthen the team?

"**WOULD** you like the shareholding more widely spread so no faction has control?

"**WOULD** you like more money injected into the club?

"**WOULD** you like to be able to buy shares in Celtic and own part of the club?

Announced

"**WOULD** you like the club to have a new board? **WOULD** you like supporters and former players to be represented on the board?

"**WOULD** you like the club run like Manchester United?

"If, as I expect, your answer to all of these questions is a resounding **YES**, then what we announced is what you have waited for.

"**WE WILL DELIVER ON EVERY SINGLE PROMISE.**

Smith's promise to fans as club looks forward to 21st Century

EXCLUSIVE
By ANDREW SMITH

"But if you answer **NO**, then I have to ask what kind of club you have in mind for the 21st Century."

Mr Smith and chairman Kevin Kelly faced a barrage of questions from the media for more than an hour in a packed Jock Stein Lounge during Friday's highly-charged conference.

They spelled out the future as a public limited company in a space-age stadium at Cambuslang.

And they also outlined plans for an issue of 25,000 shares almost immediately to raise up to £6 million to reduce borrowing and give Lou Macari money to spend.

And Kevin Kelly revealed the willingness of the current board to step aside if need be – a vow reiterated by fellow director Michael Kelly on TV on

Continued on Page Two

LOU MACARI ...cash to spend

A full two years previously, in April 1992, the club announced plans to move to Cambuslang, the preferred option among no fewer than fifteen locations, including Hampden, that were considered by the club.

As one would suspect, despite the promise of a 52,000 all-seater stadium and all the usual add-ons of a modern-day stadium complex, the news went down like a lead balloon with the faithful, because, crisis or no crisis, moving away from Paradise was not on the agenda and it certainly wouldn't be the cure for the current ills.

In November 1992 there were reports that the Cambuslang site was a toxic time bomb, but in May 1993, Glasgow District Council gave planning permission and in February, Celtic's vice chairman David Smith announced that the £20 million cornerstone funding was in place and 'Cambuslang is now a reality.'

Now, in March 1994, it was announced that the move was definitely on, although the stadium capacity had dropped to 40,000-plus. Chairman Kevin Kelly told the *View*: 'We now know we are moving to Cambuslang and that money will be available to Lou Macari. These have been the two major concerns that have worried and frustrated our supporters. Now they have been addressed and I genuinely believe we have turned the corner. Last week's announcement wasn't just the best news for Celtic Football Club, it was the best news ever for our supporters, who haven't had it easy recently. I know because I am one myself and these have been difficult times for all of us.'

The project was scheduled to be finished by August 1996 and, under the banner headline of 'Cambuslang: They said it wouldn't happen… and they were wrong!', the *View* dedicated the centre-spread to the stadium story, as well as pages one, two and three.

The centre pages announced: 'It was the day they said would never happen – the day that Cambuslang was declared a reality… At the same time as a commitment was given to turning the club into a public company and putting ownership in the hands of the fans. Deputy chairman David Smith told Friday's momentous news conference that things would never be the same again for Celtic. He was right.'

FIELD OF DREAMS ... Chairman Kevin Kelly at the Cambuslang site

Celtic VIEW

A GRAND NEW TEAM

SPECIAL SOUVENIR EDITION OF AN HISTORIC SEVEN DAYS

NO. 1446 MARCH 9 1994 £1.00 (IRL £1.40)

LOU'S PLEA TO FANS PAGE 5  **KEANE: THE MONEY MAN** PAGES 8 and 9  **OLD BHOYS SPEAK OUT** PAGE 16

PHONE FERGUS

Fans back at Ibrox – Page 10

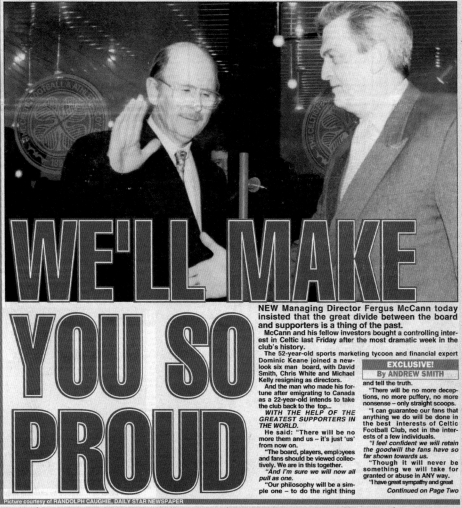

WE'LL MAKE YOU SO PROUD

Picture courtesy of RANDOLPH CAUGHIE, DAILY STAR NEWSPAPER

NEW Managing Director Fergus McCann today insisted that the great divide between the board and supporters is a thing of the past.

McCann and his fellow investors bought a controlling interest in Celtic last Friday after the most dramatic week in the club's history.

The 52-year-old sports marketing tycoon and financial expert Dominic Keane joined a new-look six man board, with David Smith, Chris White and Michael Kelly resigning as directors.

And the man who made his fortune after emigrating to Canada as a 22-year-old intends to take the club back to the top...

WITH THE HELP OF THE GREATEST SUPPORTERS IN THE WORLD.

He said: "There will be no more them and us – it's just 'us' from now on.

"The board, players, employees and fans should be viewed collectively. We are in this together.

"*And I'm sure we will now all pull as one.*

"Our philosophy will be a simple one – to do the right thing

EXCLUSIVE!
By ANDREW SMITH

and tell the truth.

"There will be no more deceptions, no more puffery, no more nonsense – only straight scoops.

"I can guarantee our fans that anything we do will be done in the best interests of Celtic Football Club, not in the interests of a few individuals.

"*I feel confident we will retain the goodwill the fans have so far shown towards us.*

"Though it will never be something we will take for granted or abuse in ANY way.

"I have great sympathy and great

Continued on Page Two

What a difference a week makes. In fact, it wasn't even a week as the previous 'Help Us Deliver' Cambuslang edition had only been warming the newsagents' stands for two days when the entire course of Celtic's history irrevocably changed.

Friday 4 March was the day that will go down in history as, with the club only minutes from receivership, Fergus McCann stepped in with money from his own pocket to save the club. The *View* stated: 'Fergus McCann has spelled out his three main objectives as he sets out in his bid to see the Celts once more scale the heights. The new managing director eased into his role on Monday and immediately vowed to: stabilise the club's finances; provide a stadium to meet the demands of the 21st century; build a team to challenge for all major honours. McCann believes major external investment is required to make this work – and initially this will mean putting into practice the £17.9 million capital package he first offered to the club in November.

'He said: "The hard work begins now. Our first job was to secure the financial position at the bank and this has now been achieved. Recapitalisation of the club will now move forward with a major input of around £17.9 million. This cash will come from ourselves, from external investors and from a shares issue aimed at the fans."' It was this proposed shares issue that consolidated the supporters' faith in McCann, as his vision was one that they shared.

It would seem that his view on Cambuslang was pretty similar to theirs, too, as he was quoted by the *View* as saying: 'You have to look at every possibility. However, I've always had very negative thoughts about Cambuslang. Nobody has shown me anything concrete or tangible to suggest that it would be the right project to pursue. My own preference remains a top-class, high-capacity stadium at Celtic Park.'

So Cambuslang, along with various other remnants of the old board, was consigned to the dustbin and the 'grand new team' sallied forth. Chairman Kevin Kelly said: 'The receivership threat hanging over the club meant that I had to act and last Thursday contacted Brian Dempsey who set the wheels in motion to put the club on a sound financial footing. I'm very pleased with the way everything has worked out and I believe by involving Fergus McCann and Mr Dempsey we have chosen the right way forward. I'd also like to welcome Dominic Keane on to the board and thank outgoing directors David Smith, Chris White and Michael Kelly for their work with the club over the years.'

IN THE FRAME ... Dominic Keane, Tom Grant, Fergus McCann and Brian Dempsey at McDiarmid Park last Saturday

Celtic VIEW

No.1254 MAY 4 1994   £1.00 (IRL £1.40)

OLD FIRM SPECIAL
WE TRAVEL WITH THE TEAM TO IBROX *Pages 2&3*

12,000 TURN UP FOR THE PARKHEAD GALA DAY *Pages 6&7*

BOOTIFUL!

Collins: I knew I'd silence Ibrox

GOALDEN Bhoy John Collins KNEW he'd bury the wonder strike that silenced Ibrox last Saturday.

Stand-in skipper Collins told me 10 minutes **BEFORE** kick-off that his

By ANDREW SMITH

revolutionary new boots would find the target.

I sat with Lou Macari's men in the dressing room and as Collins prepared to lead the side into battle, he made his amazing prediction.

He turned to me, tapped his boots, which he was wearing for only the second time, and said: "I'll **DEFINITELY** score with these on today."

He went on: "I know I didn't score against St Johnstone in midweek with them on, but I was never in any good positions.

"It'll be different against Rangers, I promise."

Collins' words could hardly have been more prophetic and afterwards he couldn't contain his joy over the glorious 29th minute free-kick that almost gave his side a memorable

JOHN COLLINS

victory against all the odds.

He beamed: "I said before the match I was going all out to silence Ibrox and I did just that.

"All four sides! It was sheer bliss."

And the battling Ibrox draw kept up an amaz-

ing run for Collins as skipper.

In the five games he has deputised for Paul McStay as captain this season, Celts have recorded three wins and two draws.

The goal also kept up his fantastic scoring rate against the Ibrox men in the last year.

Scored

He explained: "That's me scored in four of the last five Old Firm games.

"That's not bad going and I'll be going all-out to keep it up next season.

"I love these matches and it was just a wee bit disappointing that we didn't get the win at the weekend.

"Still, I think considering that we were so badly hit by injuries and the fact that we'd no fans there, we can be proud of our efforts."

YOUNG gun Chris Hay could be in line for a shock first-team debut on Saturday against Partick Thistle.

Boss Lou Macari is ready to hand the 19-year-old striker a top-team chance after his stunning hat-trick destroyed Rangers reserves at Parkhead last Saturday.

Hay could be thrown in alongside fellow teenager Simon Donnelly to fire Celts towards a European spot.

And Simon is sure his big pal will be a hit in the first team.

He said: "If he does get the chance I would just tell him to go out and enjoy himself the

LOU: CHRIS WILL MAKE HAY IN THE FIRST TEAM

way I did in my first appearance against Hibs. And I'd tell him to be confident about it.

"It would be great to play alongside Chris in the first team as we formed a partnership in the reserves and did well together.

"He's shown what he can do
Continued on Page Two

CHRIS HAY ... First team call

Continued on Page Two

It's nice to get back to talking about football for a change, but even this was football with a difference...

It was the 'fan ban' game at Ibrox when the powers that be at Rangers decided that Celtic fans wouldn't be allowed in to the game. With Rangers already eleven points ahead of fourth-placed Celtic, a win would secure the title for Rangers and the fan ban would effectively help put it on a plate for them. That was until John Collins silenced 45,000 Rangers fans with a perfectly taken free-kick in the twenty-eighth minute. The game would finish 1-1, but all the after-match talk was about that goal.

The scorer told the *View*: 'It was always in my mind that I would hit it. But I'm told that the bench were shouting for Dariusz [Wdowczyk] to take it. I just felt that it was my responsibility and I felt confident about it. I do think that the fan ban backfired a bit, as the atmosphere for most of the game was really quiet. However, I know it could have been very different if they had taken the lead. Thankfully Rangers didn't. And it was just a shame that there were no Celtic fans there to witness the brilliant strike that put us ahead!'

The *View* also stated: 'Three die-hard Celts fans really did the business at Ibrox on Saturday. High-flyers Steven Donaghy, Eamonn Taylor and Peter Beattie – all Glasgow businessmen – raised absent fans' and the players' spirits by putting up £300 to hire a private plane to fly over Ibrox before kick-off trailing a huge "Hail, hail, the Celts are here" banner. Steven said: "We wanted to show the team we were there in spirit."'

The goal was cheered, though, by over 12,000 Celtic fans who had gathered at Celtic Park to take in the reserve game. They already had a bit to cheer about when Chris Hay opened the scoring in the third minute, but around the half-hour mark there was no doubting that the twenty-two players on the park knew exactly what had happened at Ibrox as the 12,000 crowd went ballistic and kept the cheering up for a full five minutes. The 'goal' celebration only ended with a stirring but ironic rendition of 'You'll Never Walk Alone'. There was even more cheer, though, as Hay went on to score a hat-trick as the youngsters recorded a 3-1 win over an experienced Rangers side.

RESERVES

CELTIC.......3
Hay (3, 52, 68)

RANGERS...1
Wishart (74)   Att: 12,130

FAN-TASTIC....
The bhoys celebrate after hitman Hay's third goal against the sickened Gers

Celtic VIEW

No.1261 JULY 20 1994   £1.00 (IRL £1.40)

WE'RE IN SAFE HANDS

PAT BONNER

THE legend lives on!

For new Celts' boss Tommy Burns has this week confirmed that the Republic of Ireland keeper will be returning to Parkhead as a player/coach.

And that marks an amazing turn-around in the career of the 34-year-old who was freed by Lou Macari in May after 16 years at Celtic Park.

Burns explained: "I think Celtic Football Club did tremendously well in bringing over a young man from Ireland and turning him into a world class goalkeeper.

"One who has gone on to represent his country in two World Cup finals and a European Championship finals, won every domestic honour the Scottish game has to offer and has performed **TURN TO PAGE THREE**

THE TOMMY BURNS STORY

4-PAGE SPECIAL STARTS ON PAGE 7

Celts face boys from Brazil

CELTIC'S first home game of the season will be played more to the sound of the Samba beat than the Hampden roar...

And it'll all be thanks to the fans of their Brazilian opponents Flamengo when they meet on Tuesday August 2 in the first game at their temporary home.

The evening match – which has a 7.30pm kick-off – should be a cracker, with the Brazilians fired up from their countrymen's World Cup success.

Flamengo are known in Brazil as the people's team, with fans from all walks of life.

They are the best supported club in the nation, and if the fans we witnessed on our TV screens at the World Cup are anything to go by, they'll turn the game against Celtic into a real carnival night.

Sale

Flamengo may not have any World Cup heroes in their side or be as well known as some European sides, but there's no doubt they'll come to Hampden to put on a show.

Season ticket holders will gain entry with their new books while it is hoped that briefs for the game will be on sale next Monday from Celtic Park, the Celtic Supporters' Association and The Celtic Shop in Dundas Street.

Further information on this matter can be obtained by calling the Celtic Clubcall *Turn To Page Two*

The hottest ticket in town

SMILES BETTER...Tommy Burns is No.1 with the fans

NOW FANS IN SCRAMBLE FOR TOP SEATS

By *ANDREW SMITH*

TOMMY BURNS' appointment as Celtic manager has sparked the biggest ticket scramble at the club in years.

Season ticket sales are set to break all previous records and, with three to go to the big kick-off, already **MORE** have been sold than in the **WHOLE** of last term.

Selling well throughout the summer, Burns' position as the No.1 choice of the fans for the Celtic hot seat has been confirmed by an incredible upsurge in applications for season tickets since he took charge nine days ago.

Sales

Already the Celtic End of Hampden is three-quarters of the way to being a complete sell-out and anyone considering purchasing a season ticket for this section is advised to do so quickly.

The sales are a triumph for an audacious marketing campaign that has seen adverts placed in the national Press, thousands of houses leafleted and the club buy prime-time TV advertising space during Sunday's World Cup Final!

According to Acting Marketing Director Patrick Ferrell it has all had the desired effect.

He said: "We have had a tremendously positive feedback and I think it's been a case of our message really getting across while making fans aware of how good a deal is on offer to them.

"The price range of the season tickets and the ability to pay them up over a period of months have made them accessible to a great many people who'd never previously considered being season ticket holders.

"And through talking to a great many supporters over the last week about Tommy *Turn To Page Two*

FERGUS McCANN

The changes kept on coming at Celtic Park. The bulldozers were set to move in as Hampden had temporarily been commandeered for season 1994–95 and Lou Macari had been shown the door, paving the way for the arrival of Tommy Burns.

Fergus McCann said: 'I gave notice to Mr Luigi Macari that he failed to meet important obligations under his contract of employment and that as from 14 June he was dismissed from his position as manager of the club. In the opinion of the board, Mr Macari had failed to attend to his responsibilities at Celtic Park, including adequate direction and supervision of the various departments in his charge.'

On the new arrival, the MD told the *View*: 'Tommy Burns was without doubt the outstanding applicant and comes to us highly recommended. He has established himself as a successful manager, with experience at national and international level. He has demonstrated considerable leadership ability and is known throughout the sport of football for his motivational skills. I was also greatly impressed with Tommy's integrity and honesty throughout the discussions.'

The new man himself said: 'We've got to look on the season as a fresh start for Celtic. I guarantee that from the playing point of view, supporters coming along to see Celtic will see eleven guys who will compete in every game and play for the jersey and the punters in the stands. But I would like to think this will cut both ways. Because there has been a lot of cynicism – justifiable in many cases – among Celtic supporters in recent years about players, management and board.'

He added: 'Celtic's different to any other football club in the world and inspires people in a way that no other team does. It's a special animal, a breed apart from any other side, and so are the supporters who follow it. And all those people can rest assured I'll do everything in my power to put things right here. When they hurt, I'll be hurting every bit as badly.'

HAPPY BHOYS ... Paul McStay and John Collins show their delight at the return of Tommy Burns during training

Celtic VIEW

No. 1280 November 30, 1994   £1.00 (IRL £1.40)

GET BACK TO WORK

By MERLE BROWN

ROLL up the sleeves and get on with the game.

That's the message from bitterly disappointed boss Tommy Burns in the wake of Sunday's shattering Coca-Cola Cup setback.

Tommy knows that everyone will still be feeling shell-shocked after the agony of Ibrox.

But he insists the dressing-room gloom must be banished before tonight's league clash with Hibs at Easter Road.

All efforts must be well and truly focused on the three points up for grabs.

Celtic's last win in the Premier Division was against Alex Miller's men in September when they won 2-0.

Burns is well aware that the need for a victory has never been greater.

He said: "All the attention must now be on tonight's game – that's the way it's got to be.

"Obviously, everyone is desperately disappointed about what happened on Sunday.

"But I think now we've got to just get on with things and be positive, starting in this match.

"The Hibs clash and the Motherwell match on Saturday are big games.

"We all know that and we also know the importance of winning them."

Tommy looks set to shuffle the pack after the Raith defeat.

But he insists it doesn't mean he thinks any less of the players he picked for the final.

He said: "I think we need to change things around again and bring in a few different faces.

"Billy Stark and I will sit down and think about what to do.

"To be fair to the players who took part on Sunday, they played well for an hour-and-a-half, but fell out of things a bit in extra-time."

HAUNTED BY MY PENALTY HORROR

Worst moment ever says Paul

By JOE SULLIVAN

SKIPPER Paul McStay looked back on his cup final penalty miss and confessed: "It was the worst moment of my career."

Paul was inconsolable after his sudden-death spot-kick was blocked by Raith Rovers keeper Scott Thomson on Sunday.

That moment of horror saw the Coca-Cola Cup heading for Kirkcaldy after a 2-2 draw and a dramatic 6-5 penalty shoot-out.

It also means Celtic's trophy famine goes on – and no one needs to tell Paul how much the defeat means to the club and the thousands of supporters throughout the world.

He said: *"Words can't describe how I feel at the moment.*

"This is the worst I have ever felt in my professional career.

"I have got to live with it. All I've have been thinking about since then is that penalty kick and it hurts.

"As I was walking up to take the kick I was thinking 'just pick the spot and hit it'.

"I picked the corner but the keeper made a good guess and stopped the ball.

"After the five and half years we've endured without a trophy I know exactly how deeply Sunday's loss hurts every single Celtic fan.

"I was hoping before the final that it would

Turn to Page Two

MOMENT THE DREAM ENDED ... Paul McStay hits his penalty (top), Thomson gets down to save it (above) and Paul is consoled by Andy Walker (right)

TOMMY BURNS' DEAFENING SILENCE - Page 2 ● CELTS PAY THE PENALTY - Pages 4 and 5 ... Pictures courtesy of The Sun

What could have been, and perhaps should have been, the first trophy of Fergus McCann's, as well as Tommy Burns' tenure slipped through Celtic's fingers at Ibrox.

It was the League Cup final and Raith Rovers had just won 6-5 on penalties after the team drew 2-2 in regulation time and stalemated during extra-time. The *View* reported: 'The agony just goes on and on! After five and a half years of waiting for some silverware – any silverware – Celtic fans had to endure extra-time, a penalty shoot-out and then sudden-death defeat in Sunday's Coca-Cola Cup final at Ibrox. It was one of the biggest Cup upsets for years as First Division Raith lifted the first trophy of their 111-year history – a result which prolongs the seemingly never-ending run without success.

'When the teams couldn't be separated after locking horns in the shoot-out, Jason Rowbotham knocked in the first of the elimination kicks and the entire weight of Celtic's hopes and dreams was thrust upon the shoulders of Paul McStay. Raith keeper Scott Thomson will go down in history as the man who dived to save McStay's penalty to take the League Cup to the new surroundings of Kirkcaldy. But the record books won't detail the full story. The skipper was immense in midfield and played his heart out for the full 120 minutes.'

The captain himself said: 'If we had a wee bit of luck during the ninety minutes then the Cup would have been won. The fans have waited since May 1989 for a chance that Sunday's final presented us with, but the fact that we never took it is something that I will have to live with. However, I really couldn't handle Sunday night after the game. I just wanted to go home, but I went back to the park. I knew I had to face people.'

Fergus McCann added: 'We congratulate Jimmy Nicholl and Raith Rovers on their victory. Penalties are a cruel way to lose and my thoughts are with our supporters and everyone involved with the club. It was an important match for us all as a psychological morale booster. Everyone at the club is committed to the long-term success of Celtic at the highest level. Obviously we are going through a time of rebuilding and sometimes that can be painful. Personally, I didn't come here for five minutes, five days or five weeks. I am here for five years to face the many challenges the club has to meet.'

THE LEVELLER ... Andy Walker dives full length to meet Mike Galloway's knock down for Celts' opener

Celtic VIEW

No. 1287 January 25, 1995 £1.00 (IRL £1.40)

I WANT TO LIFT THE CUP AGAIN

PHIL O'DONNELL'S BIG MATCH PREVIEW - Pages 8 and 9

THANKS A MI££ION

Share delight for Celtic

THE most successful share issue EVER in British footballing history came to a close last night...

And Celtic fans proved once and for all they are without equal in the game by responding in phenomenal numbers to own part of their club.

And no-one is more delighted than the man who masterminded the campaign, managing director Fergus McCann.

The MD's delight isn't with just the overall success of the share issue ... but the manner in which it has been achieved.

For it was grass roots supporters who invested in their thousands when certain parties claimed the flotation would not succeed.

Many detractors openly stated the issue would come nowhere near the proposed £9.4 million target.

However, Celtic fan power has once again breached all expectations.

And no doubt humble pie will be on the menu at a few dinner tables today!

The MD said: "The entire

MAN THE LINES ... Tommy Burns is joined by Paul McStay, Peter Grant and Pat Bonner to help deal with the thousands of calls received for the share issue.

operation has been extremely successful and the most telling aspect is that it has been driven by the supporters, not the big institutions.

"What is even more pleasing is that the entire operation was in-house and purely a Celtic staff project.

"We didn't use advertising agencies, PR firms or slick glossy TV ads.

"Everything was achieved by telephone calls, direct mailing and information sessions.

"The Celtic supporters have proved how much Celtic Football Club means to

them despite some snide comments in the Press which have now been shown up as hollow.

"The message to these people who said the share issue was 'FLAWED' or suggested that 'the national lottery represents a better bet' is that Celtic supporters have taken the intiative."

"About such detractors methinks of a saying they have in the east - 'the dog barks but the caravan moves on!'"

McCann's four-year dream of Celtic becoming a public limited company - and a suc-

cessful one in which supporters have a say - has finally come to fruition.

It was back in the autumn of 1990 that the businessman first drew up his plans to turn Celtic around.

And in the intervening four years the MD has moved very little from those original proposals.

He said: "The plan to raise £21 million was put together when I came over to Scotland in October 1990.

"I was looking for two people with £2 million each or four with £1 million and little of that has changed from the plan I

SHARE PANDEMONIUM · Continued page 2

Stark wants new Bhoys to shine

UP FOR THE CUP

BILLY STARK wants Celtic's new faces to help them go one better than they did in their Coca-Cola Cup run.

They kick off their Tennents Scottish Cup campaign against St Mirren at Hampden this Saturday.

But the side trying to get the club to their second final of the season will be vastly different from the one that lost out on penalties to Raith Rovers in November.

In are youngsters Stuart Gray and Brian McLaughlin, new signing Pierre van Hooijdonk, along with Phil O'Donnell and Tosh McKinlay, who were cup-tied for the Coca-Cola campaign.

Skipper Paul McStay will be suspended for the tie – but assistant boss Stark reckons if Celts play as they did on Saturday against Partick

Thistle they'll come through.

He said: "The Coca-Cola Cup was a great tournament for us, right up until the last four minutes.

"We showed that we had a good cup team and I hope we can do the same in this competition.

"Celtic have a good record in the Scottish Cup. It's always been our tournament, but unfortunately we haven't done well in it recently at all.

"This time we'll be looking to change that. We have players available who will relish this competition.

"We'll miss Paul McStay without a doubt, but we'll have Phil O'Donnell and Tosh McKinlay available and Pierre van Hooijdonk up front. I hope Pierre has been

Turn to Page Two

It was branded as a pipe dream by the old board and many more who derided and gave no credence to the thought that Celtic supporters worldwide would rally to the cause and dig into their own pockets to own a small piece of the club they loved.

However, Fergus McCann's 'pipe dream' of a share issue exploded and was the most successful ever in British football, giving the MD the opportunity to quote some Eastern dogma. He told the *View*: 'The message to these people who said the share issue was "flawed" or suggested that "the national lottery represents a better bet" is that Celtic supporters have taken the initiative. About such detractors methinks of a saying they have in the east – "the dog barks but the camel moves on!"'

The cynics trumpeted from on high that Celtic wouldn't get anywhere near the £9.4 million target. However, that was surpassed and the MD added: 'The plan to raise £21 million was put together when I came over to Scotland in October 1990. I was looking for two people with £2 million or four with £1 million and little of that has changed from the plan I brought to Scotland. Only names and faces have changed, with men like Albert Freidberg and Dermot Desmond investing in the club so only small modifications have been made. Now the final part of the plan to make Celtic financially stable is in place and everything is looking good for the future.'

Reporting on a 0-0 draw with Partick Thistle at Firhill, the *View* said: 'Tommy Burns got a clear indication that Celtic supporters will never view a goal-less draw against the bottom-of-the-league club as an acceptable result – and it came from two women behind the dug-out. These irked Parkhead fans repeatedly complained to him during the game that the efforts of his side represented a poor return for their £27 admission money. Tommy remarked: "If the two females who took umbrage at our performance want to get in touch with me I'll treat them to lunch at Celtic Park and we can continue our discussion."'

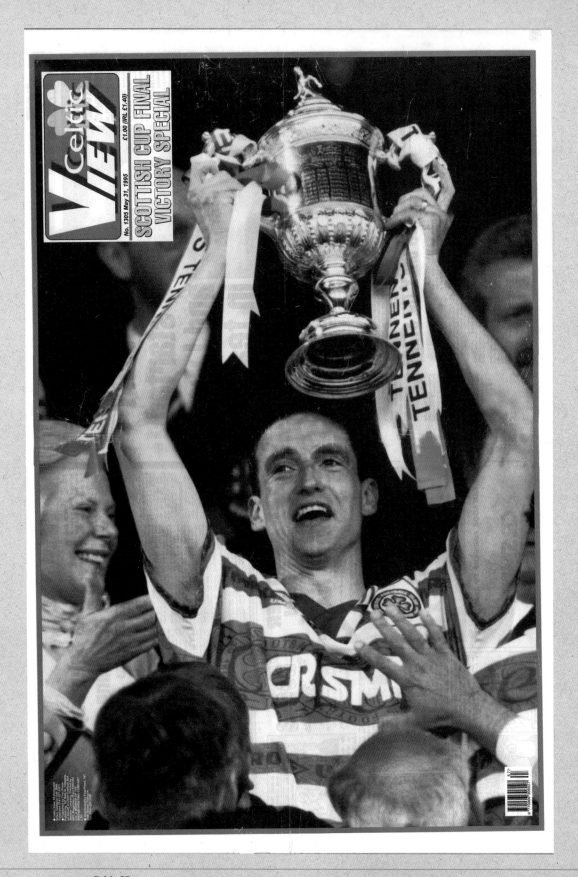

The venue was Hampden and the occasion was Celtic's first Scottish Cup final since 1990. It was the club's first opportunity to pick up silverware since 1989. It had been a long wait.

First Division Airdrie provided the opposition, but Celtic had already had their fingers burned by the Broomfield club's table-mates Raith Rovers in the League Cup final earlier that season. However, a headed goal from Pierre van Hooijdonk delivered the goods and Paul McStay finally got his hands on some silverware as captain.

The final whistle sparked scenes of unbridled joy around Hampden and beyond, and manager Tommy Burns explained the route of the coach journey back to Paradise. He told the *View*: 'I received a letter last week from a supporter who suggested it would be a nice touch if we took the same route home this time. He wanted us to travel the same road as Jock Stein back in '65 so that's exactly what we did and I'm so glad we acted upon the supporter's idea.

'Minutes after leaving Hampden, we passed Willie Haughey's Mitre bar and the bus was engulfed with fans. Then we moved further up to the Gorbals and the scenes outside the Brazen Head were nothing short of amazing – but once we turned right into the Gallowgate, absolute pandemonium set in. Baird's Bar just emptied and suddenly the Calton was full of thousands of Celtic fans…

'You should have seen it, literally thousands of them running down Kent Street from Lynch's. Honestly, it looked like Zulu Dawn. Pierre van Hooijdonk had to ask me what was going on as he was truly astonished at the scenes. Now he realises just what Celtic Football Club is all about – after coming here as a new Bhoy, he now knows that we are not simply another big club.'

The *View* carried on: 'Eventually the bus skimmed along the wet surface of London Road and turned into Kerrydale Street where hordes of the Celtic faithful had been standing for two hours in the May showers waiting for the Cup's six-year exile to finally end. And how they lapped it up – hanging from every vantage point to get a view of their heroes. Only six months earlier the same building was like a morgue in the aftermath of the League Cup final and, like that black day back in November, tears were also shed… Only this time they tasted so much sweeter!'

IT'S ONLY THE START

THIS is my first message to the supporters as the MD of a trophy-winning Celtic Football Club and it gives me great pleasure to be doing so after little more than a year in the position.

I came here with certain aims in respect to the team, the stadium and, of course, winning trophies.

And for the Scottish Cup to be captured after a relatively short rebuilding period can only give us confidence to go on and do better.

Things are changing at Celtic Park and the club is going in the right direction with the new stadium on its way to completion.

What better time then for us to use the Scottish Cup victory as a springboard to further successes.

The cup win should give the players the confidence to play open, attractive and flowing football next season.

Manager Tommy Burns and I have a couple of deals in progress and hope these will come to fruition soon.

The cup victory was very important to everyone connected with Celtic. I was delighted to see the pleasure it brought to supporters everywhere. Season 1994-95

has brought a revival in the fortunes of Celtic, the share issue bringing in more than £13million and the financial stability that involves, as well as the building of a new stadium which will be a sporting arena of spectacular style.

There was also the purchase of approximately £4 million worth of new playing talent. And now, after six years, the club wins a major trophy and at the same time qualifies for Europe.

A new era for Celtic has begun. I know that there were many supporters who didn't follow the team to Hampden, waiting to see if the changes at the club would occur.

Well, they have – and now is the time to come home to Celtic Park for the start of next season.

Then we can all work together to lead the club on to greater achievements and relive the enjoyment of Saturday's celebrations many more times in future.

JULY 9, 1997

NEW LOOK

Celtic View

The biggest, best & brightest club weekly

Issue no: 1393   Price: £1.25 (IRL £1.65)

WIN!
vip match day out at celtic park

WIN!
tickets, flights & accommodation
to see bhoys in dublin

FREE POSTER
young hoops pull-out

7UP YOUNG HOOPS

Wim's
21 Goal Salute
new coach jansen kicks off
with a bang

EASTERN SHOCK
donnelly's hoping to go west in uefa draw

48 PAGES

The first *Celtic View* of 1997–98 was special in a number of ways. New manager Wim Jansen was pictured on the front cover of the issue, which also included an exclusive interview with the Dutchman.

But fans used to the sixteen-page broadsheet newspaper-style publication were greeted by a new, forty-eight-page, full colour A4 magazine. The *View* was moving with the times and what better way to mark it than with news of a new boss.

The previous season had seen Rangers equal Celtic's nine league titles in a row and Tommy Burns had departed the club as a result. Wim Jansen's appointment was with one aim in mind – to stop the ten! And if supporters were slightly uneasy about the appointment, reassurance came from a footballing legend in the shape of Johan Cruyff. The Dutch master told the *View*: 'I have been in touch with Celtic to congratulate them on the appointment of a top-class coach in Wim Jansen. It is a massive statement of Celtic's ambition and I've no doubt that he will be a huge success.'

Simon Donnelly admits he doesn't care who Celts draw in Europe – as it can't be Batumi again!

Jansen's previous job had been in Japan, with one newspaper crassly describing the Dutchman as 'the second-worst thing to hit Hiroshima', but Fergus McCann, for one, clearly believed that Celtic had got the right man. 'Wim Jansen is a respected coach with an excellent pedigree,' McCann told the *View*. 'He will concentrate on getting the best out of the players on the training field and pitch.'

Jansen already had a connection with Celtic prior to his appointment as head coach in 1997. He had been a member of Feyenoord's successful 1970 European Cup-winning side, which had defeated Celtic 2-1 in Milan. He also played in two World Cup finals for Holland – in 1974 and 1978 – before hanging up his boots and taking up a number of coaching roles. He told the *View* he'd jumped at the chance to manage Celtic. 'I had other offers from Holland to consider,' he explained, 'but I wanted to wait for a really big club. The stadium, support and the history of Celtic attracted me and the club has always had a special place in my memories.'

Wim will inspire us to new heights

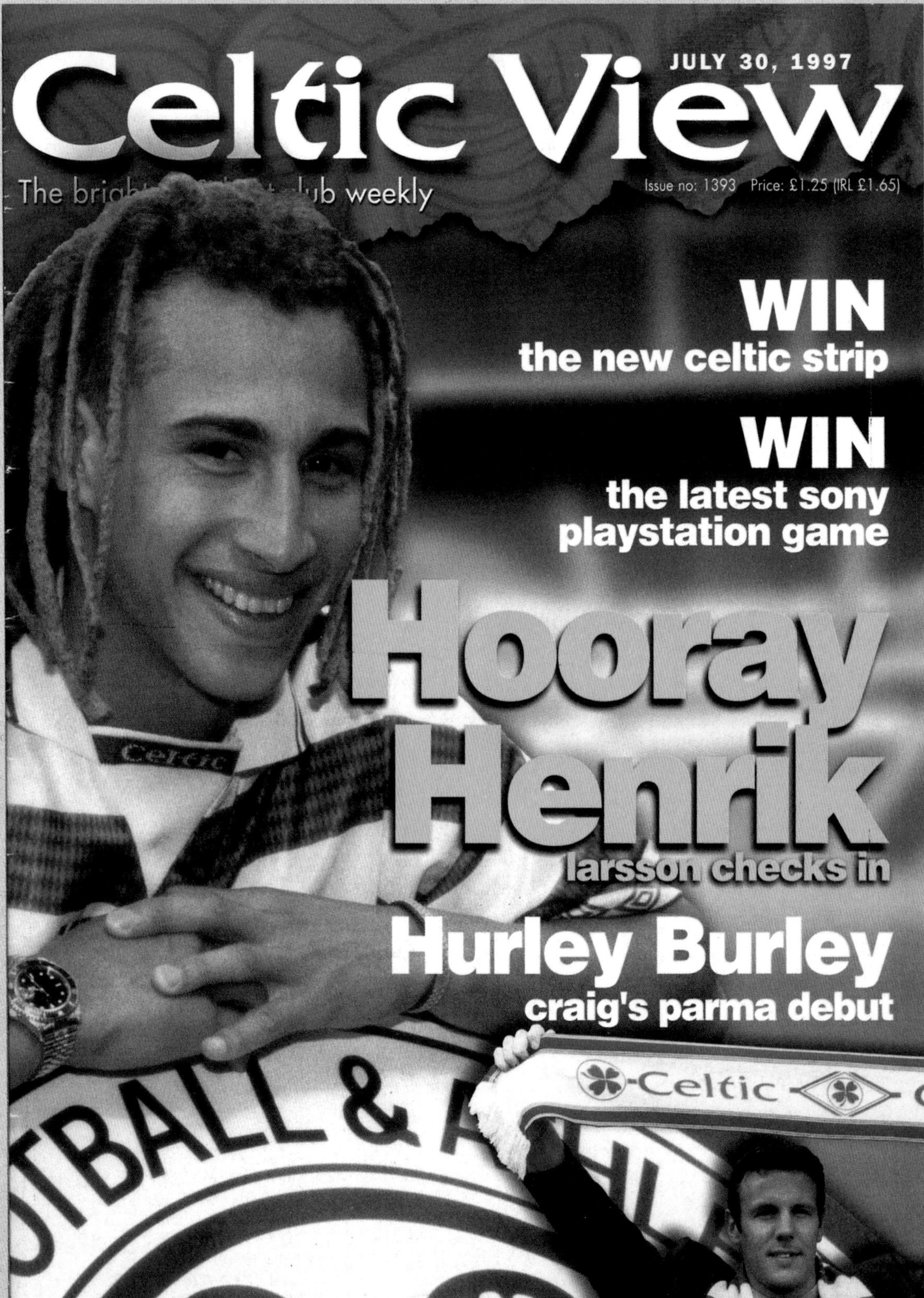

JULY 30, 1997

Celtic View

The bright... ...club weekly

Issue no: 1393   Price: £1.25 (IRL £1.65)

WIN
the new celtic strip

WIN
the latest sony playstation game

Hooray Henrik
larsson checks in

Hurley Burley
craig's parma debut

Celtic

In the nineties, trophies for Celtic were not so much like buses as blue moons. A Scottish Cup in 1995 was the first success in six years and it would be almost three years later before another piece of silverware found its way into the Celtic Park trophy room.

Wim Jansen, appointed boss of Celtic in the summer of 1997, steered his new team to glory in the Coca-Cola Cup (League Cup) with a 3-0 victory over Dundee United at Ibrox. Because of rebuilding work at Hampden, Rangers' ground was the venue for the first domestic final of the season and Celtic fans made sure they enjoyed the party there. Two quick goals from Marc Rieper and Henrik Larsson put Celtic in command and when Craig Burley added a third after the break it sparked scenes of celebration among the Celtic support. That continued with the post-match festivities which also saw the Oasis song 'Roll With It' blasted out and instantly adopted by Celtic fans as one of their celebratory anthems.

Assistant manager, former Celt Murdo MacLeod, spoke to the *View* after the game. He said: 'It is 15 years since we last won this particular trophy and I'm delighted to see it back here. And we fully intend to make sure we don't go anywhere near that long without winning it again. We don't want this to be our last trophy of the season either and the entire squad is intent on adding to this one. This final and the current campaign are all about the squad as every single one of them played a part in winning this Cup. Even the players who didn't make the side on the day were still part of the winning team.'

In a season when the main focus for everyone connected with Celtic was winning the league title – and stopping the ten – it gave a much-needed confidence boost to players and supporters alike. For a new squad, hastily assembled by Wim Jansen, it gave them a taste of success and a hunger for more, which would come to fruition just a few months later on the final day of the season.

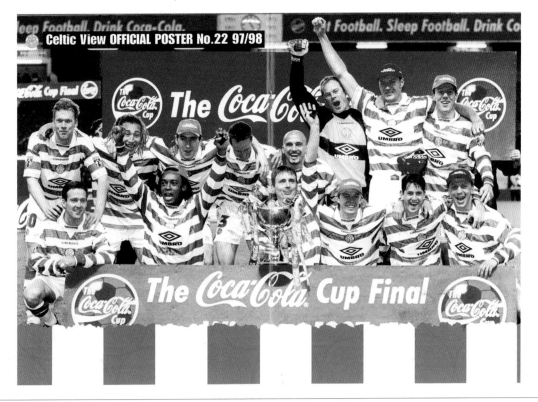

January 7, 1998

Celtic View

The brightest & best club weekly

Issue no: 1417   Price:£1.25

Happy New Year

Italian Job
rico makes his mark

Stark Truth
billy back at celtic

9 770966 306065

30>

A derby match can ensure a new year starts off in the best or worst possible manner. There is no greater feeling that beating your city rivals, though, correspondingly, defeat can plunge supporters into the depths of despair.

So for Celtic fans, 1998 began spectacularly well with a 2-0 victory over Rangers on 2 January. The win narrowed the gap at the top of the table to just one point and gave Wim Jansen's side some momentum going into the second half of the season. The goals both came after the break from the midfield duo of Craig Burley and Paul Lambert. The former scored the first on sixty-six minutes before the latter unleashed an unstoppable shot five minutes from the end of the match to secure the points for Celtic.

Goalscorer Craig Burley was understandably delighted with his goal and, more importantly, the victory. 'Last Friday was a good day for Celtic but surely it was a good day for Scottish football?' Burley said in the *View*. 'People must be fed up with Rangers winning the title all the time, and I know our fans certainly are. It's all very well saying we don't feel pressure, but we could have gone seven points behind Rangers so there was tension in the dressing-room.' It was Celtic's first victory in a New Year derby clash since 1988, when they also won 2-0 at Celtic Park.

Speaking of his spectacular goal, Paul Lambert told the *View*: 'It was just one of those you hit and hope – it was a lucky goal. But this victory will count for nothing if we don't do the business against my old club, Motherwell, this Saturday.'

The victory also provided a fitting farewell to the temporary uncovered west stand which was dismantled after that game ahead of the opening of the new south-west corner stand the following month. It reduced the capacity of Celtic Park to 47,599, though that would eventually rise to over 60,000.

FILE O' FACTS

Bell's Premier Division
Friday, January 2, 1998
Celtic Park, Glasgow

CELTIC 2 **RANGERS 0**
Burley 66, Lambert 85
Att: 49, 350

CELTIC (3-5-2): Gould; Rieper, Stubbs, Annoni; McNamara, Burley, Lambert, Wieghorst, Boyd, Larsson, Brattbakk (Jackson 84). Subs: Donnelly, Hannah.
RANGERS (3-5-2): Goram; McCall, Gough, Porrini; Gattuso (Durie 60), Ferguson, Thern, Albertz (Gascoigne 72), Cleland; Negri, Laudrup. Sub: Snelders.
REFEREE: H Dallas (Motherwell).
ASSISTANTS: G Clyde (Bearsden), J Waugh (Crocketford).
FOURTH OFFICIAL: W Young (Clarkston).
BOOKED: Celtic - Lambert (foul on Gascoigne, 81), Boyd (foul on Gascoigne, 84). Rangers - McCall (foul on Wieghorst, 39), Negri (foul on Burley, 57), Gough (foul on Wieghorst, 90).
FOULS COMMITTED: Celtic 16, Rangers 15.
ON TARGETS: Celtic 7, Rangers 0.
CORNERS: Celtic 5, Rangers 4.
CAUGHT OFFSIDE: 2, Rangers 6.
MAN OF THE MATCH: Celtic had a teamful of contenders but Tom Boyd just edged it for his rampaging runs down the left that turned the flow of the game midway through the first half.
CHAMPAGNE MOMENT: Paul Lambert's rasper of a second goal brought mass delirium inside Celtic Park.
FLAT BEER MOMENT: Fantasy flute-playing from a misguided Paul Gascoigne, anyone?

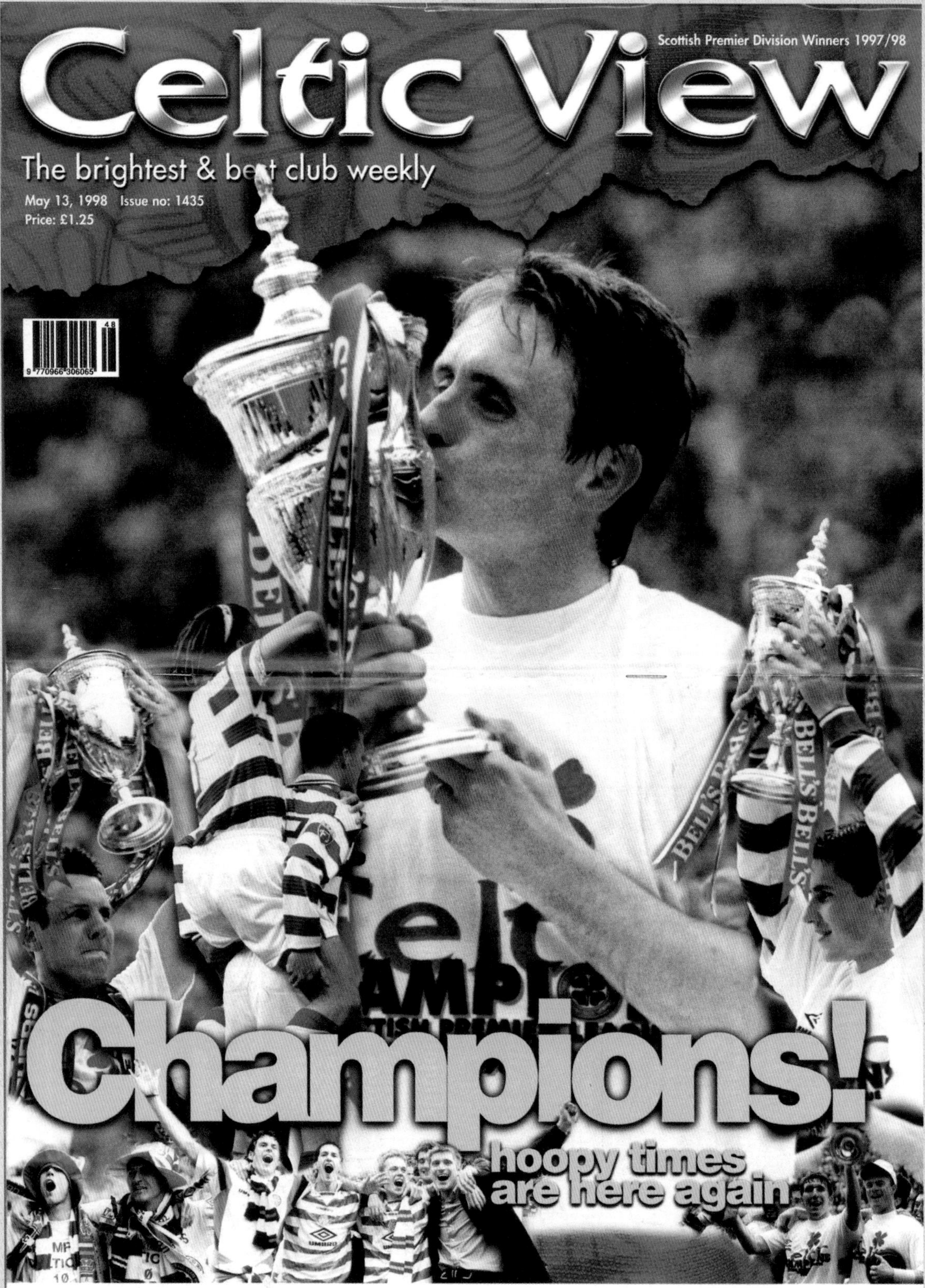

Celtic View

Scottish Premier Division Winners 1997/98

The brightest & best club weekly

May 13, 1998   Issue no: 1435
Price: £1.25

Champions!

hoopy times are here again

Celtic View, Celtic Park, Glasgow, G40 3RE.   Subscriptions - Tel: 0141 551 4263. Editorial - 0141 551 4218
Published and distributed by First Press Publishing, 197 Bath Street, Glasgow, on behalf of Celtic Football Club.   Printed by BPC Magazines (East Kilbride)

It was a long time coming – ten whole years in fact. Ten years of pain and suffering as Rangers won title after title, but on Saturday 9 May 1998 all that was wiped away as Celtic beat St Johnstone 2-0 to win the league for the first time since the centenary season. Most importantly, it stopped the ten.

The idea of Rangers surpassing the famous nine in a row was almost too much to bear for the Celtic support and so there was massive pressure on the team, managed by Dutchman Wim Jansen, throughout the season.

It all boiled down to the final game of the season and the Hoops triumphed at a tense Celtic Park. The *Celtic View* celebrated with a wraparound cover of Tom Boyd kissing the league trophy and one word that meant so much to every Celtic fan – 'Champions!'

Yet even as supporters were celebrating this triumph with street parties all over Glasgow and beyond, there was bad news on the horizon as Wim Jansen quit as boss. The news stunned fans and took a little of the shine off what had been a fantastic Celtic occasion.

A statement from Fergus McCann, published in the *Celtic View*, read: 'The decision Wim has taken is one that the board also believes is the best for the club. On behalf of everyone at Celtic, I would like to thank Wim for his time at the club and wish him all the best for the future. The nature of football now sees players and coaches changing clubs more frequently than in the past. We must all accept and embrace change as an exciting challenge and ensure that it also results in progress.

'Finally, I want to emphasise this point. All of this was not the result of the efforts of only one season, or of any one man. I want to pay tribute to all those at the club, especially the players, all of whom have worked so hard for success, some for four years or more. Individuals will always come and go but the legend that is Celtic continues.'

FAREWELL WIN... Wim Jansen's final act as head coach was to guide Celtic to a league championship triumph

July 22 1998

Celtic View

The brightest & best club weekly

Issue no: 1439
Price: £1.50

henrik larsson poster

full champions league preview

gould playing for keeps

fergus presses the issue

doctor
know
venglos just the tonic

The *Celtic View*'s headline was 'Doctor Know', though just about every newspaper in Scotland opted for 'Doctor Who?'

Having captured its first league title since 1988 and stopped Rangers' bid for ten in a row in the process, the club had been left reeling almost immediately after the trophy had been presented to captain Tom Boyd when manager Wim Jansen announced that he was leaving the club. This led to a summer of uncertainty as the search was undertaken for a new manager.

Ultimately that search led to the arrival of Dr Jozef Venglos, a sixty-two-year-old Slovak with a wealth of coaching experience built up over many years. Prior to his appointment at Celtic, Dr Jo, as he became affectionately known, had been part of FIFA's technical committee at the World Cup in France.

Speaking as the appointment was announced, Fergus McCann said: 'It has taken us some time to identify a new head coach. Although it's regrettable that we have not been able to have someone here faster, we are happy to have engaged a first-class coach for this position. He knows what it takes for a team to compete at the highest level, winning leagues and cups at national level and the European Championship with an international team, not to mention taking Czechoslovakia to the World Cup quarter-final at Italia 90.'

Dr Venglos came to Celtic Park with an impressive CV, both at club and international level, though the fact that he arrived almost as the season was set to kick off didn't give him too much time to work with his new players, something that, arguably,

would cost Celtic come the end of the season.

However, the good doctor preferred to dwell on the positives, as he told the *View*: 'Celtic is a great and very big club who I know about from playing against them as a player, and I also know about Scotland from my time as a national coach. There is a nice structure and great players here. Not many countries have ten players who have taken part in an excellent World Cup competition as with Celtic.'

LIFE AND TIMES OF DR KNOW

1936 Born on February 18 in Bratislava

1953-1955 Began a promising career as a skilful midfielder with Tatran Presov

1955-1965 Made his name with his hometown team Slovan Bratislava. Capped 25 times at junior, Olympic and B level and won one championship medal with Slovan in 1955 before being awarded a Doctorate in Philosophy at Bratislava University

1967 Appointed manager of the Australian national team

1969 Returned home to manage FC Kosice

1973 Re-joined Slovan Bratislava as manager and led them to title success in 1974 and 1975 as well as domestic cup success

1976 Part of the Czechoslovakian coaching set-up which beat Germany in the European Championship final

1978 Appointed Czech national boss and leads them to third place in the 1980 European Championship

1982 Resigned from national post after a poor World Cup in Spain

1983 Moved to Portugal to boss Sporting Lisbon

1985 Coached Kuala Lumpur state side in Malaysia

1986 Headed up a FIFA study group at the World Cup in Mexico

1990 Led Czech national team to the quarter-finals of the World Cup in Italy during a second spell at the helm

1990/91 Appointed manager of English First Division club Aston Villa

1991 Took charge at Turkish side Fenerbahce

1993 Slovakia becomes independent – with Venglos as the new national side's coach

1994 Co-ordinated another FIFA study group at the World Cup in the United States

1995 Took over the Presidency of the European Coaches Union

1998 Part of the FIFA technical committee at the World Cup in France

July 1998 Appointed the new head coach of Celtic Football Club

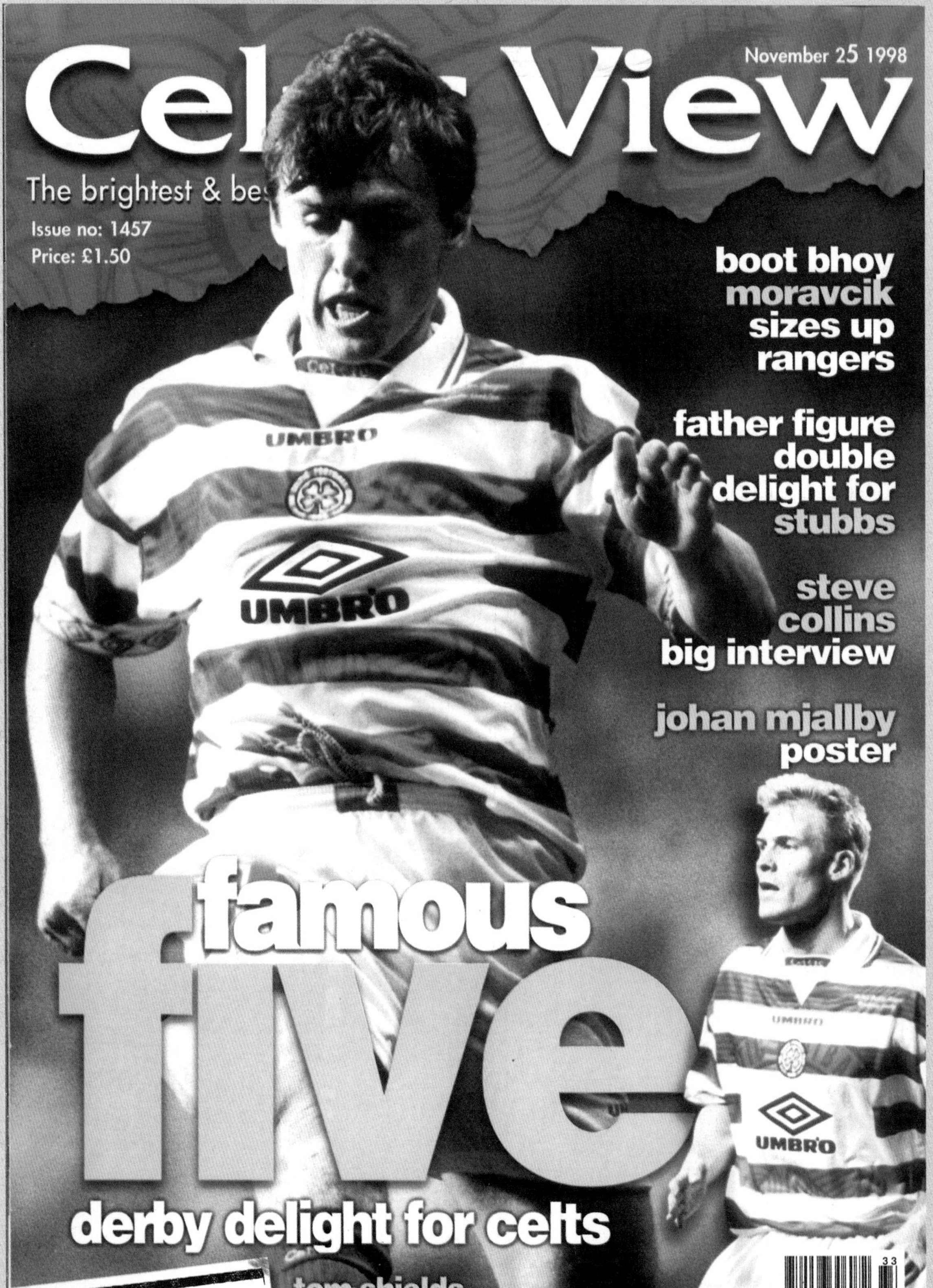

November 25 1998

Celtic View

The brightest & best

Issue no: 1457
Price: £1.50

boot bhoy moravcik sizes up rangers

father figure double delight for stubbs

steve collins big interview

johan mjallby poster

famous five

derby delight for celts

Timothy Shields

tom shields joins the view

9 770966 306072

33

Lubomir Moravcik had arrived in Scotland at the beginning of November 1998, an unheralded signing by his fellow countryman Dr Jozef Venglos. Most people had never heard of the Slovakian midfielder, in the same way that they had known little, if anything, about Celtic's latest manager.

But after just three games in the green and white hoops, not only did everyone know who Lubo Moravcik was, but Celtic supporters had discovered a new hero. Moravcik's third game for the club was against Rangers at Celtic Park and with the team already trailing their city rivals by ten points after just fourteen games, it was a must-win match for the defending Scottish champions.

It turned out to be not so much a win as a mauling, and Moravcik was at the heart of the triumph. Celtic crushed their rivals 5-1, with both Moravcik and Henrik Larsson scoring two goals each, but it was the Slovak's performance, and his finishing, which grabbed the headlines.

He scored his first goal after just twenty-three minutes and added a second four minutes after half-time, and while he was undoubtedly delighted at his goalscoring success, his slightly bemused reaction to both goals indicated a player still coming to terms with his new club and someone who was slightly overwhelmed by the atmosphere of the derby contest.

Moravcik told the *View* after the game that he'd had previous derby experience playing in France with St Etienne, 'but it was nothing like this!' He also laughed off those critics who had questioned the wisdom of signing a thirty-three-year-old player. 'For a trainer it is not a question of age when he signs a player,' said Moravcik. 'It is a question of competence. Age does not come into it. I have a lot to prove to people that I can play, but in England players like Gordon Strachan and Peter Beardsley have played a long time. Why can't I?'

The *View* also announced the signing of Johan Mjallby from AIK Stockholm, another player who would come to play a big part in Celtic's success in the seasons to come.

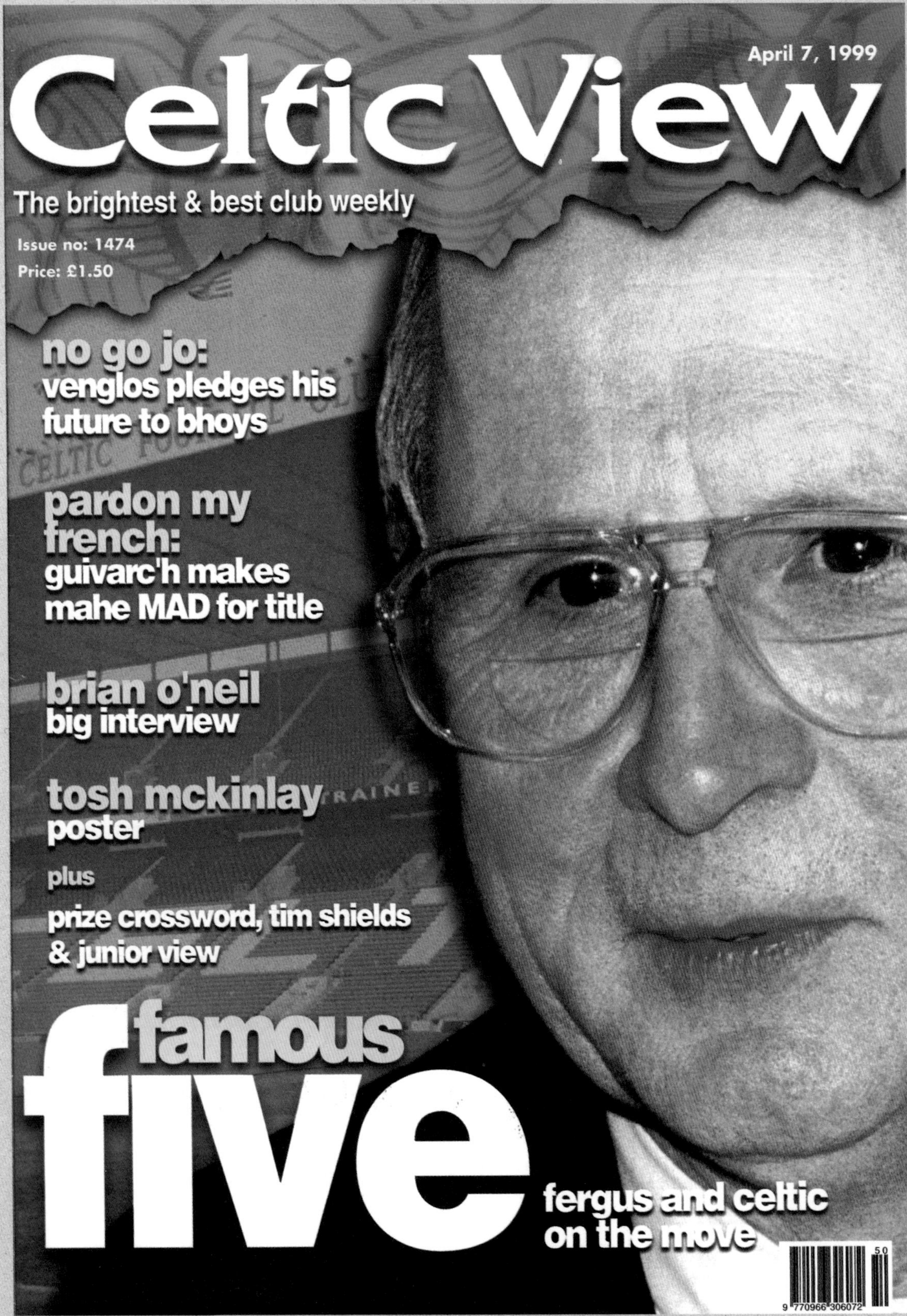

April 7, 1999

Celtic View

The brightest & best club weekly

Issue no: 1474
Price: £1.50

no go jo:
venglos pledges his
future to bhoys

**pardon my
french:**
guivarc'h makes
mahe MAD for title

brian o'neil
big interview

tosh mckinlay
poster

plus

**prize crossword, tim shields
& junior view**

famous
five

fergus and celtic
on the move

9 770966 306072

He came, he saw and he rescued the club from oblivion. Fergus McCann had arrived just in the nick of time back in March 1994 when Celtic was on the verge of going under, using his financial strength to save the club and rebuild it.

Now, five years on from those dramatic events, just as he had promised, Fergus McCann bid farewell to Paradise. In those short five years Celtic had come a long way. Indeed, the club had changed, in many ways almost beyond recognition. The imposing new Celtic Park stadium was the most visible and grandest sign of change and a lasting legacy of Fergus McCann's fantastic work.

McCann had returned home from Canada just as Celtic's debts, accrued through years of mismanagement, were about to drag the club under, and with a clear sense of what was required he quickly transformed the club. Along the way he received more than his fair share of flak, particularly from a hostile Scottish press who were perhaps uncomfortable with

the prospect of a resurgent Celtic.

However, the low point of Fergus McCann's five years in charge at the club was when some supporters booed him as he unveiled the league championship flag at Celtic Park before the start of the 1998–99 season. Those 'fans', probably swayed by the negative publicity in the press surrounding McCann, disgraced themselves and embarrassed the club. They would have done well to remember what state Celtic was in before McCann arrived, and the fact it happened on a day when the club was celebrating its first league championship in ten years only made it all the more shameful.

McCann, characteristically, shunned the spotlight when he left, slipping quietly out of Celtic Park without any fanfare and even declining a final interview with the *View*. Still, for the overwhelming majority of Celtic supporters he left with their best wishes and gratitude, and also an acknowledgement that, without him, Celtic may well have disappeared completely, leaving behind memories of a great past rather than hopes for a better future.

LARSSON WON'T REST TILL WE'VE GOT 'EM LICKED!

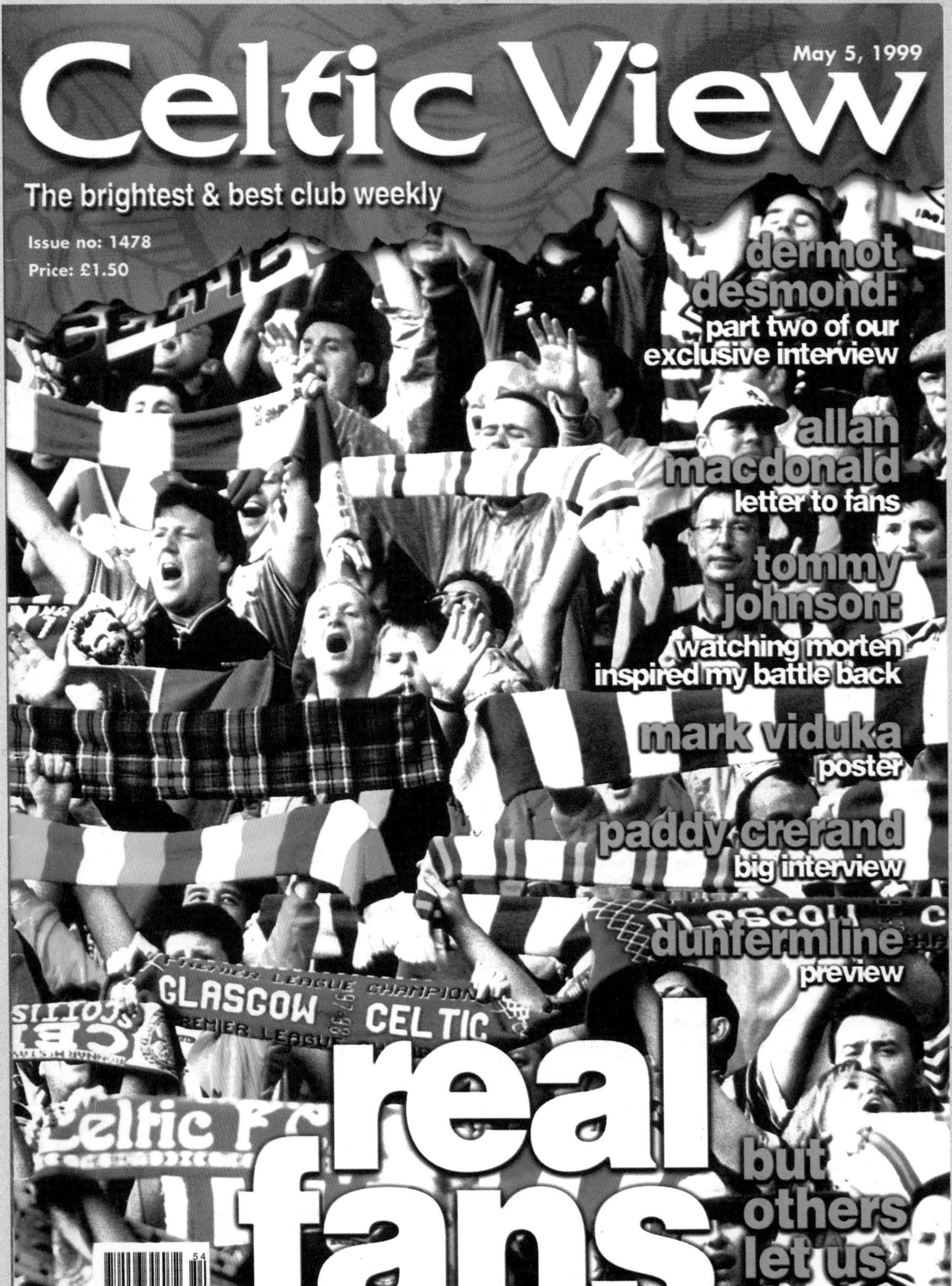
May 5, 1999
Celtic View
The brightest & best club weekly
Issue no: 1478
Price: £1.50
dermot desmond: part two of our exclusive interview
allan macdonald letter to fans
tommy johnson: watching morten inspired my battle back
mark viduka poster
paddy crerand big interview
dunfermline preview
real fans
but others let us down
GLASGOW CELTIC
9 770966 306072

The dust had barely settled on an explosive derby match with Rangers before the *Celtic View* hit the shelves.

Not only did the magazine have to report on a home defeat against their city rivals which meant that Rangers were the champions, but the club had to react to the controversial scenes at Celtic Park which saw two Celtic players sent off, referee Hugh Dallas hit by a coin, a Celtic supporter falling off the top tier of the stand and four supporters invading the pitch.

On a day of highly charged emotions both on and off the park, it didn't help matters that the Rangers players performed a mock huddle after the final whistle, which only further inflamed passions.

The stark reality for Celtic was, of course, the loss of the Scottish Premier League title, and to relinquish your grip on the trophy at your own ground, against your fiercest rivals, made it the toughest of blows to suffer. Via the *View*, Celtic's then chief executive,

Allan MacDonald, penned a letter to every Celtic supporter about the unprecedented scenes inside Celtic Park. He wrote: 'At Celtic, if you wear the name, you wear the reputation in your words and actions. The good name of Celtic and its supporters was threatened on Sunday by the conduct of a few irresponsible people. This behaviour cannot and will not be accepted.'

MacDonald concluded by saying: 'Plans are currently being formulated to re-establish Celtic as a footballing force in Europe. It is essential the behaviour of our players and supporters reflect the club's history, principles and aspirations.'

The *Celtic View* also caught up with a former player, Pat Crerand, who had played for the club in the late fifties and early sixties before his transfer to Manchester United. Crerand did not leave the club of his own accord and, as he told the *View*: 'Every day I regretted leaving and not only that day four years later when they won the European Cup.'

FULLY BOOKED: The phrase "Dallas was kept busy" ranks alongside the world's great understatements

July 7, 1999

Celtic View

The brightest & best c[...]

Vol. 35 Issue 1
Price: £1.50

kenny dalglish
- the return of the king

john barnes
big interview

dr. jo's
new bhoys verdict

tommy johnson
on stubbs scare

regi blinker
poster

marc rieper's
comeback hopes

dream team

top trio join forces to bring back glory days

'Dream Team' proclaimed the heading on the front cover of the *View*, as John Barnes took centre stage, alongside a smaller image of former Celt, Kenny Dalglish.

The *View* was certainly excited at the new managerial team appointed for the start of the 1999–2000 season. For Barnes, it was his first coaching appointment, but, with the more experienced Dalglish alongside him, what could possibly go wrong? As the opinion column in the magazine declared: 'We now have an outfit at the helm to steer us to greatness and that is all that matters. If we veer off course, we have the experience to get back on an even keel.'

Barnes became Celtic's third manager in three seasons (although his official job title was head coach) and he approached his new role with understandable optimism. 'I've been here a short time, but I already know it's not okay to finish second,' Barnes told the *View*. 'I never actually said it was, but if I speak about Celtic being in a strong position by finishing second last season I'm not saying it's acceptable, I'm merely saying that there really isn't all that much wrong at the moment.

'I think in terms of what we can achieve here and of achieving our true potential. If, at the moment, we are virtually equal with Rangers then, of course, we can surpass them, but to do that we have to find consistency of performance.'

July 1999 was a time of optimism for the Celtic support, reflected in the positive features in the *View*, and after the disappointment of losing the league the previous season under Dr Jozef Venglos, the fans

were hopeful that the league trophy would make a quick return to Celtic Park. Certainly, the players and new coaching staff – which also included former Liverpool player Terry McDermott and ex-Aberdeen striker Eric Black – believed that Celtic were in good shape for the challenges ahead.

The *View* also carried an interview with outgoing manager Dr Jo, who declared: 'I believe that the team can now become more successful as they have had a longer rest this year than they did last and everyone will work very hard.'

The CELTIC VIEW

SUE No. 1
UGUST 11, 1965
ICE FOURPENCE

COMPETITION TIME: DESIGN CELTIC'S OFFICIAL CHRISTMAS CARD FOR 2006

THE CELTIC VIEW

■ VOICE OF THE CHAMPIONS

Celticview

No. 748   **WEDNESDAY, APRIL 7, 1982**   Price 12p

THE VOICE OF THE

Celtic VI

vol.36 issue 25 £1

JULY 21 2004 vol.40 issue 2 £1.95   www.celticfc.net

Celtic View

October 8, 1997

The brightest & best club weekly

Issue no: 1406   Price: £1.25

THE CELTIC VIEW

ISSUE No. 37   APRIL 20, 1966   PRICE 4d.

No. 696   WEDNESDAY, JANUARY 14, 1981   Price

THE CELTIC VIEW

Celtic VIEW

No. 1167   APRIL 15, 1992

BRITAIN'S OLDEST CLUB NEW

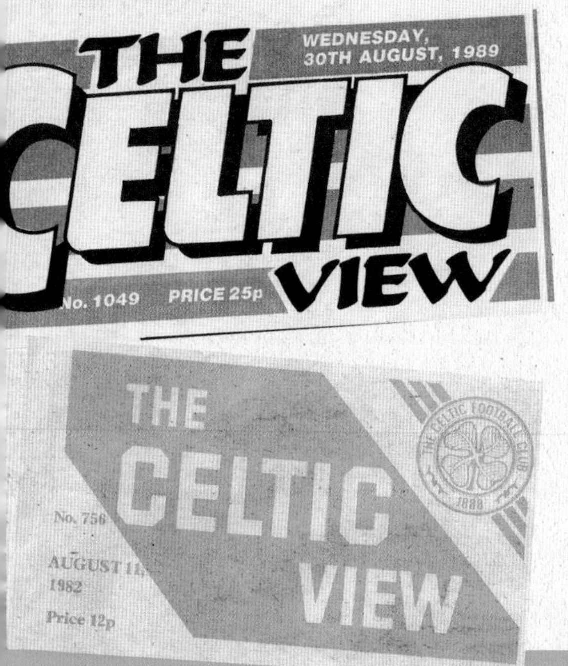

Celtic VIEW

MAY 5, 1993   80p (R.O.I. £1.20)

THE CELTIC VIEW

Wednesday August 31, 1983

No. 799 Price 15p

THE VOICE OF THE CHAMPIONS
THE OFFICIAL CELTIC WEEKLY MAGAZINE

celtic VIEW CARLING

MPIONS

THE VOICE OF THE CHAMPIONS

Celtic VIEW

www.celticfc.net

August 15, 2001
vol.37 issue 06
£1.95

THE CELTIC VIEW

WEDNESDAY, 30TH AUGUST, 1989

No. 1049   PRICE 25p

Through the decades

This is the thing that made the *Celtic View* stand out from the crowd among a forest of redtops on in the early-morning flurry of tabloid rustling. Some lasted longer than others and some of the changes were minimal, but somewhere in here is the one you were first familiar with. And although they often contained the club badge, some of these iconic images are badges within themselves.

No. 1003

THE CELTIC VIEW

Wednesday 3rd August 1988

Price 15p

THE CELTIC VIEW

No. 756
AUGUST 1982
Price 12p

Celticview

Celtic

THE CELTIC VIEW

Issue No. 99   JUNE 28, 1967   Price

No. 1089   WEDNESDAY 5th SEPTEMBER, 1990   PRICE 50p

CELTIC VIEW

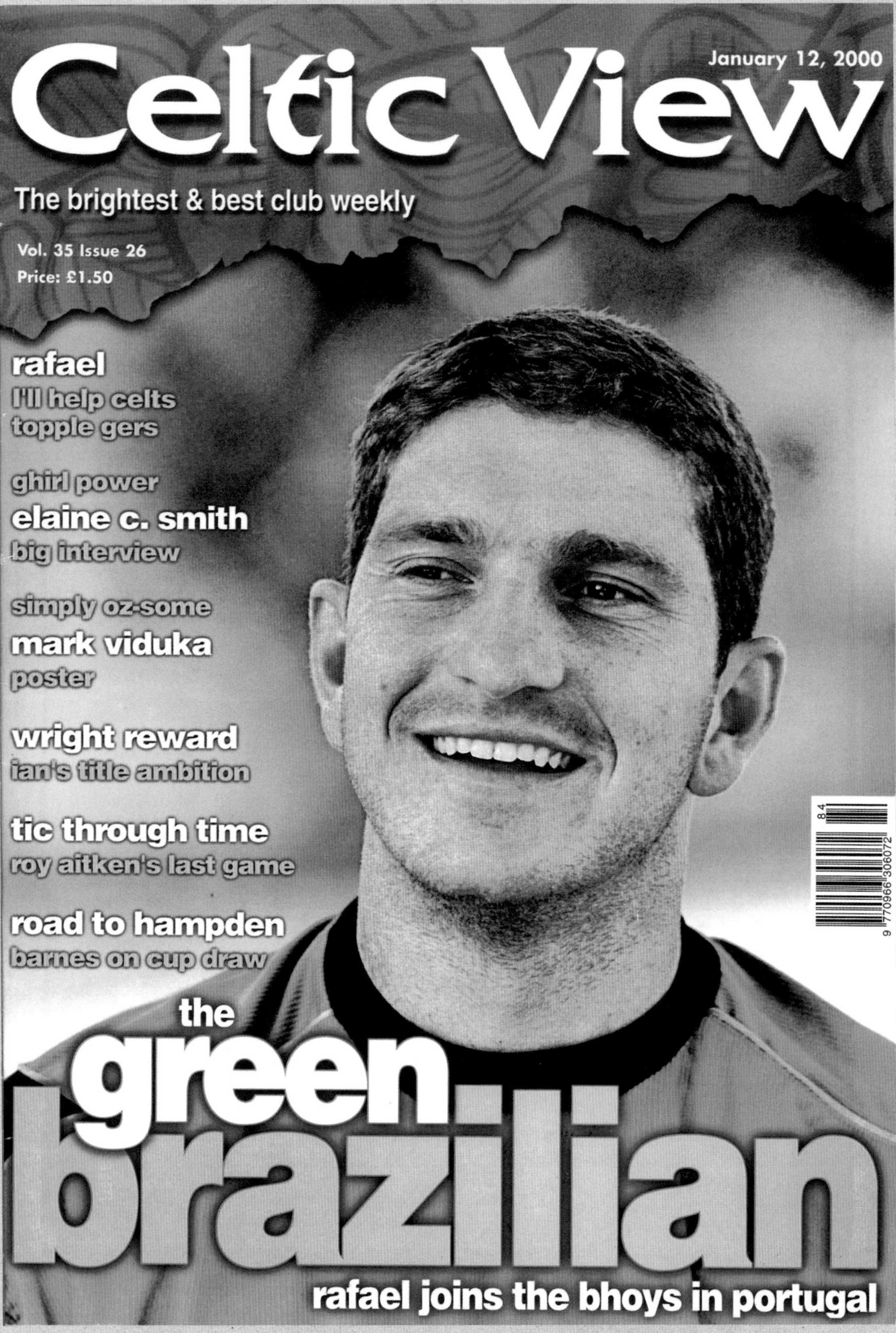

January 12, 2000

Celtic View

The brightest & best club weekly

Vol. 35 Issue 26
Price: £1.50

rafael
I'll help celts
topple gers

ghirl power
elaine c. smith
big interview

simply oz-some
mark viduka
poster

wright reward
ian's title ambition

tic through time
roy aitken's last game

road to hampden
barnes on cup draw

the
green
brazilian
rafael joins the bhoys in portugal

What's in a name? Quite a lot, apparently, when it came to the new Brazilian defender who arrived at Celtic in January 2000.

Rafael Scheidt – known to the *View* only as Rafael, but to everyone else by his surname – met up with new team-mates at a training camp in Portugal and he was clearly delighted to have joined the club. 'I have not played in two months so I am not very fit, but I will work hard both here and back in Glasgow,' he told the *View* in an exclusive interview. 'I am looking forward to playing football in Scotland and I hope to win many things. Celtic have paid a lot of money for me and made me an offer none of the other clubs could match. I don't know too much about the transfer fee but I know it was big, and I am very happy that Celtic think I am good enough. The most important thing for me is to win and I am coming here to help make Celtic the best team in Scotland.'

In the event, he played a total of six games for Celtic – two starts and four substitute appearances – and he, along with his name, became synonymous with a disappointing period in the club's history.

John Barnes also offered a warning to supporters ahead of the team's Scottish Cup clash with Inverness Caley Thistle, saying: 'You can't be complacent when there are 60,000 supporters turning up to see you, and the players will be fully focused on going through to the next round.'

In the magazine's big interview, Elaine C. Smith spoke about her passion for the Celts. Now patron of the Celtic Ladies' Academy, the Glasgow actress sang the praises of the new Celtic Park, certainly in relation to the stadia she had gone to in her younger days as a Celtic fan. She told the *View*: 'I see this new stadium of ours as very man-, woman- and child-friendly – a family stadium. Years ago I would never come to a game on my own, but now, if I had to, I would. It's fabulous and I defy any stadium in the world to match the atmosphere it has now – even Ally McCoist said that to me!'

The fan in me says 'Next year we'll win the European Cup'

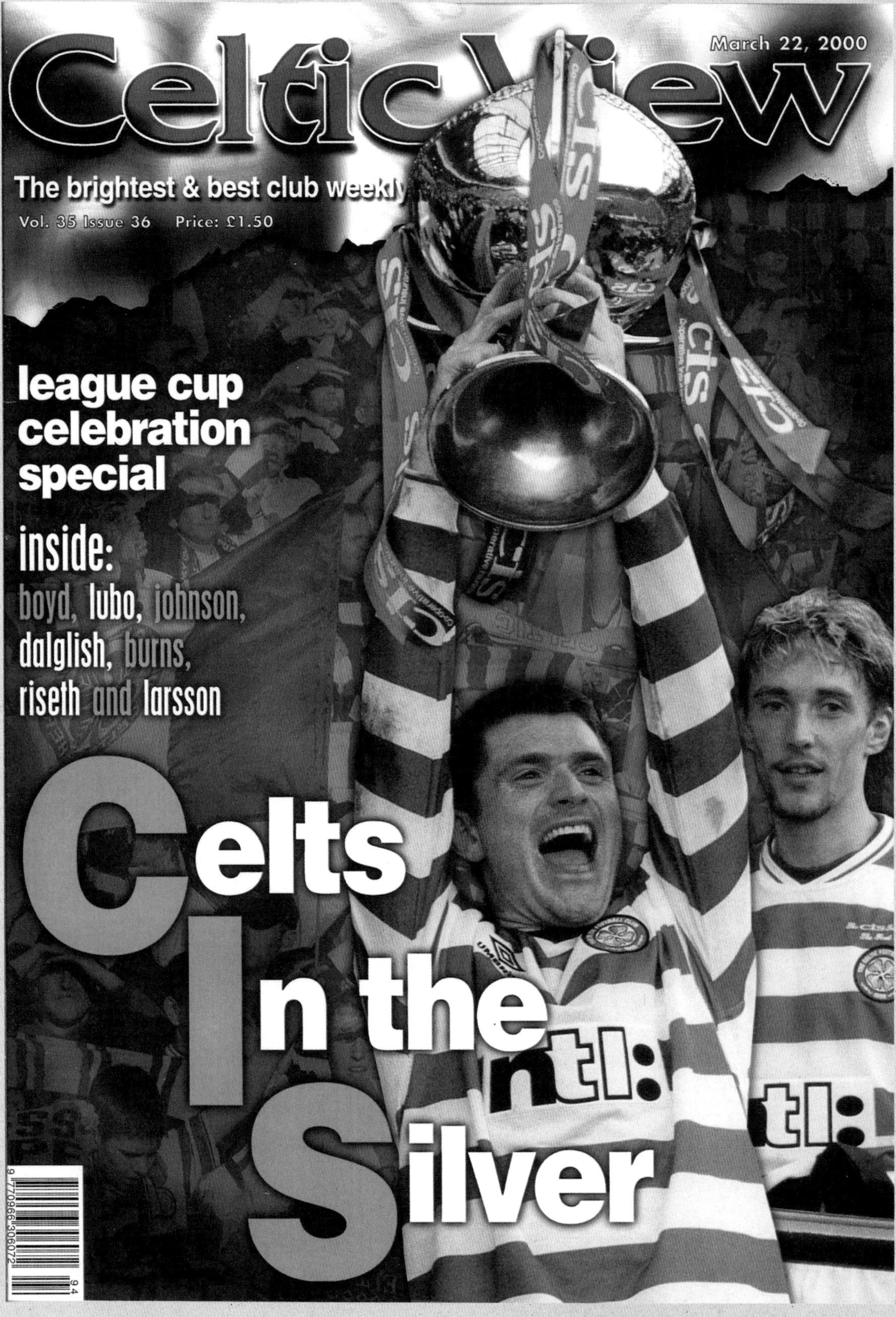

March 22, 2000

Celtic View

The brightest & best club weekly

Vol. 35 Issue 36   Price: £1.50

league cup celebration special

inside:
boyd, lubo, johnson, dalglish, burns, riseth and larsson

Celts
In the
Silver

Celtic won the first domestic silverware of the new millennium, but the CIS Cup victory in March 2000 will surely go down as one of the most low key and least heralded triumphs in the club's history.

The 1999–2000 season was a traumatic one for the club and the team was limping like a wounded animal towards the finishing line that was the end of the campaign. Trailing Rangers by twelve points and knocked out of the Scottish Cup by Inverness Caley Thistle, Celtic had already parted company with coach John Barnes by the time they faced Aberdeen at Hampden. Goals from Vidar Riseth and Tommy Johnson gave the Hoops, under the command of Kenny Dalglish, a 2-0 victory and the CIS Cup.

Speaking to the *View* after the Hampden triumph, Dalglish was keen to acknowledge the role John Barnes had played in the success, even though he hadn't been in charge of the semi-final of the competition. Dalglish said: 'It was nice to be given the chance to go back to Hampden with Celtic – I wish it could have been under different circumstances, but never in my wildest dreams would I have thought that I would get that chance. I feel very proud, although we have a lot to thank John Barnes, Eric Black and Terry McDermott for since it was their great contributions that paved the way for us to get to Hampden in the first place.'

Celtic's achievement in lifting the trophy was done, impressively enough, without conceding a single goal. Victories over Ayr United (4-0) and Dundee (1-0) were followed by a 1-0 semi-final win against Kilmarnock and the 2-0 triumph in the final.

One of the two Hampden goalscorers, Vidar Riseth, spoke to the *View* after the game. He said: 'This is my first medal with Celtic and, although I have won some cups and leagues before, this is very special.'

The *View* also looked forward to the forthcoming match against Rangers at Ibrox, which represented Celtic's last chance to peg their rivals back and give them a proper chase for the title.

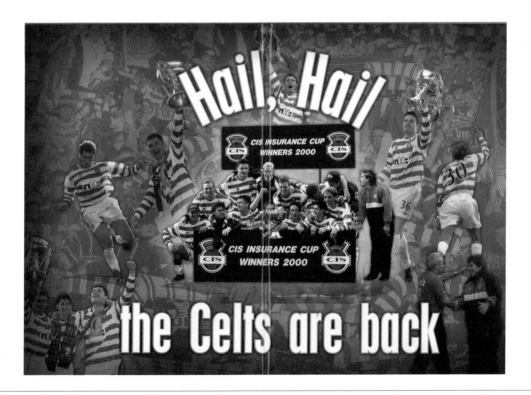

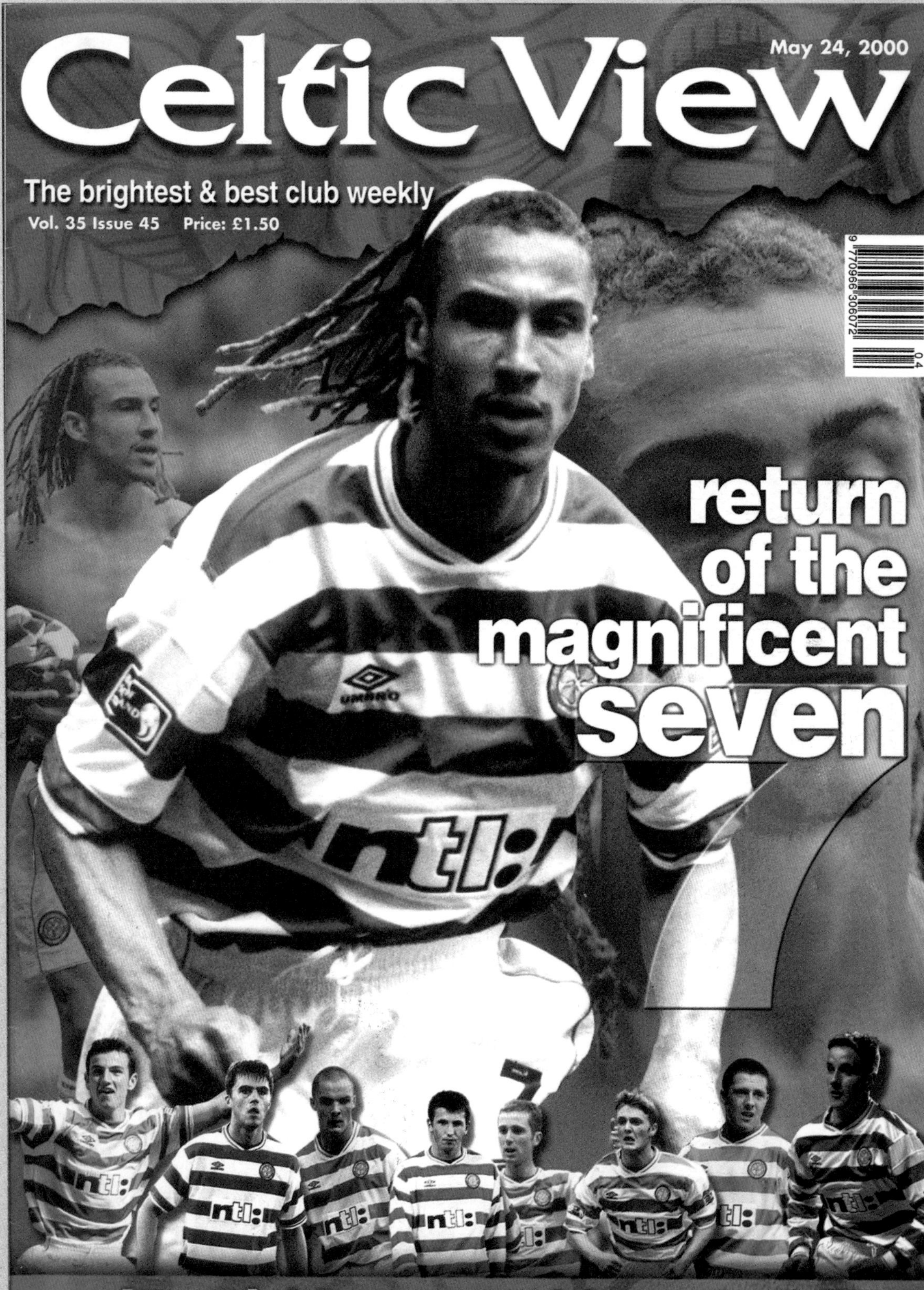

Celtic View

May 24, 2000

The brightest & best club weekly

Vol. 35 Issue 45   Price: £1.50

return of the magnificent seven

and an eightsome reel from the kids

'Return of the Magnificent Seven' proclaimed the heading on the front cover of the *Celtic View* and, after the traumas of the 1999–2000 season, it was not before time.

The campaign had begun in a spirit of optimism, with the much-heralded 'dream team' of John Barnes and Kenny Dalglish in charge. However, the season proved to be a disaster, the nadir of Barnes' Celtic tenure coming in the Scottish Cup defeat against Inverness Caley Thistle.

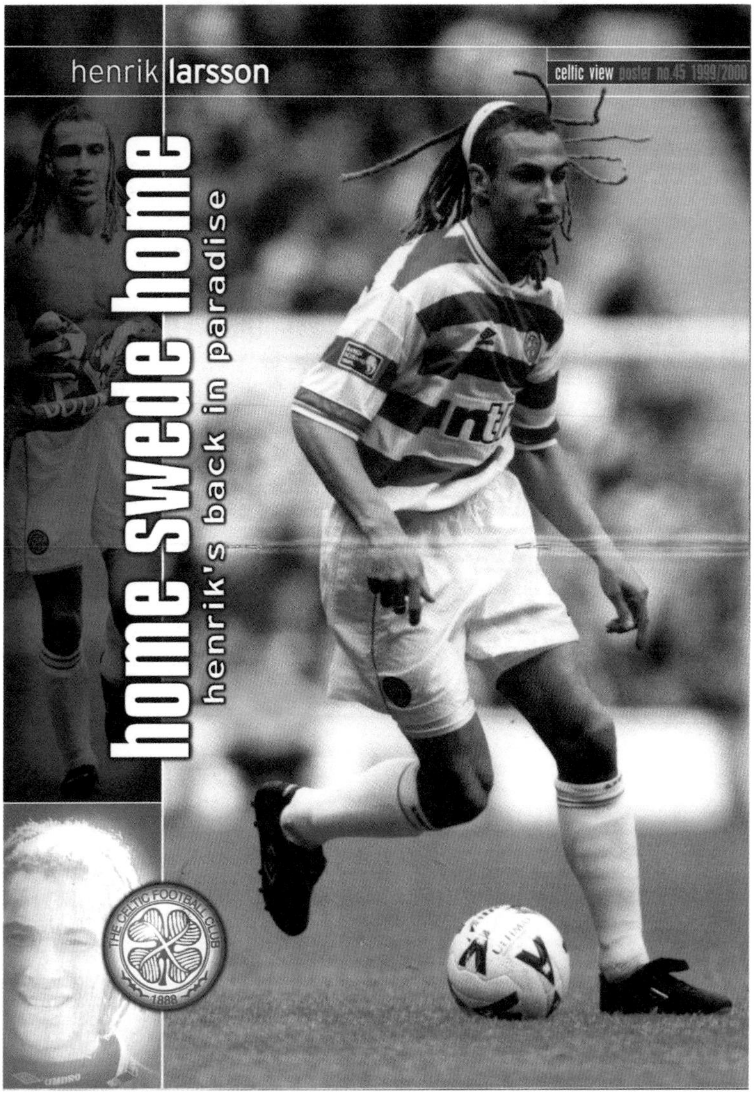

The former Liverpool player hadn't been helped in his first managerial role when Henrik Larsson broke his leg during a UEFA Cup tie against Bordeaux in France in October 1999. This effectively ruled out Celtic's top goalscorer for the rest of the season and he only made his return to first-team action for the last game of the season against Dundee United at Celtic Park. His inclusion in the first-team squad was largely to prove his fitness ahead of Sweden's participation in the forthcoming Euro 2000 competition, but on the day Larsson played the last half hour of the match, much to the delight of the Celtic support.

The player later told the *View*: 'I got a fantastic reception from the crowd even before I came on to the pitch and it was a nice feeling for me. I'm very pleased to have got back to playing, but the most important thing was that Celtic won the match. And for me personally, I have to look to the future and I'm delighted that I managed to get a run-out.'

The Celtic team that afternoon also featured eight teenagers, which gave the atmosphere at Celtic Park a further boost. The eight players were: Mark Fotheringham, John Kennedy, Simon Lynch, Ryan McCann, Brian McColligan, Liam Miller, John Convery and Jim Goodwin. John Kennedy, the only one of the eight players still at the club, spoke to the *View* after his Celtic Park debut. He said: 'It was important that we all went out and gave 100 per cent and I think the supporters saw that every one of us is prepared to fight for the jersey.'

henrik **larsson**

celtic view poster no.45 1999/2000

home swede home
henrik's back in paradise

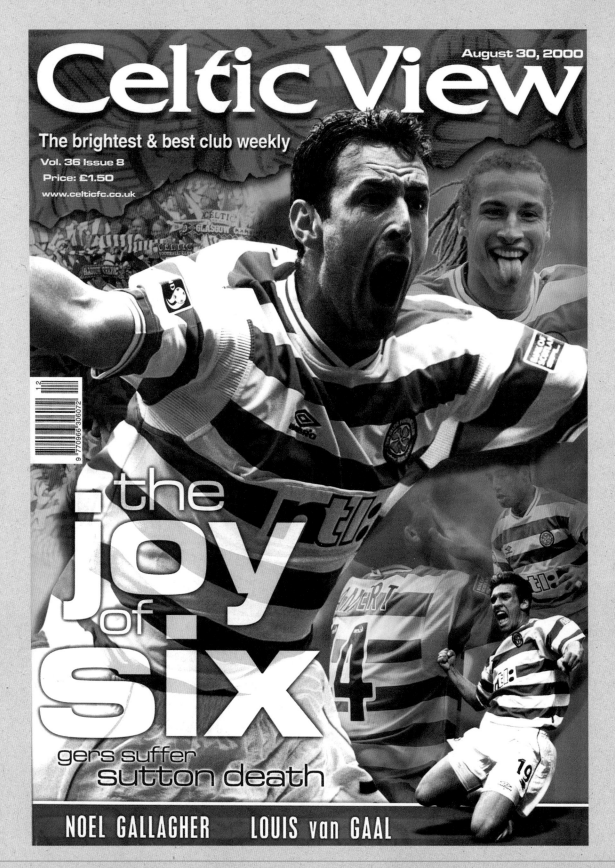

Celtic View

August 30, 2000

The brightest & best club weekly

Vol. 36 Issue 8

Price: £1.50

www.celticfc.co.uk

the joy of six

gers suffer sutton death

NOEL GALLAGHER   **LOUIS van GAAL**

It was Martin O'Neill's first test as Celtic manager and to say that he passed it with flying colours would be an understatement. While most Celtic supporters were looking for a stronger showing against Rangers than the previous season, not even the most optimistic could have predicted what would unfold on Sunday 27 August 2001.

Celtic went three goals ahead inside the first thirteen minutes of the match and when the dust finally settled on this encounter, the scoreline read 6-2 in Celtic's favour. It was truly a demolition derby and was the clearest sign that power in Scottish football was shifting back to the East End of Glasgow. There was a derby debut double from Chris Sutton, the destruction of Fernando Ricksen by 'born again' Bobby Petta and one of the most exquisite goals ever seen at Celtic Park as Henrik Larsson chipped in with Celtic's fourth goal.

Oasis frontman Noel Gallagher was also taking in his first 'live' Celtic game and he couldn't have picked a better one for his debut. Not for the last time, he spoke to the *View*, explaining the thrill he felt at seeing Celtic win and also hearing one of his own songs – 'Roll With It' – blasted out at the stadium and sung with gusto by the Hoops support. 'When the crowd were singing "Roll With It", it got to me right in the heart,' Gallagher explained. 'I'll have to get hold of a Celtic songbook to catch up on some of the other tunes though.

'I was sort of half expecting, half hoping that Celtic would win 2-1, but this is unbelievable. I'd like to get to see Celtic at Ibrox and I'd love to take in an Old Firm Cup final, but I'll definitely be back here again. After today, I wouldn't miss it for the world.'

One supporter in the crowd that day was Tony Warner, who was in goal for Celtic when they beat Rangers 5-1 back in 1998. Warner told the *View*: 'I had just about as much to do today as I did in the 5-1 game!'

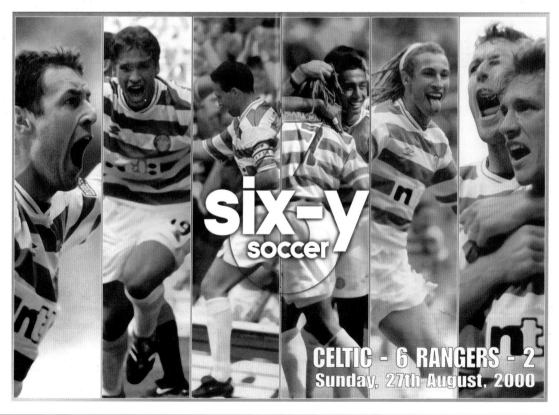

six-y soccer

CELTIC - 6 RANGERS - 2
Sunday, 27th August, 2000

vol.36 issue 33 **£1.50** £IR 2.16

March 7, 2001

Celticview

the biggest best and ...

www.celticfc.co.uk

REASONS TO BE
Cheerful

McLeod new chief's plans **Boyd** voice of experience
Connelly a reluctant hero **Shields** Spain's Old Firm

Neil Lennon scored his first goal for Celtic three months after joining the club and he rushed to the touchline to celebrate the moment with assistant manager John Robertson.

But the celebration was more than simply that of a goalscorer, as Lennon had just endured a difficult week because of where he came from. The midfielder was playing his thirty-eighth game for Northern Ireland in a friendly match against Norway at Windsor Park in Belfast. More significantly, it was his first international match since joining Celtic and a vicious minority of Northern Ireland supporters fired verbal abuse at Lennon throughout the match every time he touched the ball. It caused Lennon to question whether or not he should continue to play international football.

Speaking to the *View* after his goalscoring debut and the vocal encouragement offered by Celtic's travelling support, Lennon said: 'To me that's what football is all about and I don't get that many goals.' Lennon also revealed his reason for planting a kiss on assistant coach John Robertson in his goal celebration: 'The physios and the goalkeeping coaches were giving me loads of stick for not scoring so I was trying to run to Brian Scott but John Robertson got in the way! After the week I've had it's great to get back to football and this keeps me in the headlines for all the right reasons.'

Support for the player came flooding into the *View*, including this letter from Belfast man, James Watson. He wrote: 'I am a Protestant living in East Belfast and I feel I must write to you to register my disgust at the way Neil Lennon was treated by a few morons at Windsor Park last week. I am proud to have a player like Neil pull on the green shirt for Northern Ireland, and I would say that goes for every genuine person in the country, regardless of their religion. So, I would appreciate it if you could pass on my respects to Neil and his beliefs, and tell him to ignore the bigots we have over here.'

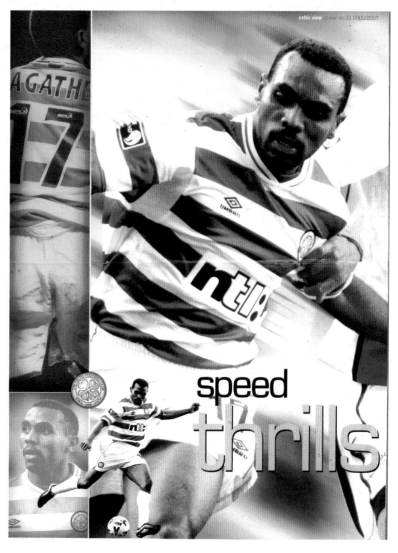

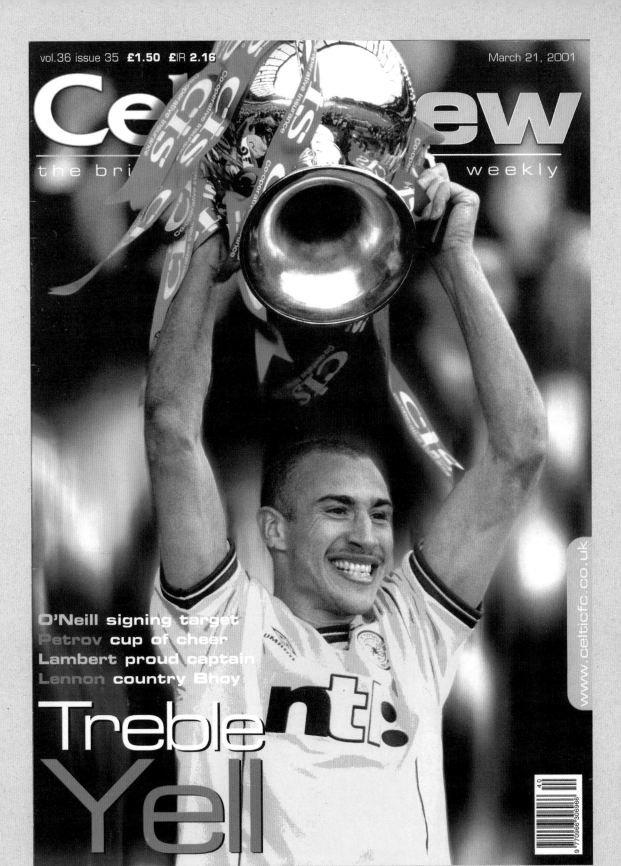

vol.36 issue 35 **£1.50** £IR **2.16**

March 21, 2001

Ce~~llic Vi~~ew

the bri~~tish~~ weekly

O'Neill **signing target**
Petrov **cup of cheer**
Lambert **proud captain**
Lennon **country Bhoy**

Treble
Yell

Celtic's first trophy under Martin O'Neill came courtesy of a 3-0 victory over Kilmarnock at Hampden in the CIS Cup final. And it was only right that Henrik Larsson dominated the front cover of the celebration issue, given that it was his hat-trick which had secured the trophy for Celtic.

The three second-half goals showed Larsson at his imperious best and even the dismissal of Chris Sutton during the match failed to take the shine off a wonderful performance. Martin O'Neill, pictured with his first silverware as Celtic manager, spoke to the *View* of his delight at the Hampden triumph: 'The scene at the end with all the green and white scarves held aloft was really fantastic and is a sight I personally will never forget,' O'Neill said. 'The crowd made the occasion very special and, if we ever needed any encouragement to go back to Hampden in another final, they provided it.

'When the Celtic fans get behind the team, it really is something to behold and I wouldn't imagine that there are many sets of supporters who can match them.

The players were all talking about the atmosphere on Sunday evening and, like me, I think every one of them got a real tingle up the spine from seeing that sea of green and white at the end.'

With Celtic having a veritable League of Nations within the first-team squad, the *View* also took the opportunity to look forward to the forthcoming World Cup qualifying games and, in particular, those which pitted Celtic team-mates against each other. Paul Lambert and Joos Valgaeren went head-to-head to discuss the forthcoming Scotland versus Belgium clash, Johan Mjallby and Ramon Vega discussed the Sweden/Switzerland game, while Neil Lennon discussed Northern Ireland's match with Bulgaria which, because of Stilian Petrov's leg break, would not see the two Celts facing each other.

'I told Stan that he'd do anything to get out of playing against me,' Lennon joked in the *View*. 'I'm obviously very disappointed for Stan because he has been in brilliant form since I came here and, from what I hear, that has been the story all season. He has recently been appointed captain of Bulgaria, which was a great honour, particularly at such a young age. We've been giving each other plenty of stick in training over the last few weeks because we were both really looking forward to the game. I'm just gutted for him because that was the last thing he needed.'

the voice of the champions

Celticview

May 2, 2001   vol.36 issue 41   £1.50

three
cheers
CELTIC'S IBROX GLORY DAY

www.celticfc.co.uk

If you're going to hit fifty goals in a season, what better place to reach that magical half-century than in the home of your arch-rivals to seal an emphatic 3-0 victory?

In truth, the performance by Martin O'Neill's champions at Ibrox was orchestrated by the irrepressible Lubo Moravcik who scored two superb second-half goals, though Henrik Larsson still managed to steal the show when he scored Celtic's third, and his fiftieth of the season, with just four minutes of the match remaining. The result was an emphatic reminder, if one was needed, of Celtic's dominance in the 2000–01 season and Larsson himself was clearly delighted to have reached fifty goals, gesturing as much to the Celtic fans in the Broomloan Road stand as he was mobbed by his delighted team-mates.

The game at Ibrox also saw a first-team debut for eighteen-year-old Shaun Maloney, who came on as a substitute. The *View* pointed out that it was an incredible moment for the player, who was pictured in the Main Stand at Celtic Park watching the first derby match of that season as Celtic beat Rangers 6-2.

The magazine also highlighted the fact that Celtic had scooped two other awards – Henrik Larsson winning the SPFA Player of the Year and team-mate Stilian Petrov winning Young Player of the Year. Manager Martin O'Neill was clearly delighted with his players' success, as he told the *View*: 'It was a great day all round, wasn't it? If I'm being honest, I was more delighted to see Stilian Petrov given his award, because I never really feared for Henrik's chances. That should give him another little boost in his recovery as, I'm sure, would just standing beside Henrik. He'll be an example to Stan of how players can come back from such a terrible injury even stronger than they were before.'

Petrov, who had endured a tough season prior to O'Neill taking over, had also suffered a leg break towards the end of the season, but his fellow professionals still acknowledged his contribution to Celtic's success.

DREAMS OF GLORY: Shaun (circled) looks on as Martin O'Neill celebrates in the 6-2 defeat of Rangers

the voice of the champions

Celtic view

64-page **special edition**

vol.36 issue 43 **£1.95**

www.**celticfc**.co.uk

May 16, 2001

Bobby Murdoch

1944 - 2001

They were the team that had put Celtic on the world footballing map. No longer were Celtic just a success in Scotland. In 1967 they became the Kings of Europe and for the next seven years the Hoops were one of the continent's top teams.

The eleven men who defeated Inter Milan on 25 May 1967 were hailed as the Lisbon Lions and became legends among the supporters. And while, in our heart of hearts, we knew that they were not immortal, it was only with the sudden and tragic death of Bobby Murdoch that it really hit home to everyone that the Lisbon Lions were, like the rest of us, mere mortals. Bobby Murdoch died in the early hours of Tuesday 15 May and although the *Celtic View* had gone to press, the magazine stopped the presses and redesigned the first five pages, including the cover, to acknowledge the passing of a Celtic great.

Fellow Lisbon Lion Jim Craig spoke movingly of Murdoch, as a player and as a man. He told the *View*: 'Bobby was a magnificent player. Strong, two-footed, with great passing ability, good vision and a powerful shot. All the other Lions would acknowledge that, when Bobby played, we all played. On a personal level, he was a quiet guy, but a real nice one. Among the Lions, he was everybody's favourite. This is a very sad day for Celtic Football Club and for the Lisbon Lions. Just 10 days before the 34th anniversary of Lisbon, we have lost one of our best men.'

Elsewhere in the *View*, there was a thirty-two-page special on Henrik Larsson in recognition of his outstanding scoring record that season. His tally would ultimately end up at fifty-three, including thirty-five in the league – enough to earn him the Golden Shoe award as Europe's top goalscorer. Among those paying tribute to a great goalscorer were then England coach Sven-Goran Eriksson, Celtic legend Jimmy Johnstone and Larsson's best friend, former Rangers player Giovanni van Bronckhorst, while in an exclusive interview with the great man himself, the *View* revealed that he had also hit a hole-in-one at Tom Boyd's testimonial golf outing. What a season! What a player!

the voice of the champions

www.**celticfc**.co.uk ■ 64-page **special edition**

Celticview

May 30, 2001
vol.36 issue.45
£1.95

sealed with a
KISS
TREBLE IN PARADISE

It was the perfect end to an unbelievable season. A 3-0 victory over Hibernian at Hampden gave Celtic victory in the Scottish Cup final and ensured a first domestic treble for the club in over thirty years.

'Let's party like it's 1969!' the *View* declared and there was no doubt that a lot of celebrating was done among the Celtic family. Team captain Paul Lambert and club captain Tom Boyd lifted the famous old trophy together and the treble was 'sealed with a kiss' of the silverware at Hampden. Both players had been part of the squad that had won the league in 1998 and 'stopped the ten', and both were important figures again as Martin O'Neill's side swept all before them. The enormity of the achievement was even more apparent given that it was only the third treble in the club's history – 1967 was the other season when Jock Stein's side won every trophy they entered.

Only one man was involved in all three trebles. John Clark won the treble twice as a player and was the kit controller when the latest one was clinched in 2001. He was surprised when the *View* told him of this fact and commented: 'It's quite a unique thing, yet I didn't even give it a thought until you told me about it! It's great to have been involved in all three trebles, but to be honest it was the furthest thing from my mind. I feel very proud to be a part of it. I've been there as a player twice and now I've been involved on the staff. It's a unique achievement and I'm proud to have played a part in it all.'

Joos Valgaeren, meanwhile, joked that the treble triumph might actually curtail John Clark's boasts about his own achievements as a player. The Belgian defender told the *View*: 'Every day, we all have to put up with Clarky telling us all about what a legend he is here. Well, now I can come back next season and tell him "I may not be a legend like you, but I'm a little bit closer than I was when I came here!"'

'We've got all the trophies'

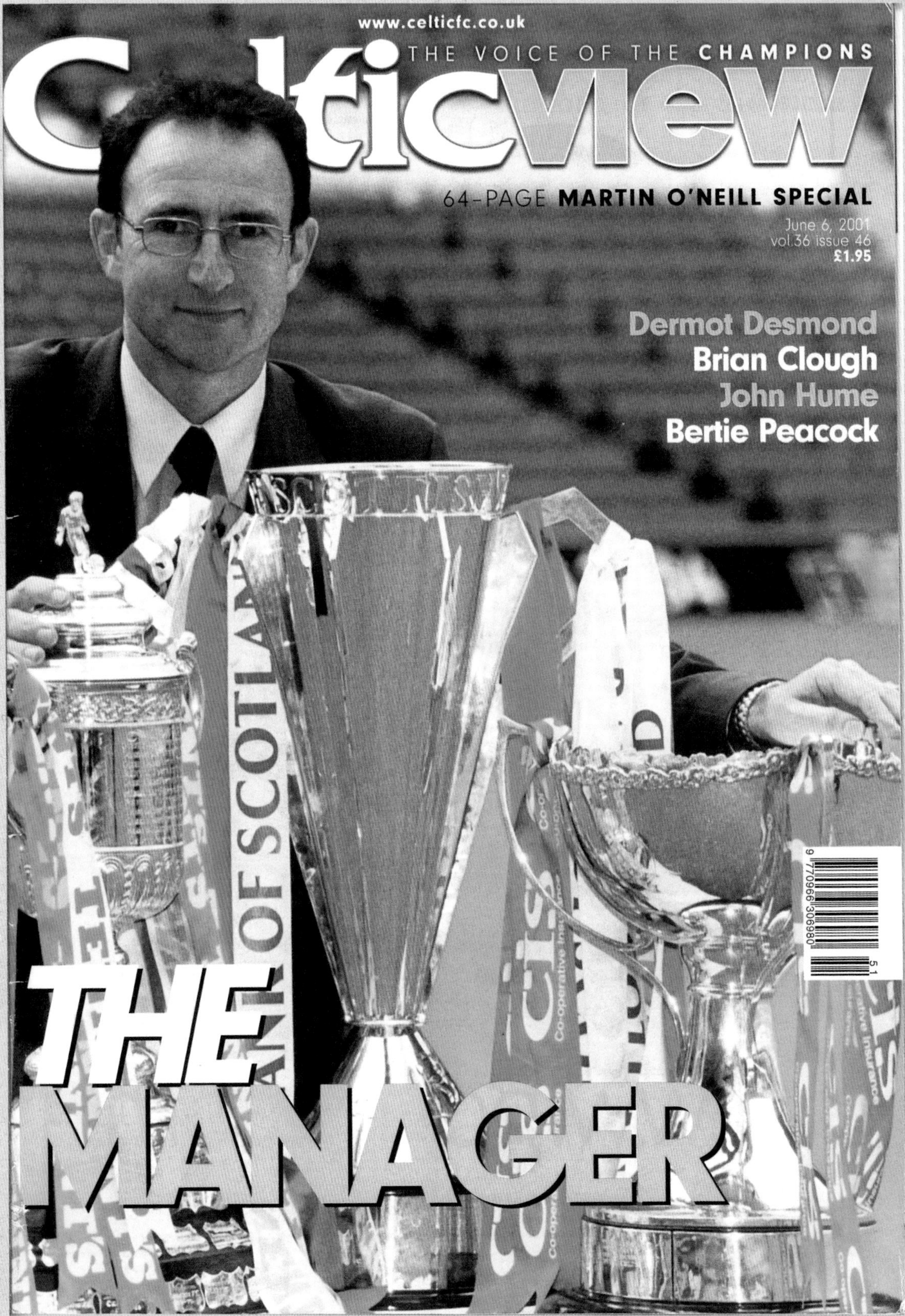

www.celticfc.co.uk

THE VOICE OF THE CHAMPIONS

Celticview

64-PAGE **MARTIN O'NEILL SPECIAL**

June 6, 2001
vol.36 issue 46
£1.95

Dermot Desmond
Brian Clough
John Hume
Bertie Peacock

THE MANAGER

When Martin O'Neill was appointed Celtic manager, he stood on the steps outside the stadium and vowed to the assembled crowd that he would do everything possible to bring success to the football club.

Twelve months later he was on the front cover of the *Celtic View* alongside the three domestic trophies his side had won. It was a remarkable achievement and represented the club's first domestic treble since 1969. Martin O'Neill, in the space of one season, had re-established Celtic's dominance in Scottish football after a long period of being second best. There were many highlights along the way, starting with the 6-2 demolition of Rangers in August 2000 and ending with a 3-0 thrashing of the same team at Ibrox in April 2001.

The final *View* of the season was a tribute issue to the man who had led Celtic to so much success. As well as an interview with the man himself, the *View* also spoke to Celtic's major shareholder, Dermot Desmond, who explained the board's confidence in their man. He said: 'Within minutes of the interview, though, it was obvious to everyone that Martin was the very man for the job. We all realised that the most important thing we had to do for the club was ensure that we got the person we wanted, and that was Martin. We knew that he would do well and was the man for the job, and there was no way that we were ever going to give up our chase for him. When you meet someone who is capable of fulfilling a professional role it leaps out at you. He was a person that we very quickly believed in and the fact that he has delivered such success this season, especially after the disappointments of last season, has been astounding.'

Others who lined up to pay tribute to Celtic's manager were midfielder Neil Lennon, brought to the club by O'Neill after previously playing under him at Leicester City, fellow Derryman and politician John Hume, and Bertie Peacock, another Irishman and someone who had made a massive contribution to Celtic in the fifties.

THE VOICE OF THE CHAMPIONS

CelticVIEW

August 29, 2001
vol.37 issue 08
£1.95

www.celticfc.net

FREE
16-PAGE CHAMPIONS LEAGUE SUPPLEMENT

MIDASTOUCH

HENRIK RECEIVES HIS GOLDEN SHOE

Henrik Larsson as the 'Golden Child'… Given that Celtic supporters were already proclaiming him the 'King of Kings' then it was hardly surprising that the *View* should attempt to deify him as well.

Some fans had voiced their objections to the song on 'religious' grounds, although it was unlikely that anyone who did sing with gusto during the game actually thought Larsson was the son of God. He was, however, Celtic's saviour, and his fifty-three goals in the 2000–01 season had gone a long way to ensuring that Celtic secured their first treble in over thirty years.

Characteristically, Larsson was most pleased with the three trophies resting in the Celtic Park boardroom and the trio of medals he won as a result, but there was also the merest flicker of personal pride at winning the prestigious Golden Shoe award. It confirmed him as Europe's top marksman for 2000–01, a fantastic achievement for any player, and the *View* joined Larsson in Monaco to pick up his award. He told the magazine: 'It's special to have won the Golden Shoe, particularly because no Swedish player has won it before. It's great to be here and I'm delighted to be picking up the prize. A lot of great players have won the Golden Shoe in the past and I'm just lucky that I've been able to reach that level.

I always believe the most important thing about the goals is that they help Celtic to victory. But obviously the award will be a nice thing to put on the mantelpiece and I'm very proud.'

Also in Monaco was Martin O'Neill, who was there for the UEFA Champions League groups stages draw, in which Celtic were taking part for the first time. He watched as his side were drawn in a tough group alongside Juventus, Porto and Rosenborg, though, as he pointed out to the *View*: 'I know the lads will be looking forward with great anticipation to playing against Juventus, Porto and Rosenborg. Who wouldn't be? I said before we began this season's European campaign that merely being in the Champions League group stages would be an achievement in itself and I stand by that.'

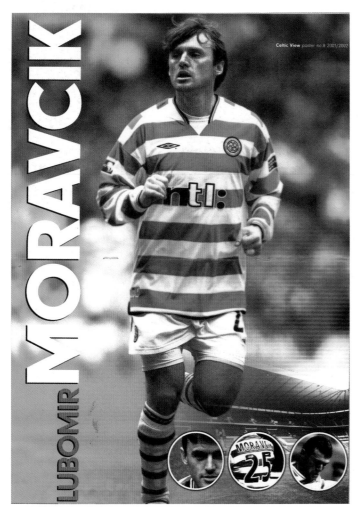

LUBOMIR MORAVCIK

THE VOICE OF THE CHAMPIONS

CelticVIEW

September 12, 2001
vol.37 issue 10
£1.95

www.celticfc.net

EUROPE

One of the most unusual front covers in the history of the *Celtic View*, the issue of 12 September 2001 featuring exclusive artwork by Scottish novelist and artist Alasdair Gray, also proved to be one of the best-selling issues of the season, hitting almost 30,000 copies.

The *View* had commissioned Alasdair Gray to produce a front cover to mark Celtic's first ever game in the UEFA Champions League – against Norwegian side Rosenborg. It was a striking image which polarised opinion – people either loved it or hated it – but it certainly stood out on the shelves.

However, the game that Gray's work celebrated did not take place as scheduled on Wednesday 12 September because of events on the other side of the Atlantic. The previous day, terrorists had launched attacks in the United States, destroying the Twin Towers in New York and badly damaging the Pentagon in Washington. Over 3,000 people died in the attacks and, while the Champions League games scheduled for 11 September took place, UEFA took the decision to cancel all subsequent games as a mark of respect for all those who had lost their lives in the tragedy.

Supporters had obviously been looking forward to Celtic's first experience of football's premier club competition, but realised that some things are more important than football. Everyone who sat glued to their TV sets, watching as the Twin Towers collapsed, was horrified by what they saw and completely understood UEFA's decision to postpone the Wednesday night games.

The fact that the game did not take place, however, did not affect sales of the *Celtic View*. Supporters, whether intrigued by the cover or wanting to keep a memento of an unsettling moment in history, snapped it up as soon as it went on sale. As one columnist in the *View* declared: 'Today, the *Celtic View* you're holding in your hands is a piece of art; it is a collector's item. It is something unique that has never been done before and might never be done again.'

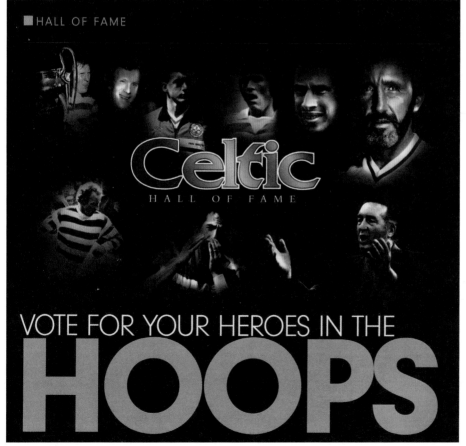

THE VOICE OF THE CHAMPIONS

Celtic VIEW

October 31, 2001
vol.37 issue 17
£1.95

www.celticfc.net

THE CELTIC FOOTBALL

1888

JUVENTUS

MARTIN **O'NEILL**
WIN **LUBO VIDEOS**
AGGIE **THE TEA LADY**
JACKIE **McNAMARA**

JUDGEMENT NIGHT

9 770966 306096

The *Celtic View* 'Halloween' issue of 2001 was published on the same day as Celtic's final UEFA Champions League game of the group stages – at home to Italian giants Juventus.

The sides had already met in Turin, where an outrageous refereeing decision in the final minute gave Juventus a penalty and a 3-2 victory. Now there was a chance for Celtic to redress that injustice and, hopefully, qualify for the latter stages of the competition, although that required Porto to lose against Rosenborg.

Speaking ahead of the game, Henrik Larsson told the *View*: 'We still have every chance in the world to get through to the second group stage, and all we can do is try to win the game and hope it's a favourable result between Rosenborg and Porto. You never want to be in the position where you are relying on other teams, but that's the way it is and that's the reality. It's our first time in the competition and you need to build up experience in order to be able to succeed. We have to wait until after tonight and then we will see how much we have learned from competing in the Champions League.'

In the event, Celtic Park was to witness one of its greatest ever European nights as Martin O'Neill's side triumphed 4-3 in a thrilling encounter. The victory included a spectacular Chris Sutton goal, though the result was ultimately academic, given that Porto managed to defeat their Norwegian opponents.

The *View* also featured one of Scottish football's unsung heroes in its 'Halloween' issue – Aggie Moffat, the tea lady from St Johnstone. Famous for putting Graeme Souness in his place after he broke a teapot in the away dressing room at McDiarmid Park, Aggie also confessed to being a Celtic fan. She told the *View*: 'I always shout for Celtic, but all the boys know that and I often get a bit of stick for it! I usually get to see the first and last twenty minutes of a game and I always come away and tell our boys whether they play well or not, but I don't suppose they bother about that.'

■ AGGIE MOFFAT

THE VOICE OF THE CHAMPIONS

CelticVIEW

January 9, 2002
vol.37 issue 25 **£1.95**

www.celticfc.net

CENTURY
BHOY

HENRIK'S HOT **100**

PLUS

MARTIN **O'NEILL**   JURGEN **KLINSMANN**   DIEGO **MARADONA**

Off the field Henrik Larsson was an unassuming character who preferred to shun the limelight. On the field, although he generally took centre stage, he would always emphasise the importance of the team over any individual achievement and while he had a trademark celebration – arms outstretched and tongue sticking out – there was still the feeling that he was exercising restraint.

Yet this particular front cover shows Larsson as a 'wild man'. The striker was caught up in the moment – this was actually taken seconds after Sweden had clinched qualification for the 2002 World Cup finals – but the *View* thought it a particularly appropriate image with which to celebrate Henrik hitting his hundredth league goal for Celtic.

That milestone was reached on Boxing Day 2001 in a dramatic match against Livingston at Celtic Park. The game finished 3-2 in Celtic's favour, with Larsson scoring the injury-time winner, but it was his goal on fifty minutes which was number one hundred.

His first goal had come back in August 1997, when he scored in a 2-0 victory over St Johnstone at McDiarmid Park. The fact that it had taken him just 133 games to reach his century was impressive, all the more so given that he missed most of the 1999–2000 season after suffering a leg break in the October.

Not surprisingly, the striker downplayed the achievement when he spoke to the *View*: 'When I finish my career that's when I'll have the chance to sit back and look at what I achieved. There's no point in sitting now and talking about what has happened. It's all in the past already and at the minute I want to focus on looking forward.'

Elsewhere in the *View*, a feature on the top ten number tens to have played football sparked furious debate, both within the *View* office and among supporters, with Diego Maradona chosen first ahead of Pele, no doubt an indication of the relative youthfulness of the writer. Bertie Auld, meanwhile, managed to make it into the top ten as the solitary Celt.

100

Henrik Larsson
and the
100 league goals

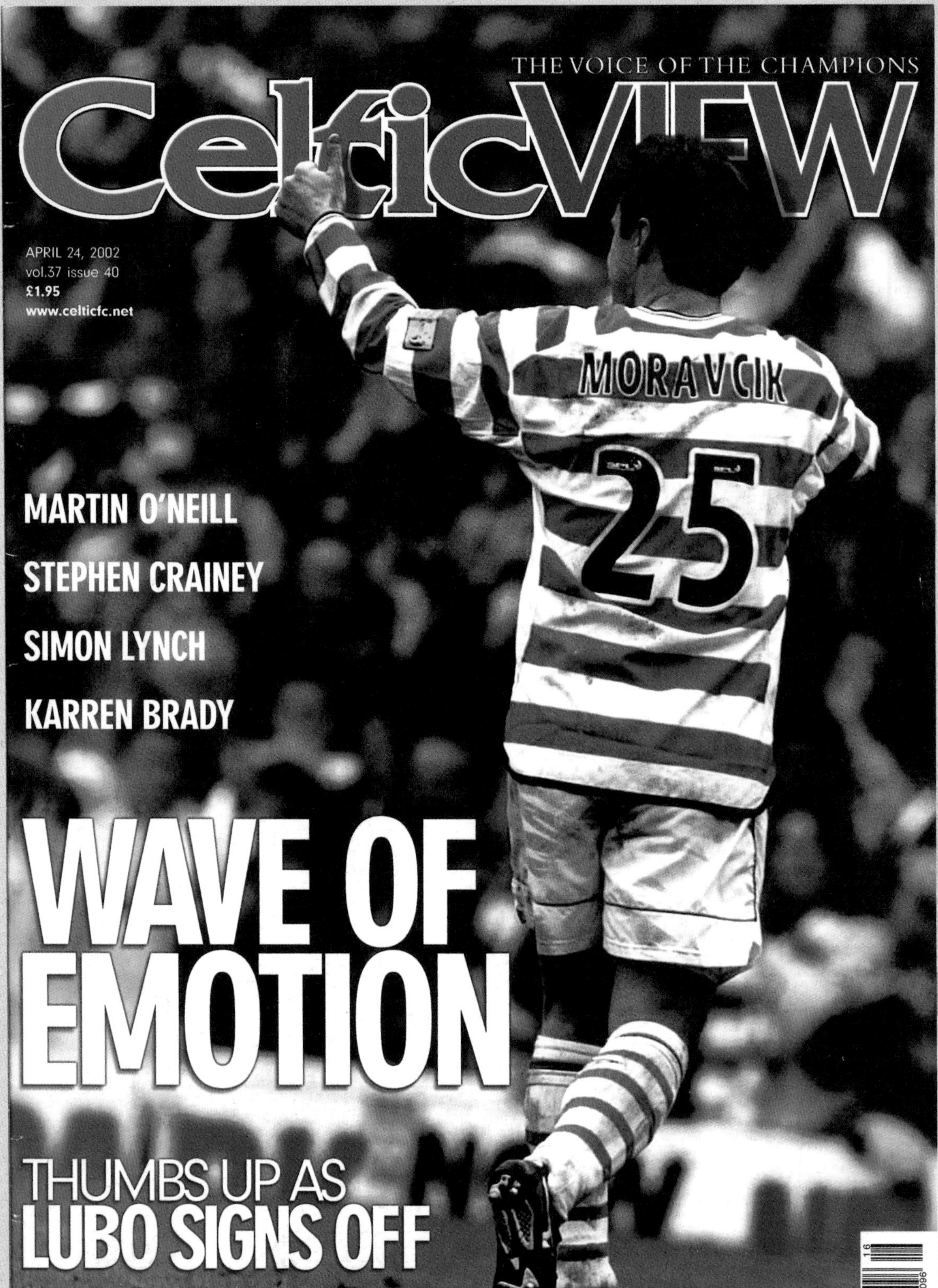

THE VOICE OF THE CHAMPIONS

CelticVIEW

APRIL 24, 2002
vol.37 issue 40
£1.95
www.celticfc.net

MARTIN O'NEILL

STEPHEN CRAINEY

SIMON LYNCH

KARREN BRADY

WAVE OF EMOTION

THUMBS UP AS
LUBO SIGNS OFF

Lubomir Moravcik had announced his arrival as a Celtic player with two goals in a 5-1 thrashing of Rangers at Celtic Park in 1998. The Slovakian playmaker made his final appearance at Paradise against the same opposition – though this time honours were even in a 1-1 draw.

Moravcik was substituted with twenty minutes of the match remaining and he gave an understated thumbs up to supporters who rose to acclaim a player who had arrived as an unknown, but was leaving a legend.

Celtic supporters were probably as guilty as anyone of asking the question 'Lubo who?' when his fellow countryman and Celtic manager Dr Jozef Venglos brought him to Glasgow. Yet even they were surprised by the level of ignorance and the ridicule levelled at the player by sections of the Scottish media. However, they were quickly forced to eat their words when the true breadth of Moravcik's ability became apparent.

In his last interview with the *View* as a Celtic player, Moravcik spoke with great pride and pleasure of his time with the club. He said: 'It is always a pleasure to receive an ovation like that at any point in your career and it is a tremendous feeling. However, football went on here before me and it will go on long after me. I have enjoyed my time here and I have very fond memories of playing at Celtic Park. It would have been nice to score a goal, but I still have the Scottish Cup final to look forward to and maybe I can do it then. It was nice to finish at Celtic Park with such a big game and although we didn't win the match I was happy because we came back to level the scores which isn't often easy when you lose a goal in the first few minutes.'

Birmingham City's managing director, Karren Brady, also featured in the *View* and admitted that, as far as she was concerned, it would be great for English football if Celtic and Rangers moved to the Premiership.

KARREN BRADY
Exclusive interview: ALISON McCONNELL

THE
BRADY
HUNCH

Birmingham City's Managing Director reveals her thoughts on the Old Firm and England

148-PAGE SUMMER SPECIAL

THE VOICE OF THE CHAMPIONS

Celtic VIEW

MAY 29, 2002
vol.37 issue
£2.95
www.celticfc.net

EXCLUSIVE
O'NEILL
REVIEW OF THE SEASON

EXCLUSIVE
KEANE
END OF A DREAM

EXCLUSIVE
OWEN
ENGLAND EXPECTS

EXCLUSIVE
MJALLBY
FULL OF EASTERN PROMISE

PLUS
TOM SHIELDS
DZIEKANOWSKI
JOOS VALGAEREN
AND LOTS MORE

WORLD BEATERS
EVERY TEAM, EVERY GAME - THE ULTIMATE GUIDE

It was an ambitious idea that gave birth to the biggest ever *Celtic View* – a 148-page summer special which looked forward to the forthcoming World Cup in Japan and South Korea.

With a special glossy cover, the magazine was perfect-bound with a spine rather than the usual stapling, and it was an impressive publication. The issue itself cost £2.95 rather than the usual £1.95 for sixty-four pages and it also had a longer shelf life than the normal seven days, with newsagents keeping it on sale for four weeks.

In terms of content, the *View* stood shoulder to shoulder with any other pre-World Cup publication. There were exclusive interviews with Roy Keane, Michael Owen, Henrik Larsson, Johan Mjallby, Paolo Di Canio and Jacki Dziekanowski among others. The *View* also offered an in-depth look at each of the teams taking part in the tournament and a series of profiles on ten World Cup legends of the past.

Among the other special, non-World Cup features in this bumper edition were ones on Celtic tattoos, an exclusive short story from top author Bernard MacLaverty, a celebration of Celtic Park as monument to the Irish diaspora and a look at the pre-match superstitions of players and manager. For good measure, the issue also coincided with the thirty-fifth anniversary of Celtic's European Cup triumph in Lisbon and the *View* spoke to goalkeeper John Fallon – the only substitute that day in May 1967.

The editorial in this issue declared: 'The *Celtic View* has always prided itself on being the most innovative football magazine in the country. We were the first ever club magazine in Britain and we have long been the best-selling club magazine as well. This week's issue continues that spirit of innovation which began back in 1965 with the first ever edition of the *View*. At 148 pages, this magazine represents a new chapter in *View* history. Not only will it stand alongside the other monthly football publications on the shelves, but the content of the *Celtic View* stands comparison with anything else you could buy.'

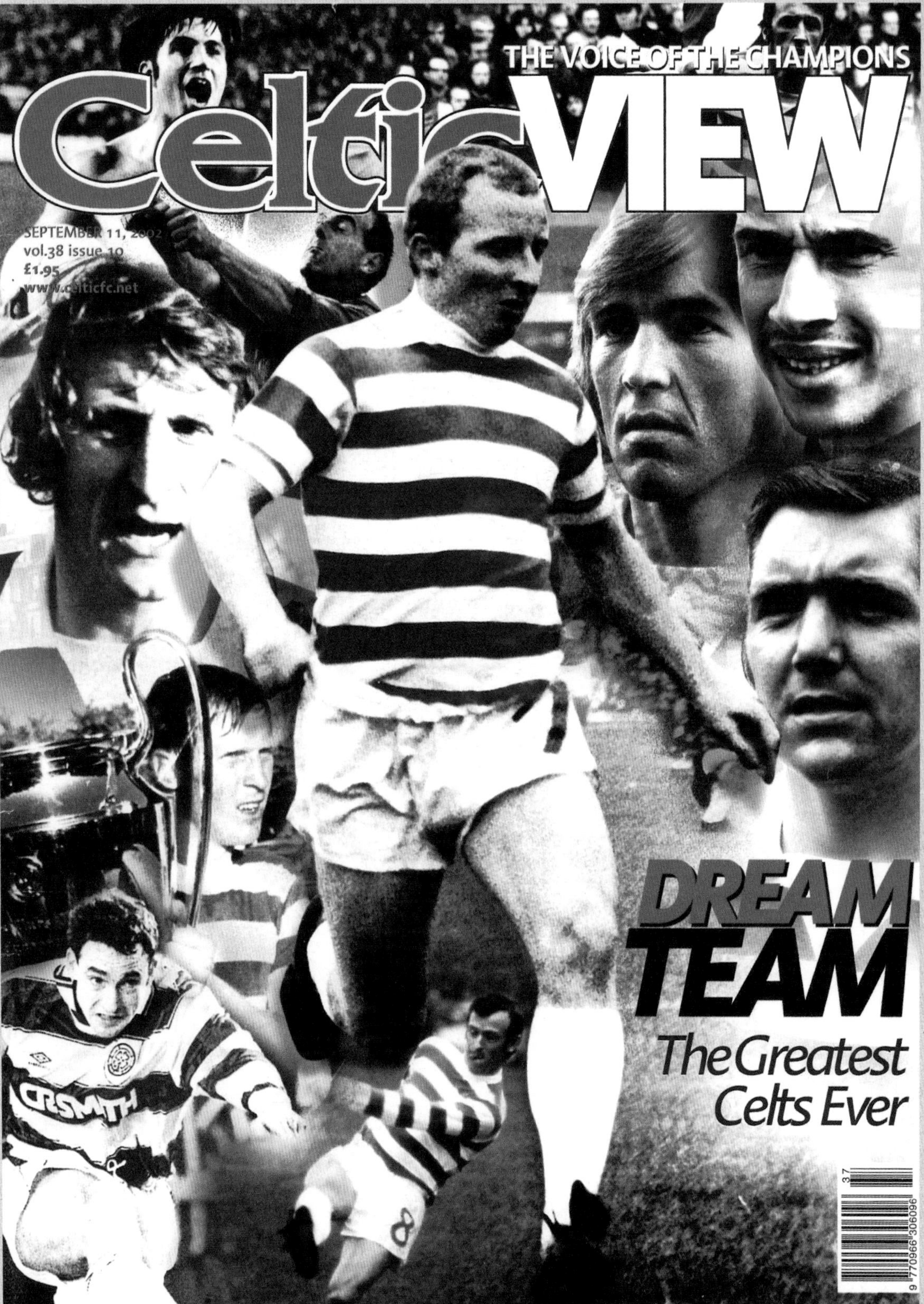

THE VOICE OF THE CHAMPIONS

CelticVIEW

SEPTEMBER 11, 2002
vol.38 issue 10
£1.95
www.celticfc.net

DREAM TEAM

The Greatest Celts Ever

Celtic

Celtic supporters had been given the chance to vote for the greatest ever Celtic team and the greatest ever Celt – and there were few surprises when the results were announced.

Taking pride of place on the front cover, a colour image standing out from the sepia-toned background, was Jimmy Johnstone. A definite choice for the greatest ever starting XI, Jinky also came out on top in the individual award.

The greatest ever Celtic team was: Ronnie Simpson, Danny McGrain, Billy McNeill, Tommy Gemmell, Bobby Murdoch, Paul McStay, Bertie Auld, Jimmy Johnstone, Bobby Lennox, Kenny Dalglish and Henrik Larsson. To celebrate this unique team, the *Celtic View* gave away a sixty-four-page greatest ever Celtic team supplement free with that week's issue.

It featured profiles on the eleven Celts who had made it into the team and a centre-page poster of ten of them at the awards ceremony. Bobby Murdoch had passed away a year and a half beforehand and, looking back at that poster, it's sad to reflect

BRADY'S BHOY:
Liam signed Tony Cascarino

BRISTOW BOY:
his game suffered like Cascarino

that the Celtic family has now lost both Ronnie Simpson and Jimmy Johnstone as well. At the time of the event, Jinky was suffering from motor neurone disease, though in accepting his award, he dedicated it to his late team-mate and friend, Bobby Murdoch.

It has often been said by the Lisbon Lions that Murdoch was the supreme talent in that team and that, when he played, the whole side did.

In the main sixty-four-page *Celtic View* that week there was an exclusive interview with Tony Cascarino, which included a picture of him in the most hideous Celtic away strip of all time.

The player himself was honest enough to admit that his time at Celtic Park hadn't been a great success, though he did recall with great fondness his goal against Rangers at Ibrox. 'I'll never forget the night after I scored at Ibrox,' Cascarino told the *View*. 'I got absolutely rotten in some Chinese restaurant in a Rangers area, I kept falling asleep and waiters would be pushing me to wake me up. My response was "I scored against Rangers" and then I sang "Who put the ball in the Rangers net, I did, I did."'

THE VOICE OF THE CHAMPIONS

CelticVIEW

MARCH 5, 2003 vol.38 issue 33
www.celticfc.net £1.95

STILIAN PETROV
Bulgarian midfielder
has his sights set on
a successful season

CELTIC CHRONICLES
We take a look back over
the Hoops' glorious history

JOHN HARTSON
The big Welshman was
on target against Hibs

MARTIN O'NEILL
looks forward to a crucial
sequence of games

ALAN THOMPSON
Previews forthcoming
Old Firm encounter

CELTS ARE FLYING
HIGH
VITAL MONTH AHEAD FOR THE HOOPS

FREE 16 PAGE JUNIORVIEW MAGAZINE

Celtic

For many people, Celtic's defeat of German side VfB Stuttgart to reach the quarter-final of the UEFA Cup was when they started to believe that something special might be happening – that Celtic's name was on the UEFA Cup.

In a two-minute spell early in the first half of the game, Alan Thompson and Chris Sutton gave Celtic a 5-1 aggregate lead, and although the Germans won the match 3-2 on the night, it was Martin O'Neill's side who progressed to the last eight of the competition. 'It is exciting days at the club,' said the manager. 'These are massive matches for us and it isn't often in Celtic's history that we have had five such massive games crammed together. We play Rangers-Liverpool-Rangers-Liverpool, and then, would you believe it, Inverness Caley Thistle. Given the recent past, the Scottish Cup tie adds yet more spice to the run of games that we are on the brink of.'

Alan Thompson also looked forward to the forthcoming clash with Rangers and the prospect of grabbing a goal against Celtic's city rivals, telling the *View*: 'My old man might stick a couple of quid on it, he likes a bet on me. It would be nice to score, but it's not the be all and end all and I'd be more than happy just to come out the game with a victory.'

The ongoing problem of supporters leaving early from games was also debated in the magazine, with two fans giving opinions on the subject – one for and one against. It is an issue that continues to divide supporters, although the view that Celtic fans should stay and support their team for the full ninety minutes was given credence at Celtic's home game against Hibernian, when Johan Mjallby popped up in the ninety-third minute to give the Hoops a 3-2 victory. No doubt the cheers that echoed up from the stadium to the streams of fans leaving the ground would have been a painful reminder of the error of their ways. The *View*, of course, stayed neutral on this whole issue!

Celtic Chronicles

70-year wait for cup

As we mentioned in our last edition, the match organised by local club Ferencvarosi Torna in Budapest between Celtic and Burnley for a special trophy in the summer of 1914 ended in confusion.

With the score 1-1 at full time on a blazing hot day, the referee wanted 10 minutes extra time but the players had had enough and came off.

Eventually, officials of both clubs reached an understanding. They tossed for the cup and Burnley won. The sponsors, though, would not agree to hand it over until the deciding game had been played, at Glasgow, Burnley or on neutral ground.

The match was eventually played on September 1, 1914 at Turf Moor four weeks into the First World War and Celtic won 2-0! However, no Budapest Cup was presented. It had apparently been won by a professional wrestler in a raffle run by the Austrian Red Cross during the early days of the war!

For the happy sequel to this sad tale we have to fast forward more than 70 years.

Ferencvaros officials, aware of Celtic's centenary and realising that their victory over the English Cup winners Burnley had never been properly marked, decided to set matters right.

A party from Hungary flew over to watch Celtic's League title-clinching match against Dundee at Parkhead in April, 1988 and presented the club with the fine trophy (left).

THE VOICE OF THE CHAMPIONS

CelticVIEW

MARCH 26, 2003
vol.38 issue 36
www.celticfc.net
£1.95

ANFIELD SPECIAL
Souvenir pull-out of Celtic's glory night in Liverpool, including exclusive interviews with Henrik Larsson and John Hartson

ROCKET MAN
Alan Thompson reflects on his stunning strike

O'NEILL
UEFA clash was, "One of our greatest results ever."

Walk On
CELTIC BOOK THEIR PLACE IN UEFA CUP SEMI-FINAL

Celtic

John Hartson had probably never scored a better goal before or since and his strike confirmed Celtic's victory over Liverpool in the quarter-final of the UEFA Cup.

The Welshman, a childhood Liverpool fan who idolised his fellow countryman Ian Rush, scored Celtic's second goal to give Martin O'Neill's side a 3-1 aggregate victory. More importantly, it put Celtic within 180 minutes of a European final. The victory was also greeted with a sigh of relief from the thousands of supporters who had already booked tickets and flights for the final in a rash burst of optimism following the previous round's victory over VfB Stuttgart.

Describing his goal to the *View*, Hartson said: 'You hit one or two of them in your career. I supported Liverpool as a kid mainly because Ian Rush was my hero and to come here, score a goal like that, such an important goal as well, is a dream come true for me, especially after the weekend. It wasn't in front of the Kop, but it was in front of the Celtic fans and it was a brilliant feeling.'

It had been an interesting few days for supporters because, having enjoyed the high of the Anfield victory, they were brought right back down to earth with a shock Scottish Cup exit at the hands of Inverness Caley Thistle. Admittedly, Martin O'Neill had fielded an under-strength side, but the defeat denied fans an end-of-season jaunt to Hampden and, ultimately, led to a trophy-less season.

Letters to the *View* that week, however, concentrated on one subject and that was the news that there were to be no charges brought by Northumbria Police against any Celtic player in connection with alleged incidents the previous year. At the time the *Daily Record*'s infamous 'Thugs and Thieves' headline attacked the Celtic players, much to the fury of supporters, who gleefully pointed out in letters to the *View* just how wrong the tabloid had been. A club statement said: 'We look with interest to see if they [the *Record*] have any proposals to apologise and attempt to put the "record" straight.'

UEFA CUP QUARTER-FINAL 2nd leg
ANFIELD STADIUM, THURSDAY 20 MARCH 2003

LIVERPOOL 0 v 2 CELTIC

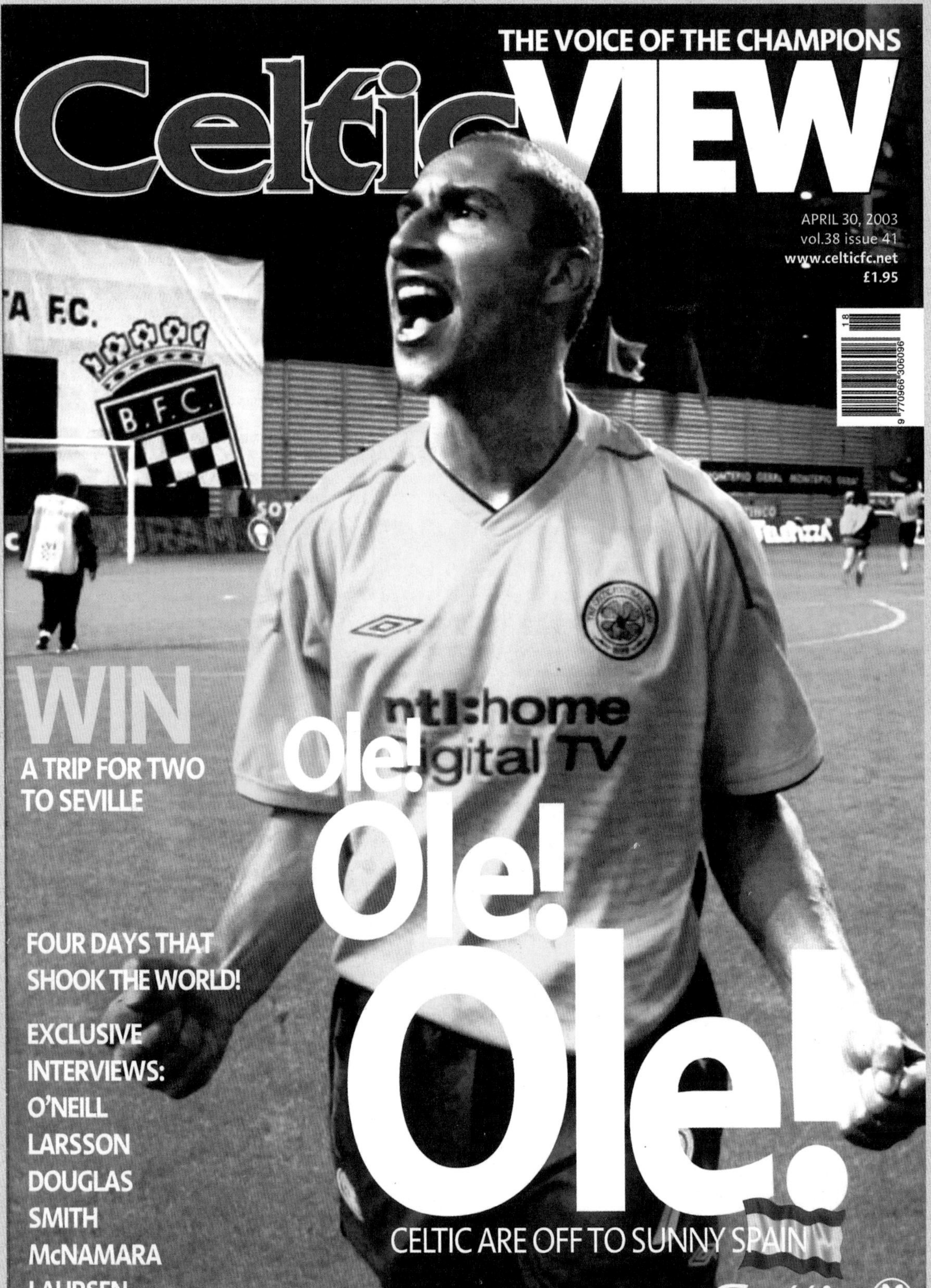

THE VOICE OF THE CHAMPIONS

Celtic VIEW

APRIL 30, 2003
vol.38 issue 41
www.celticfc.net
£1.95

WIN

A TRIP FOR TWO TO SEVILLE

FOUR DAYS THAT SHOOK THE WORLD!

EXCLUSIVE INTERVIEWS:
O'NEILL
LARSSON
DOUGLAS
SMITH
McNAMARA
LAURSEN

Ole! Ole! Ole! Ole!

CELTIC ARE OFF TO SUNNY SPAIN

Celtic

The *Celtic View* declared on its front cover that it had been 'Four Days That Shook The World!' Admittedly, it was really only the Celtic world, but still... reaching a European final and beating Rangers at Ibrox in the space of a few days was certainly dramatic.

Henrik Larsson deservedly took centre stage on the cover, having scored the vital goal in Portugal which put Celtic into their first European final for thirty-three years. However, he did leave it late, popping up with just twelve minutes of the match remaining to fire home the only goal of the tie and send hundreds of thousands of Celtic supporters around the world into raptures and on to the Internet to book their flights to Spain.

Larsson spoke to the *View* after the game to give his reaction to the stunning victory. He said: 'This is massive. I woke up on Friday morning with a big smile on my face and it is such a tremendous feeling. I can only speak about the years that I have been here and in those seasons we haven't really performed all that well in Europe, with the exception of last season, so it is great to reach the UEFA Cup final, but we can't be satisfied with that. Now we want to do something on the day, but we don't need to be told that it will be very difficult because Porto are an excellent team. Without a doubt, though, Thursday's goal was definitely the most important of my career – so far.'

The subsequent victory over Rangers at Ibrox was almost lost in the euphoria of the European triumph, although it remains memorable for the deluge of beach balls that rained down on Ibrox as the teams emerged from the tunnel.

The *View* also contained a couple of unusual features – a special TV guide for 'what you'll be missing while you're in Seville', while Señor Antonio Hamilton came up with twenty-one things to do until the UEFA Cup final, including, 'Get yourself a huge Spanish moustache (ladies as well) and make sure it's big enough to nest small animals in. It's important that we don't look like tourists when we get there.'

THE VOICE OF THE CHAMPIONS

CelticVIEW

MAY 14, 2003
vol.38 issue 43
www.celticfc.net
£1.95

UEFA CUP FINAL 7 DAYS TO GO

Don't forget your
BEACHBALL

Celtic ✲

Celtic's first game after reaching the UEFA Cup final was a clash against Rangers. And supporters showed a tremendous sense of humour when they showered the Ibrox pitch with beach balls as the teams came out of the tunnel.

There was a real party mood in the derby game that day – certainly among the Celtic support – and the 2-1 victory only added to the occasion. In advance of the UEFA Cup final, the *Celtic View* decided to give away a free beach ball with every copy of the 14 May issue. It was a great idea. The only problem was trying to source 30,000 beach balls in seven days. After much blood, sweat and tears, the task was finally completed successfully and the issue was a sell-out as supporters made sure they got their free gift to take to Seville.

With just one week to go until the game against FC Porto in Seville, there was a real sense of anticipation among all Celtic supporters and the *View* carried a travel guide for the tens of thousands of fans intending to make the trip to Spain, regardless of whether they had a ticket for the final or not. As is always the case, however, the travel information from the club contained this important proviso: 'Please do not travel to Seville if you do not have a ticket for this match.'

There was also cultural advice to Celtic supporters who did have a ticket for the match and intended travelling to Spain. The Museo de Bellas Artes, according to the *View*, 'is a gorgeous old convent housing one of the best art collections in Spain', while supporters were urged to 'try to get to Teatro Lope de Vega for big name flamenco stars'. It's unclear whether many did, in fact, experience the thrills of flamenco dancing or the sophistication of Seville's premier museum, but the Bhoys still enjoyed themselves!

Elsewhere in the *View*, Lisbon Lion Jim Craig had a moving interview with Kathleen Murdoch, the widow of Celtic legend, Bobby.

CelticVIEW

MAY 17, 2003
vol.38 issue 44
www.celticfc.net
£1.95 / 3.6EUROS

CELTIC FC v FC PORTO
UEFA CUP FINAL
ESTADIO OLIMPICO, SEVILLE
WEDNESDAY, MAY 21, 2003

9 770966 306096
21

UEFA
UEFA CUP

Celtic ✤

It was a cover full of optimism and hope, one that promised so much... that painful feeling of so near yet so far comes flooding back into the pit of the stomach every time one looks at the front of this particular *View*.

Breaking with tradition, the *View* published its pre-UEFA Cup final souvenir issue on a Saturday, just four days before the game against FC Porto in Seville. There was to be no *View* on the day of the game – Wednesday 21 May 2003 – because everyone was in Seville! So the preview issue was designed almost like a match programme, with contributions from a whole host of big names from the world of football and showbiz. Martin O'Neill, Neil Lennon, Henrik Larsson and Alan Thompson all anticipated the game, while Ian Rush, Alan Rough and Fredrik Soderstrom gave the 'neutral' view. And for good measure, Oasis guitarist and songwriter Noel Gallagher spoke to the *View* about his love for the

Hoops... again! It was an issue that looked forward to the game and, such was the optimism within the Celtic family, the staff were geared up to produce the post-Seville celebration issue, too.

Manager Martin O'Neill spoke for everyone when he told the *View*: 'We're there and as the week progresses we'll give it more thought. I'm sure the Celtic fans will party whether we win or lose the game, but we're not going there to make up the numbers. We want to try and win the game. It's a hard game, it's exciting to be in it and with 20 minutes to go against Boavista, if you had said to me then that I'd be getting ready for the final I'd certainly have taken it. The goal finally came and then it was the longest 12 minutes of all our lives and it was great to see it through and now we can go to Seville and enjoy it.'

Those were heady, heady days and over 80,000 supporters would head to the south of Spain, full of hope that Celtic would bring home a European trophy.

The road to Seville

1st Round
CELTIC v FK SUDUVA
agg: 10-1

2nd Round
CELTIC v BLACKBURN ROVERS
agg: 3-0

3rd Round
CELTIC v CELTA VIGO
agg: 2-2 (celtic win on away goals)

4th Round
CELTIC v VfB STUTTGART
agg: 5-4

Baile Seville
SEVILLE   2003KM

Quarter-Final
CELTIC v LIVERPOOL
agg: 3-1

Semi-Final
CELTIC v BOAVISTA
agg: 2-1

> "Celtic fans were getting used to Euro travel – there were fewer guys in the aisles of planes shouting 'Hat for the driver!'"

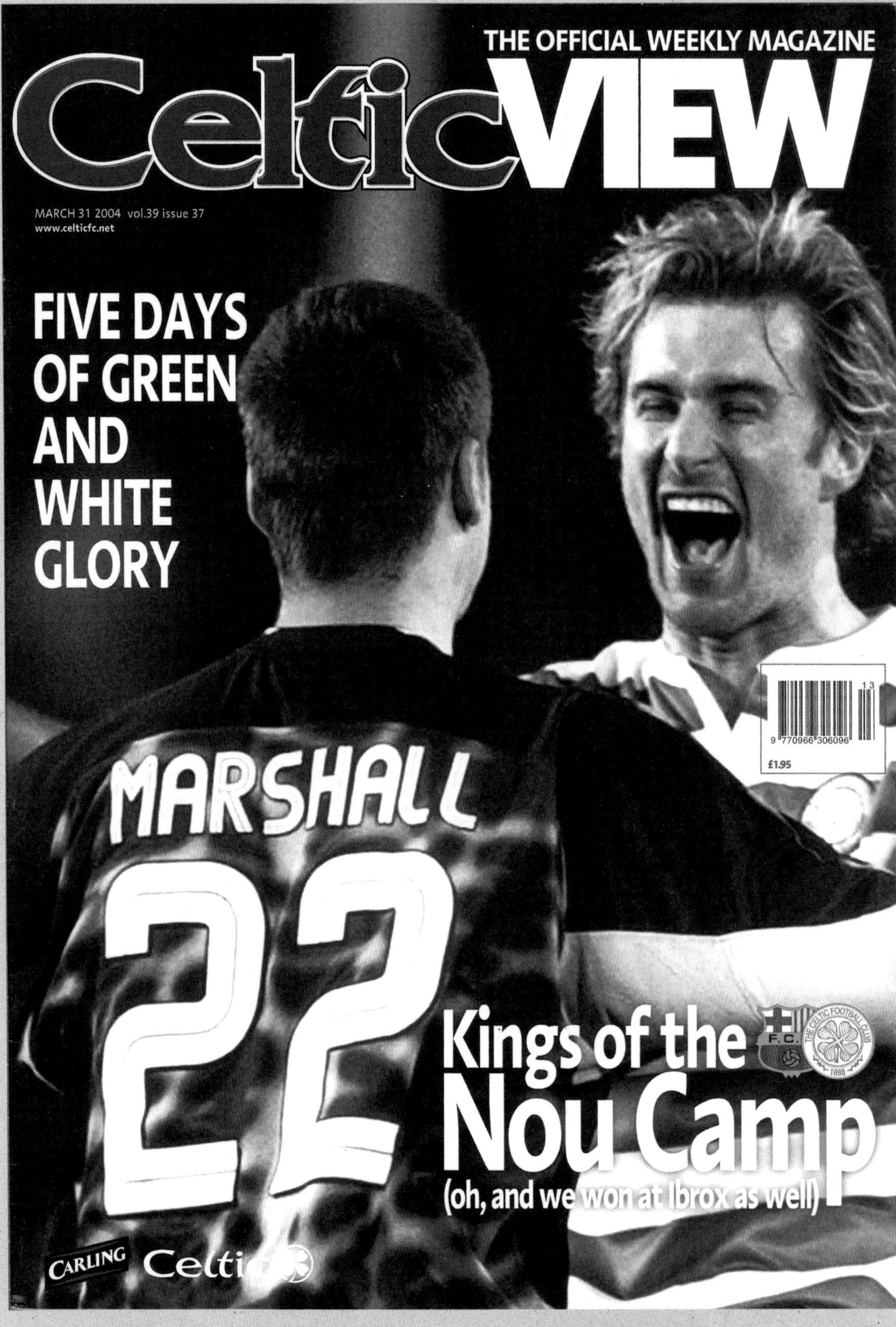

THE OFFICIAL WEEKLY MAGAZINE

Celtic VIEW

MARCH 31 2004 vol.39 issue 37
www.celticfc.net

FIVE DAYS OF GREEN AND WHITE GLORY

MARSHALL

22

£1.95

Kings of the Nou Camp
(oh, and we won at Ibrox as well)

CARLING Celtic

Celtic's re-emergence as a European force continued with a momentous victory over Barcelona in the UEFA Cup. And with memories still fresh from the Seville experience of the previous season, the Nou Camp triumph had supporters dreaming of another European final.

Martin O'Neill's side had travelled to Catalunya with a 1-0 lead to defend, but they knew it would be the toughest of tasks, not least because teenage goalkeeper David Marshall would be in the starting eleven following Rab Douglas' red card in the first leg at Celtic Park. And Marshall certainly earned his place on the front cover of the *View*, as well as in the history books, with an incredible display of goalkeeping which prevented Barcelona scoring.

Also in the side that night for Celtic was defender John Kennedy, who followed up a masterful display against Barça with another strong showing in the subsequent victory at Ibrox the following weekend.

On the day of the *View*'s publication, Kennedy spoke of his delight at having broken through to the Celtic first team. He also looked forward to winning his first senior cap for Scotland that night at Hampden against Romania.

Kennedy, as everyone knows, suffered a terrible knee injury in that game, which would keep him out of first-team action for three years, so his words to the *View* that day have a certain poignancy: 'Football is always going to be full of ups and downs because that is the nature of it and right now I am just delighted that it all seems to be highs. It has been an amazing week and, because it has been one thing after another, with the Barcelona game, my first Old Firm start and then the Scotland call-up, I've not had a chance to think about it all. I would never even have thought a few weeks ago that this is where I would be at the minute, so it's amazing really. It's hard to take it all in, but this is what football is all about and all I can hope is that I grasp the chances that I have.'

UEFA Cup 4th Round, 2nd Leg, Thursday March 25, 2004, Nou Camp

BARCELONA 0 V CELTIC 0

NERVE-WRACKING it most certainly was, but after holding firm in the Nou Camp Celtic will face Villarreal in the UEFA Cup quarter-final after Alan Thompson's first leg goal was sufficient to see Martin O'Neill's side progress in a competition they fared so well in last season.

Irrespective of what happens next, this result will be remembered as one of the most momentous in Celtic's history. A 0-0 draw in the imposing environment of the Nou Camp, with shots raining down on an inexperienced 19-year-old keeper and minus key personnel, the elimination of Barcelona is equal to any achievement Celtic have made in recent years.

VOICE OF THE CHAMPIONS

Celtic VIEW

APRIL 28 2004 vol.39 issue 41
www.celticfc.net

£1.95

MARTIN O'NEILL
Manager looks forward to end of a long hard season

AIDEN McGEADY
Youngster keeps his feet on the ground

RONNIE SIMPSON
Legends pay tribute to the Lisbon Lion

Trophy time

SPL silverware comes back home to Paradise this Sunday

CARLING   Celtic

After a season as the 'official magazine of Celtic Football Club', the *View* was able to reclaim the title 'Voice of the Champions' after Martin O'Neill's side had won the Scottish Premier League title at a canter.

It was something of a relief to be able to put the league trophy back on the front page of the *View*, announcing its impending return to Celtic Park that weekend. This issue of the magazine was also significant for a number of reasons. Firstly, it recorded the first-team debut of one Aiden McGeady, whose exploits at Tynecastle, which included a goal in the 1-1 draw, had already hit the headlines. McGeady told the *View*: 'My phone was ringing off the hook on Sunday night with everyone calling up to congratulate me, but I didn't mind. It was just such a great day, not only for me, but for my whole family, and especially my mum and dad. I think they're pretty proud of me, and everyone I've spoken to have been really encouraging. To be honest, it's not really sunk in yet.'

More poignantly, the *View* also recorded the sad passing of Ronnie Simpson. The Lisbon Lions' goalkeeper, known affectionately by his team-mates as 'Faither' because he was the elder statesman of the squad, was a familiar face around Celtic Park on matchdays and a long-time friend of the *View*. His friend and former team-mate Jim Craig led the tributes in the magazine with a moving obituary, which was complemented by a number of contributions from other former team-mates.

Ronnie Simpson could rightly be regarded as a Celtic great – one of the best goalkeepers the club has ever had – and his crowning glory was 25 May 1967, when he helped Celtic win the European Cup. Among the many comments from supporters which were printed in the *View* was one from James O'Rourke of Ontario, Canada, who wrote: 'I was privileged to meet Ronnie Simpson several times when he travelled with the rest of the Lions to our North American Convention. He was a true gentleman, and a wonderful ambassador for the club. You will be greatly missed Ronnie. My thoughts and prayers go out to his wife and family.'

Ronnie Simpson 1930 - 2004

THE VOICE OF THE CHAMPIONS

CelticVIEW

MAY 12 2004 vol.39 issue 43
www.celticfc.net

Green &
Whitewash

Celtic

CARLING

£1.95

Ninety minutes were already on the clock when Chris Sutton produced a sublime chip to give Celtic a 1-0 victory over Rangers in the final derby match of the season. In the process he ensured that Celtic won all five games of the 2003–04 campaign against their city rivals – four league games and a Scottish Cup tie.

It was also the first time that any Celtic side has won all its league games against Rangers since 1971–72 and even then that was when there were only two a season. In fact, you would have to go all the way back to the early years of the twentieth century, when, between 1912 and 1914, Celtic went on an unbeaten run in their fixtures against their old adversaries, to find the last time the Hoops had such a hold over the Ibrox side.

Judging by Chris Sutton's reaction on the cover of the *View*, he was quite pleased with his goal, which also increased the gap at the top of the table to a massive sixteen points. It reaffirmed Celtic's dominance in this derby fixture and showed that, as far as Martin O'Neill's men were concerned, there was no such thing as a meaningless match against Rangers.

By a wonderful coincidence the normally reticent Chris Sutton was also the main interview in that week's magazine. The big Englishman preferred to avoid the media spotlight, though on this occasion the *View* did manage to pin him down. Sutton, as ever, was uncomfortable talking about himself, preferring to lavish praise on his team-mates, including Henrik Larsson, John Hartson and Didier Agathe, among others. However, he did look ahead with great optimism to the future at Celtic Park, telling the *View*: 'I've really enjoyed the last four years here – that's why I signed the contract – and hopefully the next two or three will be just as good. I'm getting a bit older, but hopefully I can still do a good job for the team and win some trophies here. That's all I'm looking to do, really.'

Chris Sutton scores Celtic's late winner against Rangers

The Crying game

HENRIK'S TEARS IN PARADISE

It's surprising in the West of Scotland to see one grown man cry, but when there's a stadium full of them then you know that something quite extraordinary has occurred.

And it was all Henrik Larsson's fault. He may have made us happy when skies were grey, but when it came to his final competitive appearance at Celtic Park there wasn't a dry eye in the house. After seven magnificent years, Larsson was calling time on his Celtic career and for the game against Dundee United on 16 May 2004 he was given the captaincy.

Celtic had long been crowned champions and the supporters who gathered at Celtic Park for the final league game of the season were there to pay homage to the Super Swede. True, there was still the Scottish Cup final and a farewell fiesta game against Seville, but this was the last competitive match at the stadium where he had excelled for so many years.

The game, however, looked to be heading towards a goalless draw when Larsson popped up with two goals inside the last ten minutes of the match. The emotion of the occasion even got to the normally ice-cool player, who broke down in tears after scoring his second of the afternoon. And there were more to follow when he reappeared on the pitch after the final whistle for a long, emotional and tear-filled standing ovation from a devoted Celtic support.

The two goals Larsson scored against Dundee United brought his tally in the green and white hoops

to 240 from 314 games (he would bag another two in the Scottish Cup final), and this total propelled him into third position in Celtic's all-time top goalscorers' table, behind Bobby Lennox in second place and the legendary Jimmy McGrory in first place.

Captain Jackie McNamara paid his own tribute to the Magnificent Seven in the *View*, saying: 'I'll look back with a lot of pleasure on the experience of being

in the same team as Henrik. He's been different class, certainly the best player I've played with during my time here. He's also added so much to his game during his time here, and I can't speak highly enough of the contribution he's made to this club.'

THE VOICE OF THE CHAMPIONS

Celtic VIEW

NOVEMBER 24 2004 vol.40 issue 20 £1.95 www.celticfc.net

We shall not be moved

Manager's support for Neil Lennon after sectarian abuse at Ibrox

OLD FIRM Martin O'Neill on the hypocrisy of the press ... Peter Lawwell on the hysterical criticism aimed at the manager ... Fans on the match, including the embarrassing antics of Peter Lovenkrands

This is a picture of solidarity between manager and player as Martin O'Neill gives his support to Neil Lennon, after the Irish midfielder had suffered a torrent of sectarian abuse during a match against Rangers at Ibrox.

The Celtic manager strode on to the pitch after the game, which Celtic lost 2-0 with both Alan Thompson and Chris Sutton sent-off, and walked with Lennon back towards the Celtic supporters, amassed in the Broomloan Road stand. It was a visible sign of the close bond between manager and player and it was O'Neill's way of saying 'enough is enough'.

Almost from the moment that Neil Lennon signed for Celtic, he had been subjected to sectarian abuse and his manager argued, rightly so, that in twenty-first-century Scotland it was unacceptable.

What was even more saddening in this day and age was the reaction of the Scottish press, who pilloried the Celtic manager rather than condemning the bigots. As O'Neill himself pointed out to the *View*, it was in marked contrast to the way the English press had condemned a handful of racist fans at Blackburn who had abused Dwight Yorke. 'It's laughable,' he said. 'Here we are with this ferocious outcry about Dwight Yorke getting stick at Ewood Park, and there's no doubt that it was shocking and something we all want to see wiped out of football. But Neil Lennon goes to Ibrox, and pretty much every other away ground in Scotland, and gets racially abused from start to finish, and people say: "Oh, it's alright. He's big enough to take it."

'Now, this is a player who has received death threats, been abused and assaulted in the street and at his home by sectarian louts, and who takes dreadful stick week in, week out, only because of what he is. And that's alright? No, it's double standards, nothing else.' Such was the strength of feeling among Celtic supporters regarding the issue that there were four pages of letters in the *View* that week, all of them offering support to Martin O'Neill and Neil Lennon.

EMBARRASSING: Peter Lovenkrands' disgraceful behaviour during the Old Firm game led to Alan Thompson's sending off, and Celtic have announced their intention to appeal against the red card given to the Englishman

Celtic VIEW

THE VOICE OF THE CHAMPIONS

MARCH 16 2005 vol.40 issue 35 £1.95 www.celticfc.net

CARLING · Celtic

IF YOU KNOW THE HISTORY

Celtic's hand of friendship to refugees and asylum seekers

O'NEILL Full of praise for the top scorers in the SPL Championship | **BEATTIE** Delighted to be back in first-team and amongst the goals | **BELLAMY** On form and with his sights set on a double triumph

If ever a cover summed up just what Celtic Football Club is all about, then it was the *Celtic View* of 16 March 2005.

A group of refugee and asylum-seeker children, wearing the green and white hoops, posed for a photograph along with manager Martin O'Neill in the main stand at Celtic Park. The heading underneath read 'If You Know The History' and it served as a timely reminder to every Celtic supporter of where they and the club had come from.

It was the day of a game against Dunfermline, yet Martin O'Neill still took time out from the pre-match preparations to meet the children. The group of kids from ten different countries had already enjoyed a two-hour coaching session with the club's community coaches and the club were delighted to be involved in the project run by New Roots Scotland.

What made this cover so poignant, and timely, was the fact that it came in the middle of a general election campaign in which some politicians attempted to demonise refugees and asylum seekers in a crude attempt to win votes from the prejudiced and narrow-minded.

Celtic Football Club was formed specifically to raise money to help feed the Irish immigrants in the East End of Glasgow. It also quickly became a source of pride for those immigrants as the new club achieved success on the field of play. The club has never forgotten that and neither has the overwhelming majority of the Celtic support.

However, it was important for the *Celtic View* to reiterate this, reminding fans that, as the descendants of nineteenth century refugees and asylum seekers, we should not only reject the politics of prejudice, but we should do everything we possibly can to oppose it. For a football magazine to put such a powerful, non-football image on its front cover was something that took a lot of courage. The fact was, it was the right thing to do and was, as the editorial explained, 'another way of the club remaining true to its roots'.

Celtic ✪

Stilian Petrov celebrates after he grabs the Hoops' fifth against Dunfermline

primus.

Celtic's Official Fixed Line Telecoms Partner

Celtic VIEW

THE VOICE OF THE CHAMPIONS

APRIL 27 2005 vol.40 issue 41 www.celticfc.net £1.95

CARLING Celtic

PETROV Ibrox goalscorer pays tribute to a great team effort | **BILLY CONNOLLY** His ONLY interview and it's with the *View* | **HARTSON** Striker wants more trophies to add to Players' Award

Craig Bellamy looks a picture of serenity, the camera capturing him lost in prayer. The stunning image was taken at Ibrox just seconds after he'd scored against Rangers, putting Celtic 2-0 up, and the emotion of the moment was clearly overwhelming for the Welsh striker.

Hindsight would have us wish that Bellamy had also offered up a prayer for a successful conclusion to the league campaign given that, after the victory at Ibrox which put Celtic five points clear of Rangers with just four games remaining, Martin O'Neill's side still contrived to lose the title with a final-day collapse at Fir Park.

In an almost prophetic end to his interview with the *View* after the Ibrox victory, the Celtic manager said: 'We've won the match against Rangers and allowed ourselves an opportunity and we must take that opportunity. We've allowed ourselves a slip along the way and I am convinced there will be a few more twists and turns along the way. Let us be absolutely up for the game.'

At the time the *View* was happy to celebrate what we, and everyone else, thought was the decisive moment of the league campaign. The image of Bellamy on his knees in prayer was so powerful it did not need any headlines to supplement it. Indeed, it also featured as the poster in the centre pages of the magazine.

Bellamy, unfortunately, injured his hamstring during the game at Ibrox and his absence from the next game, at home to Hibernian, was instrumental in Celtic losing that match 3-1 and allowing Rangers back into the title race.

This was also an issue full of celebrities, with an exclusive chat with comedian Billy Connolly – his only interview during a tour of Scotland – and a feature on rock band, Kasabian. Although fans of Leicester City, the band also had a strong affection for Celtic, not least because of the presence of Martin O'Neill and Neil Lennon at the club, both of whom were able to meet the band and pose for photographs.

"PLAYING YOUR HOME TOWN CAN BE A BIT SCARY – LIKE TRYING TO BE FUNNY TO YOUR AUNTIES OR UNCLES"

A MAN FOR ALL SEASONS: Billy has revelled in Celtic's successes over the years – including the prize-laden Martin O'Neill years – but doesn't stress over any dips in fortune

CelticVIEW

JUNE 1 2005 vol.40 issue 46 www.celticfc.net £1.95

Celtic

CARLING

Dawn of new era

Gordon Strachan speaks exclusively to the *View*

O'NEILL An emotional farewell as Celtic win the Scottish Cup | **LAWWELL** New boss will build on the success of last five years | **McNAMARA** On a special weekend for the Celtic team and the captain

Gordon Strachan stares pensively at the camera, his first picture for the *View* in what was the final issue of 2004–05. He also spoke to the magazine for the first time ahead of the press conference which would announce him as the new Celtic manager.

However, his excitement at the new managerial challenge ahead was tempered by the circumstances under which it had occurred. Celtic Park had been under a cloud since the final day of the season when a defeat to Motherwell had seen the championship snatched away from the club. The mood wasn't helped when, just days later, Martin O'Neill announced that he was stepping down as manager because of his wife's ill health. Even victory in the Scottish Cup final against Dundee United proved to be an emotional rather than an exhilarating experience, because of those circumstances.

It was into this atmosphere that Gordon Strachan stepped, knowing that there was a tough act to follow,

but also aware that drastic surgery was needed on an ageing squad. The *View*'s tribute to Martin O'Neill, detailing the successes of the previous five seasons, clearly highlighted the benchmark set by the Irishman, and the new man in charge admitted as much.

He told the *View*: 'The circumstances are a problem to me, though obviously a bigger problem to Martin. And it's very hard to celebrate taking this job. Someone said to me the other day about having a drink to celebrate and I said I couldn't really celebrate just yet. Once we know Martin's wife is getting better, and they're comfortable and alright, then maybe we can do that, but at the moment if I could swap places and put Martin here and his wife healthy, then I would do that. I think we all wished that Geraldine was fine and the status quo could have remained, but life's not always that fair so I have to step in and do this job. It's not easy taking over from a legend, but I'm willing to do it. I'm excited about it and I'm not scared to do it, but it's a kind of surreal appointment.'

Celtic – Tennent's Scottish Cup Winners 2005

Celtic view

www.celticfc.net, November 9th 2005, Vol.41 Issue.18, £2.25

EXCLUSIVE INTERVIEW: STRIKER CHRIS SUTTON TALKS TO THE CELTIC VIEW

 THE OFFICIAL CELTIC WEEKLY MAGAZINE

FOUNDING FATHER

Brother Walfrid statue unveiled at Celtic Park

INSIDE THIS WEEK'S VIEW

Strachan, Falconer, McStay + lots more

WIM JANSEN
The former Celtic boss played against the Hoops at Paradise

JOHN HARTSON
View poster marks his 100th goal for Celtic

BATTLE STATIONS
Remembering the 1967 World Club Championship

9 770966 306102

Another memorable *Celtic View* front cover records a momentous event in the club's history.

Just one day short of the 118th anniversary of the meeting in St Mary's Church Hall, Calton, Glasgow, which gave birth to Celtic Football Club, a statue was unveiled outside the front of Celtic Park of the club's founding father, Brother Walfrid. The idea for the statue, as well as the funds to erect it, came from Celtic supporters and the decision to honour Brother Walfrid was an acknowledgement of where the club and its supporters had come from and why Celtic was formed in the first place.

Celtic is more than just a football club and for the supporters who gathered outside the stadium on Saturday 5 November 2005 for the unveiling ceremony were certainly reminded of this. Speaking at the event, chairman Brian Quinn described how Brother Walfrid's vision had seen the benefits of a football club to help his charitable activities financially. The chairman said: 'He also saw this as a means of bringing together the Scottish as well as the Irish strands in Glasgow's disadvantaged population. From the very outset Celtic Football Club commanded the passionate support of the communities it was intended to represent. This was something with which, in their deprived conditions, they could identify with and from which they could draw inspiration, a sense of self-worth and some kind of positive response to those who did not make them welcome.'

The chairman concluded by saying: 'I started my remarks by asking why Celtic have grown and flourished over a period of 118 years, from a local Glasgow club into a global presence. We often describe ourselves as a family and we are, right down to the occasional keenly felt squabbles. But we are more than that. We are a movement, founded on principles established by a quiet, determined man who set out to bring out the best in people and promote a generosity of spirit that endures today.'

During the event, the Celtic chairman was presented with a special Celtic cross by the Archdiocese of Glasgow, which had been carved from the rubble of the recently demolished St Mary's Church Hall, the birthplace of Celtic Football Club.

THE OFFICIAL CELTIC WEEKLY MAGAZINE

Century Bhoy

Celtic view

www.celticfc.net, February 22nd 2006, Vol.41 Issue.32, £2.25

CARLING · NIKE

THE OFFICIAL CELTIC
WEEKLY MAGAZINE

EXCLUSIVE INTERVIEW!

ROY KEANE
ON LIFE
AT CELTIC

8 MAGIC MOMENTS

Zurawksi leads goal charge as Lennon gets in on the act

JOHN KENNEDY
Defender takes it one step at a time on the road to recovery

SEASON TICKETS
It's your chance to win a pair for 2006/07 for yourself

GORDON STRACHAN
Manager was delighted with the performance against Dunfermline

Neil Lennon's goals are not so much like buses, but more like Halley's Comet: if you're lucky enough to see it once, you know you're unlikely to see it ever again.

Okay, so that's a little harsh on the Irish midfielder, but with just three strikes in 304 appearances for Celtic, a goal was still a rare occurrence, so when Lennon scored his third – and what ultimately proved to be his final – goal for Celtic the *View* thought it was worthy of a front cover celebration.

Lennon's goal came four minutes from time in an 8-1 rout of Dunfermline and, even amidst a four-goal show from Maciej Zurawski and a spectacular Shaun Maloney strike, the Irishman's shot from the edge of the box still managed to steal the show. Incredibly, it meant that Lennon had scored twice against Dunfermline at East End Park, with Hibernian the other victims.

Talking to the *View* after the game, manager Gordon Strachan spoke for everyone when he said:

'I'm still in shock. He got a standing ovation for the shot alone. But I think you can file that one away now. We won't be seeing another one of them for at least another four years!'

The player himself was still smiling the day after the game when he sat down with the *View* to look back on his three goals for Celtic. 'A JFK moment' was how the midfielder jokingly referred to his latest goal. 'I remember the last time I scored, Martin O'Neill said he was pencilling another one in for 2006 and I thought "cheeky get". But he was spot on and, to be honest, I don't know when the next one will come.'

That issue of the *View* also featured an exclusive interview with Roy Keane, who spoke about settling into life at Celtic Park. It had something for softies, too, because *View* reader Mick Mooney won the ultimate Valentine's prize for his girlfriend Pamela Marshall courtesy of T-Mobile: a day of pampering and shopping followed by a candlelit dinner at Paradise. Now who says the age of romance is dead?

T··Mobile·

LOVE IS IN THE AIR FOR OUR T-MOBILE WINNER
PAMELA ENJOYS THE ULTIMATE VALENTINE'S DAY THANKS TO HER ROMANTIC BOYFRIEND

CELTIC VIEW reader Mick Mooney from Glasgow won the ultimate Valentine's prize for his girlfriend, courtesy of T-Mobile.

Mick, aged 28, was the lucky winner of the T-Mobile Valentine's Day Competition we ran in the View.

And Mick's fantastic prize meant that his girlfriend Pamela Marshall received the full 'footballer's wife' treatment on Tuesday 14th February.

On Valentine's morning, the T-Mobile taxi arrived to chauffer Pamela into town where she was given £200 to splash out on the perfect outfit.

Next stop was top Glasgow salon Taylor Ferguson where the lucky lady enjoyed a champagne lunch followed by an afternoon of pampering with VIP hair and beauty treatments.

To round off the day in style, T-Mobile arranged a romantic Valentine's Day meal for Pamela and Mick within one of Celtic's finest hospitality suites.

Truly a Valentine's Day to remember! Having enjoyed the whole experience, Pamela told the View: "It was I fantastic day, I thoroughly enjoyed it. I was very, very impressed with the meal at Celtic Park and T-Mobile really pulled out all the stops to make this an absolutely fantastic day."

And Mick was just as delighted. He said: "It was a brilliant day, absolutely superb. Cheers to T-Mobile."

Celtic view

CARLING | NIKE

www.celticfc.net, March 15th 2006, Vol.41 Issue.35, £2.25

THE OFFICIAL CELTIC WEEKLY MAGAZINE

JIMMY JOHNSTONE
1944-2006
'YOU'LL NEVER WALK ALONE'

The black masthead would have warned the few Celtic supporters who did not already know that there was sad news to relate.

This *Celtic View* front cover was a sombre one, the only colour image that of Jimmy Johnstone in green and white hoops. The words underneath were short and to the point:

Jimmy Johnstone
1944–2006
'You'll Never Walk Alone'

After a brave and lengthy battle with motor neurone disease, the Greatest Ever Celt sadly passed away on 15 March 2006. Supporters knew him as 'Jinky', the mercurial talent at the heart of Jock Stein's greatest ever team. They also knew him as one of their own and very quickly the front of Celtic Park became a shrine to the player and the man.

Jim Craig, a former team-mate and long-time friend of Jinky's, led the tributes in the *View* which included reflections from the rest of his Celtic team-mates, along with other ex-Celts, including Tommy Burns, Danny McGrain and Henrik Larsson.

The Swedish striker, who had worn the number seven with the same distinction as Jimmy Johnstone, and who had developed a friendship with the former Celt during his time in Glasgow, said: 'I always got on well with him from the start and, whenever I saw him, he would always be smiling. That's how I'll remember him.'

The *View* also reprinted the last interview Jinky ever game to the magazine, in July 2005. Like his contemporaries, he was always happy to speak to the *View* and he looked back fondly on his career, from a young footballer in Viewpark, Uddingston, right through to the triumph in Lisbon.

Gordon Strachan, who had always cited Jinky as one of his heroes, told the *View*: 'I enjoyed Jimmy's company and he was a true, true great. He was a brave man, on and off the pitch.'

Amidst the outpouring of grief, Celtic did have to prepare for a CIS Cup final against Dunfermline, which became the Jimmy Johnstone final, and at which every Celtic player would wear the number seven on their shorts in tribute to the Celtic legend.

Celtic view

www.celticfc.net, March 22nd 2006, Vol.41 Issue.36, £2.25

THE OFFICIAL CELTIC WEEKLY MAGAZINE

JIMMY JOHNSTONE
THE VIEW LOOKS BACK ON AN EMOTIONAL WEEK FOR THE CELTIC FAMILY

CIS Cup triumph dedicated to the Greatest Ever Celt

WE WON IT FOR JINKY

Celtic's first trophy under Gordon Strachan was overshadowed by the sad death of Jimmy Johnstone just a few days before the CIS Cup final at Hampden. Yet amidst the unprecedented outpouring of grief from the Celtic family, the players and the management still had to prepare for the game against Dunfermline.

It could be argued that the fact that the match became the 'Jimmy Johnstone final' added to the pressure on the Celtic players, but they responded magnificently, cruising to a 3-0 victory, and while it was a first trophy as manager for Strachan and as captain for Neil Lennon, the *View*'s headline told the story of who took centre stage at the National Stadium. 'We Won It For Jinky' the magazine declared, and it was certainly an emotional afternoon at Hampden.

Speaking in the *View*, the manager explained: 'The thing about Jinky is that he was loved and appreciated throughout this club and it was nice that, by our performance, we allowed ourselves to celebrate his memory in the proper way. The atmosphere at the end was fantastic and it goes without saying that the wee man would've enjoyed it all and respected what we'd achieved.'

The magazine also contained a special tribute to Jimmy Johnstone, allowing supporters to register their own words of tribute to a Celtic legend and also looking at ten of Jinky's greatest ever games in the green and white hoops. Dr Cameron Munro from Aberdeen wrote: 'I am a Dundee United fan, but today I feel very sad at the passing of a true Celtic great. In my mind Jimmy Johnstone was a world class player, a great entertainer and a brave man both on and off the pitch. It's a cliché, but I really doubt if we will see his likes again. God bless, Jimmy.'

The *View* also carried an interview with teenage Irish defender Darren O'Dea, who explained that he would consider a loan move in the 2006–07 season if he thought it would help his Celtic career. Nearly a year later, O'Dea would be starring for the Celtic first-team against AC Milan in the San Siro.

Celtic view

Celtic ✦

CARLING · Nike · www.celticfc.net, April 12th 2006, Vol.41 Issue.39, £2.25

VOICE OF THE CHAMPIONS

WIN CHANCE TO BE PART OF TROPHY CELEBRATIONS

ALL THE REACTION TO CELTIC'S LEAGUE TRIUMPH

CHAMPIONS

John Hartson's goal brings the title back to Paradise

Sometimes a single word can tell the whole story and in this case 'Champions' says it all.

It took Celtic just four minutes to score the goal which would clinch the league title. In truth, everyone had known for months that the Scottish Premier League trophy was returning to Paradise, but the 1-0 victory over Hearts courtesy of that early John Hartson goal confirmed the fact. It ensured that Gordon Strachan was a title winner in his first season in charge at Celtic, a tremendous achievement given the upheaval in the squad since the previous season and the shaky start to the 2005–06 season.

For John Hartson, it would prove to be the crowning moment of his final season in the Hoops and a poignant one at that, as he scored the title-clinching goal on his thirty-first birthday. A few days later the Welsh striker admitted to the *View* that he had not yet seen a replay of the goal. He said: 'It maybe wasn't the greatest goal I've scored, but I managed to get a really good, clean contact on it and I was just delighted to see it go in, especially early on in the game. I feel that goal got the crowd up and got us playing really well for a while. When I hit it, I didn't really think it would go in, but I thought that the keeper would at least have to work to get it and I don't think he expected it to come in so early.

'But do you know what?' added Hartson with a broad grin. 'Believe it or not, I haven't even seen the goal yet! I am giving you my first insight into it, but I'd like to see it again. I went straight out after the game for a bit of a birthday party on Wednesday night and then the next day I just looked at a couple of papers. I haven't even seen it on the news. I haven't even watched the telly and, honest to God, I haven't seen the goal yet, but I will have a look back on it.'

THE OFFICIAL CELTIC WEEKLY MAGAZINE

SCOTTISH PREMIERLEAGUE
CHAMPIONS 2005/06

Celtic view

www.celticfc.net, May 17th 2006, Vol.41 Issue.44, £2.25

CARLING

VOICE OF THE CHAMPIONS

Celtic ✿

BE PART OF THE CROWD – RENEW YOUR SEASON TICKET BY JUNE 2

WORLD CLASS

Green light for Celtic's new state-of-the-art training facility

DOUBLE DELIGHT AS UNDER-19s WIN YOUTH CUP

With hard-hat and shovel in hand, Celtic chairman Brian Quinn was happy to pose for the *View*'s front cover picture, because he was standing on the site of the club's new multi-million pound, state-of-the-art training complex.

Brian Quinn described the new facility at Lennoxtown as 'a very important and significant milestone in the history of Celtic Football Club'. Work had just started on the complex and it would take a year to complete. The club was hopeful that it would be operational for the 2007–08 season, although the chairman also acknowledged the fact that the existing facility at Barrowfield, just a few hundred yards from Celtic Park, had done a great job over the years in producing successful teams.

Initial plans for the new sports academy and training facility at Lennoxtown included: three natural grass, full-size, UEFA-standard pitches; one artifical, full-size artificial UEFA-standard pitch; an indoor training area; goalkeeping training areas; a state-of-the-art gym and fitness suite; hydrotherapy facilities incorporating a hydro-pool; physio and medical facilities; a sports science and development facility; extensive changing facilities; a classroom; a parents' viewing area; football administration offices; and media facilities.

The club, still basking in the glow of the league triumph in Gordon Strachan's first season in charge, were delighted with this new development, as was the manager. He said: 'I have already visited the site and seen the plans for the new training facility and academy at Lennoxtown, and the whole project looks very exciting. Clearly a club of Celtic's size and stature requires quality facilities to match and the new development will certainly deliver these.'

This issue of the *View* also looked forward to the UEFA Champions League final in Paris between Barcelona and Arsenal. It pointed out to supporters that a Barcelona victory would be best for Celtic, not just because Henrik Larsson was playing for the Catalan giants, but because a Barça victory would ensure Celtic's entry to the group stages of the following year's competition, guaranteeing at least three top European nights at Celtic Park.

HENRIK'S LAST TANGO IN PARIS

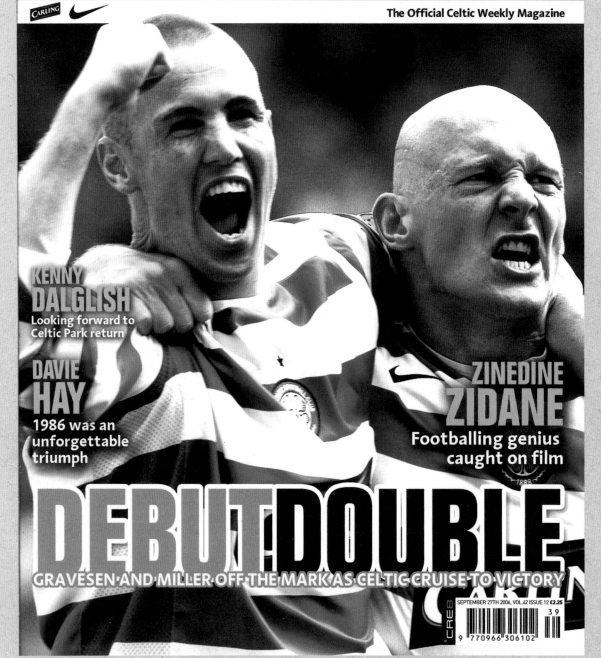

PARADISE FOUND: JAN VENNEGOOR OF HESSELINK IS LOVING LIFE WITH THE HOOPS

☐ VOICE OF THE CHAMPIONS

Celticview

The Official Celtic Weekly Magazine

KENNY
DALGLISH
Looking forward to
Celtic Park return

DAVIE
HAY
1986 was an
unforgettable
triumph

ZINEDINE
ZIDANE
Footballing genius
caught on film

DEBUT DOUBLE

GRAVESEN AND MILLER OFF THE MARK AS CELTIC CRUISE TO VICTORY

SEPTEMBER 27TH 2006, VOL.42 ISSUE.12 £2.25

9 770966 306102

Any victory over Rangers is always worth celebrating and, traditionally, the *Celtic View* has seen an upturn in sales on the back of a derby win. Gordon Strachan's side emerged triumphant from the first meeting between the sides of 2006–07 and it was two of the manager's summer signings who sealed the 2-0 win.

Thomas Gravesen opened the scoring after thirty-four minutes and Kenny Miller sealed the victory with seventeen minutes of the game remaining. For Miller, in particular, it came as something of a relief, having gone nine games without a goal. The former Rangers striker could never be faulted for his efforts in every game he played for Celtic, but, like every forward, he would be judged on his goals, and to score his first one for the green and white hoops against Rangers certainly went down well with supporters.

Kenny Miller told the *View*: 'Maybe it was meant to be. Every week has been the same – I've been thinking I am going to get my first goal in this game, or the next one. But this was a big win for us and it was great for me to get off the mark for Celtic. Of course it is a relief, because the longer it goes on, the more people talk about it and write about it. As much as I knew I had been contributing to the team, you want to get goals as a forward and against Rangers I obviously managed to get one, so I'm absolutely delighted.'

The win put the Hoops seven points clear of Rangers after just eight games and it was already promising to be a good season in the Scottish Premier League for the reigning champions.

The *Celtic View* had also, over the previous three years, been commissioning and publishing exclusive short stories by new and established writers. In this issue, Professor Willy Maley of the University of Glasgow, a former *View* columnist, contributed the wonderfully titled 'Buckfast at Timoney's'. Zinedine Zidane also popped up in the pages of the *View* as we reviewed a new film about the great Frenchman – *Zidane: A 21st Century Portrait*.

Kenny Miller

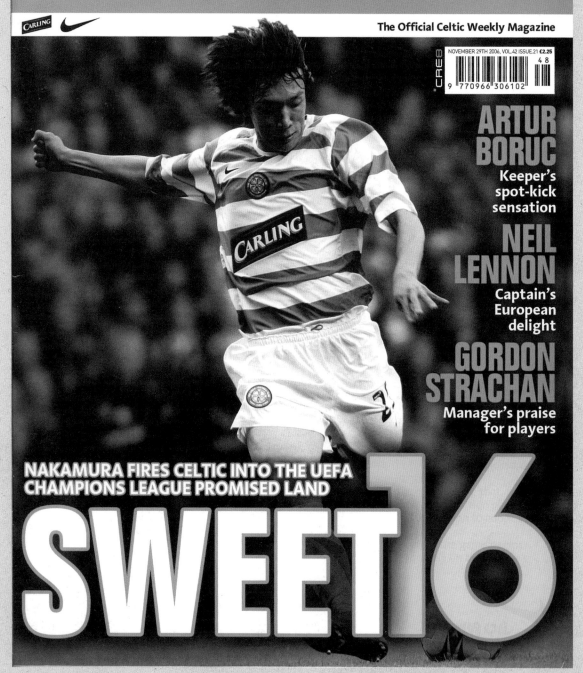

EXCLUSIVE INTERVIEW: BARRY FRATELLI OF THE FRATELLIS SPEAKS TO THE VIEW

□ **VOICE OF THE CHAMPIONS**

Celtic view

THE CELTIC FOOTBALL CLUB 1888

CARLING ✓

The Official Celtic Weekly Magazine

NOVEMBER 29TH 2006, VOL.42 ISSUE.21 £2.25

9 770966 306102

48

ARTUR BORUC
Keeper's spot-kick sensation

NEIL LENNON
Captain's European delight

GORDON STRACHAN
Manager's praise for players

NAKAMURA FIRES CELTIC INTO THE UEFA CHAMPIONS LEAGUE PROMISED LAND

SWEET 16

For many Celtic supporters, the highlight of the 2006–07 season was the victory over Manchester United at Celtic Park in the UEFA Champions League.

That choice was based not only on the fact that the Scottish champions had beaten one of the Premiership's finest, but also because the victory ensured that Celtic would be playing in the last sixteen of club football's most prestigious competition for the first time ever. As the *Celtic View* front cover proclaimed, it was 'Sweet 16' for Celtic, and it was Shunsuke Nakamura who proved to be the goal hero, cementing his place as the club's most gifted player.

The Japanese midfielder's free-kick nine minutes from time sent Celtic Park into raptures, although there was more drama at the end of the game when Artur Boruc saved a Louis Saha penalty. No one in the ground was aware at first that the victory had ensured qualification for the last sixteen, but as word came through of Benfica's victory over FC Copenhagen, the reality dawned on supporters. The

ever modest Nakamura, speaking to the *View* after the game, said: 'I was very pleased to score and it was nice it was at Celtic Park, but I also made a lot of mistakes and I have to think about that too. It was probably the most important goal of my career, because it was such a big game.'

The letters page of the *View* contained some unexpected words of praise under the heading 'Congratulations From The Other Side Of The Divide'. The correspondent, one Jimmy Johnston, wrote: 'Well done to the Celtic on a marvellous win over Man Utd. The defence was excellent and they took their chance when it was presented to them. As a Rangers fan it was good to see that passion, determination and belief in the jersey can produce success.'

Elsewhere in the magazine, Lisbon Lion John Clark was on the spot in the popular 'That's Entertainment' feature, though his choice of Hylda Baker as his celebrity dream date certainly caused some amusement, or should that have been bemusement, among the *View* staff?

Heartache as Manchester United are awarded a penalty

Jubilation as Artur Boruc saves Saha's penalty and Celtic win

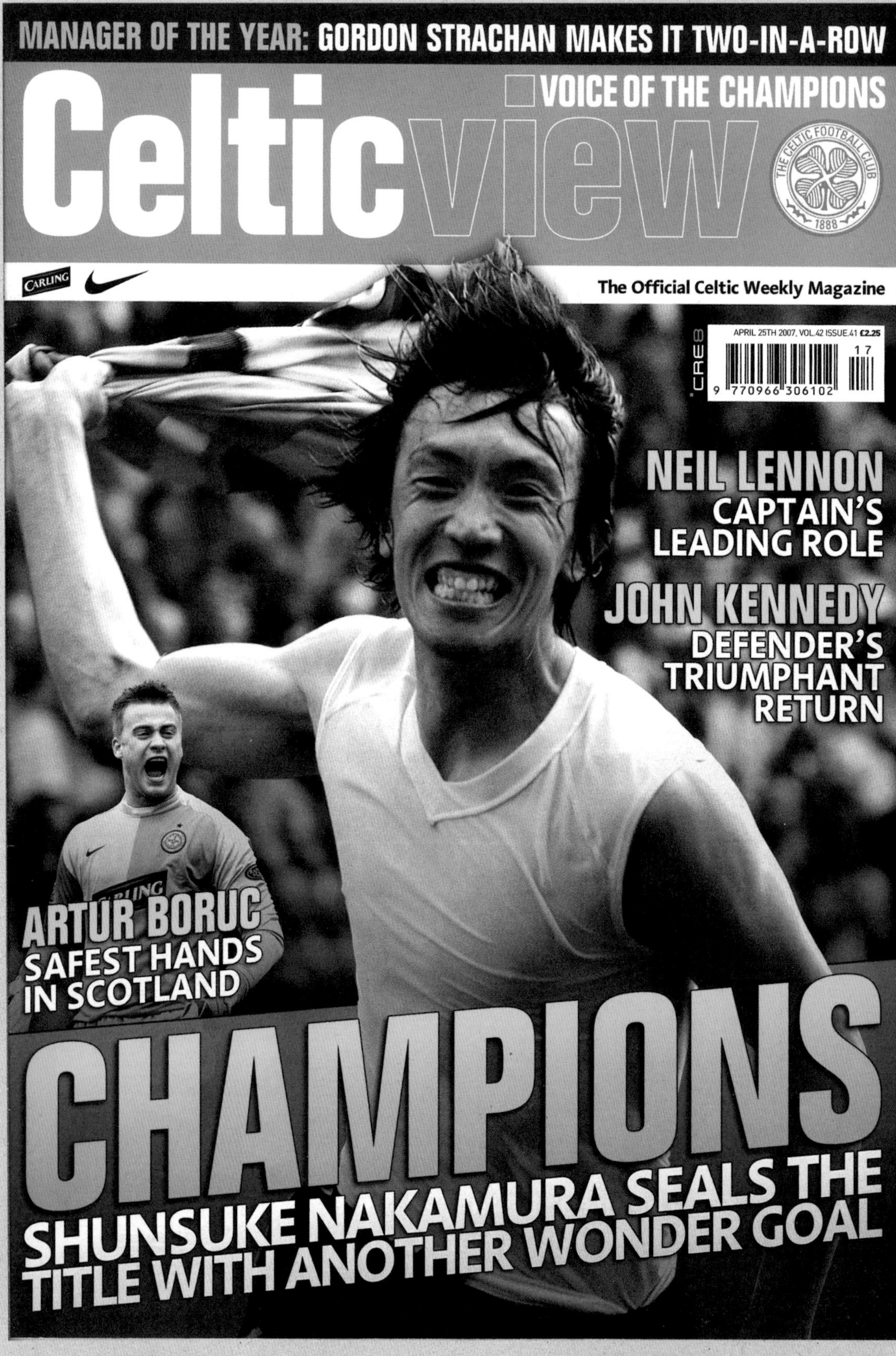

MANAGER OF THE YEAR: GORDON STRACHAN MAKES IT TWO-IN-A-ROW

☐ VOICE OF THE CHAMPIONS

Celticview

THE CELTIC FOOTBALL CLUB 1888

CARLING ✔ NIKE

The Official Celtic Weekly Magazine

APRIL 25TH 2007, VOL.42 ISSUE.41 £2.25

9 770966 306102

17

NEIL LENNON
CAPTAIN'S LEADING ROLE

JOHN KENNEDY
DEFENDER'S TRIUMPHANT RETURN

ARTUR BORUC
SAFEST HANDS IN SCOTLAND

CHAMPIONS
SHUNSUKE NAKAMURA SEALS THE TITLE WITH ANOTHER WONDER GOAL

It's highly unlikely that 'simmits' will ever become the height of fashion in Japan. Let's face it, they've never achieved that status in Scotland, but Shunsuke Nakamura's celebration after scoring the goal which secured the 2006–07 league title did reveal the undergarment of choice for the Scottish Premier League's top player.

The Japanese midfielder had impressed supporters with his talents in his first season at Celtic, but his second campaign proved to be an extraordinary success story. He scored the goal that won the league, scored the goal that put Celtic through to the last sixteen of the UEFA Champions League for the first time and scored the Scottish Premier League goal of the season – a sublime chip in a 2-2 draw with Dundee United at Celtic Park on Boxing Day 2006. That would be enough for most players, but Nakamura also managed to scoop every single Player of the Year award going, from Celtic supporters, Scotland's sportswriters and his fellow professionals.

As for his goal against Kilmarnock at Rugby Park,

which won the title and sparked his uncharacteristically emotional celebration, Nakamura was back to his naturally modest self in explaining how it had occurred: 'I saw the movement of the goalkeeper at the previous free kick,' he said. 'So this time I knew he would move to the near post, which is why I sent the shot to the far post.' Sounds simple, doesn't it?

There was much for the *View* to celebrate as Gordon Strachan's side retained the Championship. Captain Neil Lennon made his 300th appearance for the club in the title-winning game, although just a few days later the Irishman announced that he was calling time on his Celtic career at the end of the season.

More poignant was the appearance in the starting eleven at Rugby Park of defender John Kennedy, after an absence of just over three years. The twenty-three-year-old defender had last played for Celtic on 28 March 2004, before suffering an horrendous knee injury, and his return was a fantastic sight for all Celtic supporters. 'To return on a day like this really is a fairytale,' Kennedy told the *View*. It was certainly one with a happy ending.

CALLING ALL YOUNG CELTS: CHECK OUT OUR SPECIAL JUNIOR SECTION
Celtic view
VOICE OF THE CHAMPIONS
THE CELTIC FOOTBALL CLUB 1888
The Official Celtic Weekly Magazine
A TALE OF TWO TROPHIES
MAY 23RD 2007, VOL.42 ISSUE.45 £2.25
SCOTTISH CUP FINAL PREVIEW
Gordon Strachan
Jan Vennegoor of Hesselink
The Road to the Final
EUROPEAN CUP 40TH ANNIVERSARY
Billy McNeill
Lisbon Lions' memories
Tribute to Jock Stein

While the *Celtic View* was born almost two years before Celtic's greatest triumph, its creation coincided with an unprecedented upturn in the club's fortunes.

Billy McNeill has often talked about there being a fairytale element to the Celtic story and while the creation of an official club publication was not necessarily the stuff of fairytales, its arrival at the same time as Jock Stein certainly seemed fated. Forty years on from that day in Lisbon, the club, and the *View*, marked the event. An anniversary banquet with marquee on the Celtic Park pitch was organised for over 1,500 people, with the surviving Lisbon Lions naturally the guests of honour.

The *View*'s celebration was slightly less ostentatious – the magazine opted for a twenty-eight-page pull-out led by an interview with 'Cesar'. The Lisbon Lions are the most famous team in the club's history, yet remain the most down-to-earth group of people you could ever hope to meet. Most importantly, they are all good Celtic men and have always been fantastic supporters of the *View*; always happy to speak to the

magazine whenever a request is made.

As well as McNeill's memories, the *View* also spoke to his team-mates – Jim Craig, John Clark, Tommy Gemmell, Bobby Lennox, Bertie Auld, Stevie Chalmers and Willie Wallace – and paid tribute to the three players who have sadly passed away – Jimmy Johnstone, Bobby Murdoch and Ronnie Simpson.

Older readers, or those with spectacular memory recall, may well have recognised a couple of other 'Lisbon' features. An interview with the German referee from the 1967 European Cup final – Kurt Tschenscher – was reprinted and, probably to the dismay of Jim Craig, Herr Tschenscher maintained a stout defence of his decision to award Inter Milan a seventh-minute penalty. 'At the time there was no doubt in my mind that the award was correct,' Tschenscher said. 'Today, I have no reason to view this decision differently.' The magazine also reprinted a poem by supporter John Mulligan, entitled 'The Great Day', which had first been published in the *View* on 19 May 1968 to celebrate the first anniversary of the Lisbon victory.

☐ VOICE OF THE CHAMPIONS

Celticview

The Official Celtic Weekly Magazine

NEW BHOY
Scott Brown talks to the View

HAMPDEN HERO
Joe Doumbe sinks the Pars

DOUBLE JOY

NEIL LENNON'S SILVER LINING

The last *Celtic View* of the 2006–07 was able to celebrate another double – the fourteenth in Celtic history – after Gordon Strachan's side beat Dunfermline 1-0 at Hampden in the Scottish Cup final.

However, while the main image was of Neil Lennon holding aloft the famous old trophy, the front cover also gave an indication of things to come as Scott Brown signed on at Celtic Park. The midfielder, who joined from Hibernian in the biggest ever transfer between two Scottish clubs, gave his first interview to the *View* and revealed that it was Neil Lennon who had welcomed him to the club and had given him a guided tour. That also included some words of advice from the outgoing captain, as Brown revealed. 'I talked to Neil last Monday and he's the nicest man in the world,' the new signing said. 'On the field things are different. Everyone wants to win and Neil said to me, "Make sure you never lose that." He showed me around the stadium and took me upstairs for some lunch. It was nice of him to do that and I'll always remember what he said to me.'

The Irishman had shown over seven seasons, in words and deeds, that he was a winner and the Scottish Cup final victory at Hampden was his eleventh winner's medal as a Celtic player. That triumph came courtesy of an unlikely goalscorer – on-loan Cameroon defender Jean-Joel Perrier-Doumbe, who popped up with just five minutes remaining to score the only goal of the game.

The last issue of 2006–07 also had a strong international flavour to it. A project sponsored by the Celtic Supporters' Association to help build wells in Africa – named Walfrid Wells in reference to the club's founder – was featured, as was a story on the worldwide charitable destinations of old Celtic strips. A South African journalist enlightened readers on the phenomenon that is Bloemfontein Celtic Football Club, who also wear the hoops. And to round off the season's 'Celebrity Celts' feature, Glasgow actress Kathleen McDermott took the hot seat, revealing that two of her grandparents had played for Celtic in the twenties and thirties.

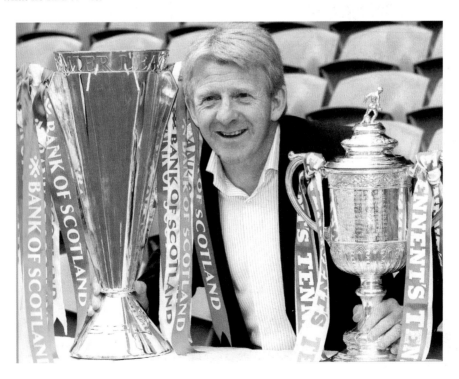

THE VOICE OF THE CHAMPIONS
THE OFFICIAL CELTIC WEEKLY MAGAZINE

celtic view

CARLING · NIKE

THE ITALIAN JOB
MASSIMO DONATI JOINS THE SCOTTISH CHAMPIONS

WIN
EXCLUSIVE SIGNED MASSIMO DONATI CELTIC SHIRT

LIVING THE DREAM
SCOTT McDONALD ON LIFE AT PARADISE

MAGNIFICENT SEVEN
CELTIC'S GREAT EUROPEAN OCCASIONS

GORDON STRACHAN
GEARING UP FOR THE NEW SEASON

TEDDY BJARNASON
TARGETING A FIRST-TEAM SPOT

EXCLUSIVE: CELTIC LEGEND ROY AITKEN ANSWERS FANS' QUESTIONS

JULY 11TH 2007, VOL.43 ISSUE.01 £2.25

9 770966 306102

As the *Celtic View* entered its forty-third year, the magazine returned to the shelves with a new look for a new season. The cover also featured a new face in the shape of Massimo Donati, the Italian midfielder who signed for Celtic from AC Milan during the close season.

As is the case every year, the *View* spent the close season planning ahead and a number of new features appeared in the first issue of the new season. The 'Magnificent Seven' series kicked off with a look at seven 'magnificent' European moments in Celtic's history. 'The Captains' looked, appropriately enough, at Celtic's captains through the years, beginning with the very first one, Jimmy Kelly. And the 'First & Last' feature put Celtic players on the spot as they answered questions about everything, from the first goal they scored to the last CD they bought.

However, as has always been the case, the core ingredient of the *Celtic View* was the team and the players, and with a seventy-two-page magazine to fill every week, there is certainly scope to feature a number of members of the first-team squad. Two of the new faces graced the front cover of the first *View* of 2007–08 – Scott McDonald and Massimo Donati. The Australian and the Italian, who both joined Celtic during the close season, spoke to the *View* about their respective transfers and their ambitions for the future.

There was also an older and perhaps more familiar face in the pages of the magazine as Celtic legend Roy Aitken answered supporters' questions on a range of subjects, from his favourite Celtic memory to the time he was 'adopted' by the club.

The *Celtic View* continues to go from strength to strength. It is the oldest weekly club magazine in football and remains the biggest and the best. Its history, as told through these front covers, is also a history of Celtic Football club since 1965 and the *View* will continue to report on the major events at the club through its pages.

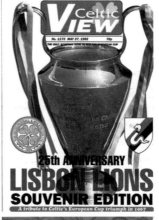

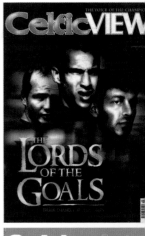